The Final Flight

The Crash of Polish Air Force 101 and the Death of a President

Linda M. Boris

Copyright © 2016 Linda M. Boris.

All rights reserved. No part of this book may be reproduced, stored, or transmitted by any means—whether auditory, graphic, mechanical, or electronic—without written permission of both publisher and author, except in the case of brief excerpts used in critical articles and reviews. Unauthorized reproduction of any part of this work is illegal and is punishable by law.

ISBN: 978-1-4834-5661-4 (sc)
ISBN: 978-1-4834-5662-1 (e)

Because of the dynamic nature of the Internet, any web addresses or links contained in this book may have changed since publication and may no longer be valid. The views expressed in this work are solely those of the author and do not necessarily reflect the views of the publisher, and the publisher hereby disclaims any responsibility for them.

Any people depicted in stock imagery provided by Thinkstock are models, and such images are being used for illustrative purposes only.
Certain stock imagery © Thinkstock.

Lulu Publishing Services rev. date: 08/18/2016

A wreath and a Polish flag are laid against the empty chairs that would have seated the President and his contingent at the 70th Anniversary Katyn ceremony

Contents

Author's Note ix
Prologue xi

1   First Foreshadowing 1
2   Second Foreshadowing (Setting the Stage) 5
3   Katyn 14
4   "Pamiętamy" (We Remember) 18
5   Preparations 23
6   The Cockpit Crew 26
7   Before the Flight 38
8   The Precurser Flights 45
9   The Final Flight 54
10 Aftermath 73
11 Preparing for Return to the Homeland 87
12 Why? 97

Epilogue 113
Appendix 119
Bibliography 293
About the Author 305

Author's Note

Before sitting down to write this book, I did as thorough an internet search as I could to determine if there had been any books written in the English language about the crash of PLF-101 in Smolensk. I could find none, with the singular exception of a book entitled: "Smolensk Air Crash 10-4-10: Official Facts, Scientific Analysis" by Dr. Mark Laskiewicz published September 8, 2015. When I found this book I downloaded it and began reading it. From my brief perusal the first part of this book, it seemed to me to be a product of the conspiracy theory party which can be found rather prominently on any internet search of the subject of the crash and so I dismissed it as not useful to my research.

My research on this book was based in three main sources of information: the Final Report from the examination of the aviation accident no. 192/2010/11 (the Polish report), the Interstate Aviation Committee Air Accident Investigation Committee Final Report (Russian MAK report), and internet articles and videos. Both the Russian and Polish investigation reports were available in English so I downloaded these and had them printed so I could more easily highlight and bookmark. Probably about 95% of the internet articles and videos dealing with this incident were in Polish. Since I speak and read very little Polish, I am heavily indebted to "Google Translate" for getting me started on the rough translations of on-line articles, blogs, and other resources. Polish is a tricky language whose sentence structure is different from ours. Additionally, there is a very sparse use of articles and pronouns (the, a, he, she, it, we, ours, yours, etc) which made the task of translating these sources into meaningful and accurate English versions more difficult. I used other on-line translation sites when

"Google" failed me, and often resorted to my good old fashioned Polish-English dictionary to aid me in tough spots.

I am also indebted to Andrzej Nejman, an English teacher in Poland, who I found when I appealed to my Polish Genealogy Email Group (PBS) for help. Andrzej is the cousin of the husband of one of the PBS members. She connected us and Andrzej was very kind and gracious in agreeing to assist me. I relied on Andrzej for those most difficult translations (often because of Polish colloquialisms) that I just felt I had to get exactly right. When I could find no English translation of Jacek Sasin's words to the people gathered at the Katyn Cemetery waiting for the Polish President to arrive, I downloaded and edited a You Tube video of the people gathered there as they began to get word that the President's plane had crashed and, unsure if perhaps I was asking too much, I sent it to Andrzej. He immediately translated it for me. Thank you, Andrzej!

I have no background or expertise in aviation, so for those portions of the book which deal with specific actions of the pilot and the plane, I relied almost exclusively on the Russian and Polish aircraft investigation reports, and a little bit of on-line research. I hope the reader will pardon anything of a technical nature that I have written which may not seem quite right. The most important factors in this disaster were human ones, so fortunately, I did not have to rely heavily on technical explanations.

The crash of PLF-101 (for Americans a rough equivalent to our Air Force One) is highly instructive from the standpoint of aviation safety and certainly a cautionary tale. But more than this, it was a devastating event not just for the family and friends of the almost 100 people who perished in the crash, but for an entire nation. It is for this reason I that I wrote this book for an American, English speaking audience. For it does not matter if the country is yours. Human tragedy is universal. We can all relate as human beings not only the suffering of an individual, but the suffering of a nation.

...any man's death diminishes me, because I am involved in mankind, and therefore never send to know for whom the bells tolls; it tolls for thee." –John Donne

Prologue

April 10, 2010 started out just like any other Saturday morning for me. I slept in as I usually did on a Saturday morning and when I finally decided to get out of bed, I took my morning shower and made my way downstairs to the kitchen to make breakfast. As usual, I turned on the TV. There was rarely anything interesting to watch on a Saturday morning, so I flipped on CNN.

I caught it in the midst of a report:

> *"......the plane, a Russian made Tupolev, Tu-154 was on a flight to the western Russian city of Smolensk and the Polish foreign ministry officials say it hit some trees on approach to the airport and caught fire. A Russian official says there was fog at the time of the crash and as we heard from our Richard Quest, we need to make the point that this particular aircraft has a remarkably good safety record. Now, as we've been reporting, Polish President Lech Kaczynski was on his way to that memorial service in Katyn when he was killed in today's plane crash. The service was to mark the 70th anniversary of the Katyn massacre during World War II and there were no survivors. Polish Prime Minister Donald Tusk is convening an*

emergency cabinet meeting and former President Lech Walesa calls the crash an inconceivable tragedy…" [1]

I froze where I stood in the kitchen. Forgetting now about breakfast, I went to my lap top and began searching the internet for more information. Surprisingly, there wasn't that much from American sources, so I tapped into my Polish news links which I had bookmarked some time ago. I plugged the URLs into Google translate to be able to read the rough translations and get some idea of what had happened.

From these sources I quickly learned that this plane crash not only took the lives of Polish President Lech Kaczynski and his wife, but of a considerable number of people in the highest levels of the Polish government. In addition to the four crew members and three flight attendants, on board the Tupolev-154M on April 10th were the following: The President and First Lady, the Former Polish President in Exile, five members of the chancellery (office of the President), the Undersecretary of State, the Undersecretary of State for Defense, the Undersecretary of State in the Ministry of Foreign Affairs, the Undersecretary of the Ministry of Culture, Secretary General of the Council for the Protection of Monuments to Struggle and Martyrdom, the Chief of the National Security Bureau, the Ombudsman and Civil Rights Commissioner, two members of the Ministry of Foreign Affairs Diplomatic Protocol office, one translator, the President's personal physician, all four military service chiefs, (Air Force, Land, Navy, and Special Forces) and the Chief of the General Staff of the Armed Forces, the Commander in Chief of the Warsaw Garrison, and the Operational Commander of the Armed Forces, seventeen members of the Polish Parliament, nine members of the Polish Government Protection Bureau(BOR), ten representative of civilian and military clergy, twelve representatives of Katyn families and Katyn Family support organizations, fourteen representatives of Polish organizations and culture including the Presidents of the Polish National Bank, Bar Association, Olympic Committee, Home Army Veterans' Association, and the Institute of National Remembrance.

---

[1] *CNN Crash Kills Polish President 10 Apr 2010 You Tube video* <u>https://www.youtube.com/watch?v=4yzRj9rmxO8</u>

How could such a thing happen? Why were all these important people even on the same plane together? This was incomprehensible to me. Lech Walesa had called it exactly right: the tragedy was inconceivable. And yet it had happened.

As I went about my life in the next hours and days, I was incredulous that no one else seemed even the least bit interested, much less shaken as I was, by the catastrophe and its magnitude. The 24-hour news cycle stations were covering it but not with any real intensity or urgency. It was just a side story. No one around me was talking about it or even mentioning it and everyone just went on with their everyday lives seemingly oblivious to the historical and monumental tragedy that had just occurred.

That night, unable to find any solace or anyone I could talk to about this terrible event, I sent an email to my new friend in Poland, Halina Z. Only three weeks before, through a message board on a family history website I had made contact with Halina, a Polish historian with family from the same small Polish town of Przedecz as my great-grandparents. We had started corresponding by email back in late March with the help of on line translation resources (she didn't speak English, I didn't speak Polish). By April 10th, we had been of great help to each other in finding information and documents on our ancestors and had already become good friends. Noticing the similarities in our appearance when we exchanged photos, I began referring to her as "my Polish sister" and her to me as "my American sister".

That night, I sent Halina the following email:

> *From: Linda*
> *To: Halina*
> *Sent: Sunday, April 11, 2010 1:06 AM*
> *Subject: A sad day for Poland and all of Polonia*
> *My dear friend Halina:*
> *I'm terribly sorry to hear about the plane crash that killed the Polish president and other officials! It feels to me very much like part of my family is gone.*
> *The irony is that they were traveling to the monument for the soldiers who were shot in the Katyn*

forest. I wish you and all the Polish people comfort at this terrible time.

Though it was now in the very early morning hours in Poland, Halina immediately replied:

> *Linda my friend*
> *Thank you, that you wrote to me, thank you ;-(*
> *crying and sadness,*
> *the whole office of the president -- dead*
> *Polish army generals-- dead*
> *political parties, people-- dead*
> *representatives of the families of Katyn-- dead....*
> *Why the pilot tried to land at any price?*
> *Weather conditions should have led the pilot to land at another airport.*
> *Experts asked why the pilot had acted in this way, answered: -The celebration of Katyn is a special day. It was the pressure, the vision of great ceremony. Perhaps this was the reason for the disaster.*

Over the next few days, my only solace was to be found in the Polish news media reports and my "Polish sister", Halina.

On April 14, I wrote:

> *Dear friend Halina:*
>
> *How are things going there? I have been watching the Polish news on the internet since there is not much on our news here in the USA about the Poland tragedy. I am happy that President Obama will be going to the funeral on Sunday. I hope they show some of it on our news here.*
> *I am reading a book now about the Katyn massacre. I wonder if there is a film in English about it? It is surprising to me that we know so much about the Holocaust and extermination of Jews during WWII,*

but little is known here about how the Poles were similarly treated.

    Please email and tell me how things are going there.

Linda

Halina replied:

Linda ;-(

    Putin announced today is the day---
They are showing the video of Wajda's {Polish
director}, "Katyn", on television in Russia
And I as a historian, prepare the Przedecz
presentation on the victims of Katyn --about LEON
KULESZA Polish Army officer;-(
All I know about this man,
He also went for him, our President Kaczynski.
Linda I KNOW THAT YOU UNDERSTAND ;-(
so will send you information on the victims of Katyn
of the patriots who died ;-(
    LINDA My dear friend
ESPECIALLY FOR YOU I looked for video about Katyn,
with the English language subtitles.
YOU ARE THE PERSON. YOU are very sensitive
BIG HEART ;-)
I am very happy that I have met YOU ;-)
if you can read, see a movie, you understand it now,
in April 2010 what happened ...
Why they went to the 70th anniversary of Katyn.
Russia, our partitioning, recently when Walesa was
President
It was time Soviet soldiers withdrew from our country.
Now you know how it was in 1945!
Poland was in captivity!

> *I send you a page where there is a short film about mourning.*
> *In Warsaw, there are 2 caskets with the bodies of the President*
> *Another 32 bodies today come from Russia await further identification.*
> *On Sunday, OBAMA and others come.*

Halina gave me the link to watch the funeral services for Poland's first family live and their subsequent interment in Krakow. On Sunday, April 18, I watched the entire service on my lap top computer, streaming live from Poland. The American media covered very little. I watched as the couple's caskets were driven at a slow pace through the streets of Warsaw, passing Warsaw's city hall and a museum dedicated to the 1944 Warsaw Uprising. The caskets were then flown to Kraków. I watched the funeral mass from Krakow's St Mary's Basilica, with thousands of mourners packing the church and gathered outside. I understood very few of the words that I heard, but I understood the depth of emotion, of sadness, of shock, in the reporting. I watched the live stream for hours. It was important for me to be there where the magnitude of this tragedy was understood, deeply felt, and endured.

As if there were not enough profound ironies in this tragic event, yet another strange twist of fate--the eruption of the Eyjafjallajokull volcano in Iceland-- served to mar the commemoration of the dead. At the very time of the Smolensk crash and its aftermath, including the planned April 18th funeral for President Kaczynski and his wife, the ash spewed from this volcanic eruption caused the closure of the controlled airspace of many European countries resulting in the largest air-traffic shut-down since World War II. The closures caused millions of passengers to be stranded not only in Europe, but across the world. With large parts of European airspace closed to air traffic, many more countries were affected as flights to and from Europe were cancelled. Poland shut down its entire airspace on April 16. The disruption affected the funeral but family members decided not to postpone it even though it would most probably mean that other countries' dignitaries would be unable to attend.

President Barack Obama, Prince of Wales of the United Kingdom, President of Ireland Mary McAleese, Spanish King Juan Carlos I, Spanish Prime Minister Jose Luis Rodriguez Zapetero, South Korean Prime Minister Chung Un-chan, Prime Minister of Canada Stephen Harper among others were all forced to cancel their planned attendance due to the volcanic ash. German Chancellor Angela Merkel was stranded somewhere between Lisbon and northern Italy, so Germany was represented by President Horst Köhler and Foreign Minister Guido Westerwelle, who travelled to Poland in a helicopter. In the presence of the dignitaries who were somehow able to make their way to this important ceremony, and, more importantly, in the presence of the families and friends of those who had lost their lives in the crash, and the citizens of a grieving nation, the services were carried out.

At the coverage of the ceremony for the Polish President and his wife, I watched intently as the camera slowly panned the crowd. As the camera zoomed in on a man in a dark suit standing solemnly and sadly at the memorial I gasped. How is it that President Lech Kaczynski could be standing there at his own funeral? It was like seeing a ghost. I had not known until that point that Lech Kaczynski had an identical twin brother, Jaroslaw, who, even at the age of 60, was virtually indistinguishable in appearance from his brother. Even after I learned this fact, I was still taken aback every time the camera fixed on him. It was yet another strange twist in this most incredible story.

In the European community, much has been written about the Smolensk crash. Thousands of articles can be found on line in the course of internet searches. There is as of yet no book that I am able to find written in the English language about this disaster with the singular exception of a book entitled: " Smolensk Air Crash 10-4-10: Official Facts, Scientific Analysis" by Dr. Mark Laskiewicz published September 8, 2015. When I found this book I downloaded it and began reading it. After about two pages I realized it was a product of the conspiracy theory party which can be found rather prominently on any internet search of the subject of the crash. The deceptively named website "SmolenskCrashNews", is another such source promulgating the theory that there was and is a huge cover up as to the "real" cause of the crash.

Many conspiracy theorists arose from the ashes of this disaster. Most pose a theory that a nefarious Russian plot brought down the plane. Or that Kaczynski was "assassinated" by his political opponents. I understand how conspiracy theorists work and how they spring up with incredible passion in the wake of such events. We certainly are far from immune to them in our own country. But I was surprised and almost shocked, to see than even now, in 2016, Lech Kaczynski's twin brother, chairman of Poland's right-wing Law and Justice party (PiS), is seeking to reopen the investigation of this crash, resurrecting the theory that the plane was actually brought down by an explosive device. I have read and watched so much about this tragic plane crash since it occurred in 2010. The only thing that I can wonder, given all the factual evidence, is not **why** this plane crashed, but **why wouldn't it?** This plane did not need an explosive to bring it down; nor did it need an underground plot to undermine the Polish government. So many mostly human factors conspired to do this; it is inconceivable that, given the myriad of details and circumstances present at the time, that this flight could have ended in any other way than that which it did.

I emailed Halina about my undertaking to write of the Smolensk crash and my amazement that Jaroslaw Kaczynski was actually proposing to reopen this investigation, six years later. In her inimitable and passionate style, she replied:

> *My Dear Linda ;-)))*
>
> *Kaczynski is crazy. He DESTROYS the guidance of SOLIDARITY leader Walesa*
> *This is a despicable man*
> *Linda, Smolensk catastrophe is a combination of events:*
> *lack of organization, adverse weather conditions*
> *horrible Russian military airport; - (((((*
> *terrible airport conditions!!!!!!!!!!!!*

> *and the fact that Polish President Lech Kaczynski wanted at all costs to land in Smolensk*
>
> *This decision was the fault of the Kaczynski brothers*
>
> *They hated Prime Minister Donald Tusk (he is now the head of the European Council)*
>
> *God that day did not give a chance, and therefore all died !!!!!!!!!!!!!!!!*
>
> *In Poland, there are two camps, those who believe in the assassination !!!!!!!!!! (PiS party)*
>
> *Those who believe that it was a big accident !!!!!!!!!!!!! (the rest of the community)*

Personally, I believe the crash was a terrible accident—although entirely preventable. Human factors played the largest role in the crash.

I want to tell the story of this doomed flight for an American, English speaking audience. I want to tell the story from the standpoint of the people involved. The crew, the passengers, the families, the Polish people-- all victims of a catastrophic event, perhaps preventable, but more likely destined to happen. The entire history of Poland and the Polish people can be summed up as one of "destiny". And too often, a sad and tragic one. The Smolensk crash was just another episode in the fateful drama that has consistently played out in the entire course of Polish history. It is ingrained in the very fabric of the Polish people, who, like Sisyphus are forced to roll an immense boulder up a hill, only to have it roll back down, repeating this action for eternity.

CHAPTER ONE

FIRST FORESHADOWING

The Spanish made CASA-295M Polish transport plane was beginning its descent into the Miroslawiec Polish Air Base. It was just after 7:00 pm on Wednesday, January 23, 2008. They were making their third of five stops to discharge passengers—all high ranking Polish Air Force officers returning from the 50th Annual Aviation Safety Conference in Warsaw. Ten attendees had deplaned at Powidz Air Base; fifteen more at Poznán-Krzesiny. Sixteen passengers remained on board. After Miroslawiec, the plane was scheduled to make one more stop at the Swidwin Air Base, home of the 40th Aviation Squadron before returning to their home base--the 13th Aviation Squadron in Krakow. [2]

The majority of the remaining passengers were from the Swidwin Air Base, and included Brigadier General Andrzej Andrzejewski, Commander of the 1st Tactical Air Brigade. Five officers from Miroslawiec Air Base also remained on board and were preparing to disembark. These included the Base Commander, Colonel Jerzy Pilat and LtCol Dariusz Pawlak, Squadron Commander.

Weather at Miroslawiec was poor with a ceiling at 300 feet and a visibility two statute miles in mist. The crew was cleared for a PAR (Precision Approach Radar) approach to runway 12/30. At an altitude of

---

[2] "Plane Crash Kills 20 Polish Officers" Associated Press January 24, 2008 http://www.military.com/NewsContent/0,13319,160664,00.html

less than 100 meters directly above the cloud layer, visibility was so limited the four man crew could not see the ground. [3]

When the plane was at an altitude of about 260 meters, the Miroslawiec Air Traffic Controller told the pilot: *"You're perfectly in the axis. Do you see the runway lights?"* Four seconds later, the pilot responded: *"No, I don't see the lights yet"*. [4]

Now the crew was forced to abort their first landing attempt.

During the second approach, controllers gave the pilot of the CASA six commands to come left onto the correct glide path, but failed to give them any indication as to height. At 2.8 kilometers from the runway the aircraft was 390 feet too high, but controllers reported: *"019, you are exactly on glide path"*, prompting the crew to disconnect the autopilot and make a seven degree bank to the left. The bank continued to increase, unnoticed by the crew. They were busy looking out of the window trying to spot the runway lights and preparing to land and had lost their spatial orientation. During the final stages of their approach, the aircraft continued to bank and began to lose altitude. No one in the cockpit was watching their altitude or artificial horizon indicators. [5]

The aircraft was equipped with a ground proximity warning system (EGPWS) which would have sounded as the plane's bank exceeded 40 degrees, but the system's audio warning was turned off. The flight crew had missed the EGPWS test before departure from Warsaw, even though it was a checklist item, and never corrected the problem--the warning system remained switched off. The pilot was not familiar with the system having never before this time flown a CASA C-295M that was so equipped. [6]{2}

The aircraft reached a bank of 76 degrees at 175 knots before its left wing struck the ground. It hit the ground in a wooded area 1300 meters from the runway and 320 meters left of the runway centerline. About 4.6 meters of the end of the left wing broke off. In another 16 meters, the rest of the left wing crashed into a railway embankment. Just across the tracks

---

[3] "Protokol badania katastrofy lotniczej pod Miroslawcem" 23 Jan 2008 https://pl.wikisource.org/wiki/Protokół_badania_katastrofy_lotniczej_pod_Mirosławcem_-_23_stycznia_2008

[4] Ibid.

[5] Ibid.

[6] Ibid.

there was a collision with the ground resulting in the total destruction of the left side of the hull and breaking off of the left side of the chassis. The right wing and right engine were torn from the aircraft and, sliding along the ground, the remainder of the aircraft collided with a stand of trees 20-30 centimeters in diameter. [7]

The aircraft was totally destroyed. All four crewmembers and all sixteen remaining passengers returning from the aviation safety conference were killed.

In the wake of the accident, the remainder of Poland's nine C-295M's were immediately grounded pending the outcome of the investigation.

The Commander in Chief of the Polish Air Force, General Andrzej Blasik, held a solemn news conference in Warsaw which he began by reading out the names of the men who were killed. "I knew all of them ... and some of them were my friends," he said. [8] In less than two years time, General Blasik would join his friends as he himself would die in the Smolensk crash.

The investigation found that the CASA-295M - one of the air force's two newest C-295s (having just been procured the previous year) and assigned to its 13th Air Transport Squadron, - was fully serviceable at the time of the accident, and that a mix of bad weather, air crew inexperience, and air traffic control failings led to its loss near the Miroslawiec air base.[9]

The investigation concluded that the pilot was performing his first flight with the latest version of the CASA-295, while his co-pilot was not fully trained to operate under instrument flight conditions, and blamed a "temporary" training standard and inadequate documentation. The instrument landing system at Miroslawiec was also inoperative, and its controllers were not trained to handle aircraft types other than the Sukhoi Su-22. [10]

---

[7] Ibid.
[8] "Plane Crash Kills 20 Polish Officers" Associated Press January 24, 2008 http://www.military.com/NewsContent/0,13319,160664,00.html
[9] "Protokol badania katastrofy lotniczej pod Miroslawcem" 23 Jan 2008 https://pl.wikisource.org/wiki/Protokół_badania_katastrofy_lotniczej_pod_Mirosławcem_-_23_stycznia_2008
[10] Ibid.

As a result of the investigation, the airport commander at Miroslawiec, two air traffic controllers and an officer from the Air Operations Centre were dismissed, along with 13th Squadron's commanding officer. Several dozen other personnel also faced losing their jobs.

The accident prompted new procedures under which no force commander would be permitted to travel together with his deputy and any military flight with more than 10 personnel on board must be approved by the chief of the general staff. The new rule did not apply to civilian flights. [11]

Inexperienced pilots. Poor weather conditions. Inaccurate direction from air traffic controllers. Inoperable or overridden warning systems and equipment. High ranking passengers. An aircraft whose crew was so busy looking outside their windows to visualize the landing strip they failed to monitor their altitude. An aircraft that, on a left bank, slammed into trees and crashed just short of the runway. The CASA-295 crash was an eerie foreshadowing of what would happen less than two years later. But when that time came, the ante would be greatly "upped" and the consequences would be even more disastrous.

---

[11] "Polish Flight Skirted Military Protocol" by Marc Champion, 15 Apr 2010 http://www.wsj.com/articles/SB10001424052702303348504575184330003561878

CHAPTER TWO

SECOND FORESHADOWING (SETTING THE STAGE)

In August of 2008, a clash between the former Soviet republic of Georgia and separatists in the South Ossetia and Abkhazia regions, backed by Vladimir Putin's Russian government under the guise of "peacekeeping" drew the attention of the international community. The brief 2008 war was the first time since the fall of the Soviet Union that the Russian military had been used against an independent state, demonstrating Russia's willingness to wage a full-scale military campaign to attain its political objectives.

It was only seven months since the CASA-295M crash.

On the morning of August 12, 2008 a Polish Air Force Tu-154M from the special regiment assigned to fly the President and other VIPs, transported the presidents of Lithuania and Estonia and the Prime Minister of Latvia to Warsaw where Polish President Lech Kaczynski joined the prestigious group on board the VIP plane. The contingent was headed to Tbilisi to attend a rally in support of the Georgian President Mikheil Saakashvili. Captain Gregory Pietruczuk of the 36th Aviation Regiment, a special aviation regiment of the Polish Air Force whose most important mission was the transport of Polish politicians and Ministry of National Defense highest officials, had gotten the nod to head the crew of this multinational mission. His co-pilot was Captain Arkadiusz Protasiuk; his navigator, Captain Robert Grzywna. These two would later be the pilot in command, and the co-pilot, respectively, of the doomed Smolensk flight.

The plane was scheduled to fly from Warsaw to Simferopol in the Crimea to pick up Ukrainian President Viktor Yushchenko. The final leg of the flight plan was to Ganja, Azerbaijan where the VIP contingent was to take ground transportation, provided by Tbilisi's mayor, the 300 kilometers to the Georgian capital for the rally.

Flying with the heads of state, were Polish ministers Wladyslaw Stasiak (Chief of the Chancellery of the President of Poland—who would later die in the Smolensk crash) and Maciej Łopiński (Chief of the President's Cabinet) and members of the presidential security teams and members of the media.

In Simferopol, while the plane was refueling and the dignitaries waited in the VIP lounge, Minister Stasiak came on board the aircraft. Stasiak informed Captain Pietruczuk that, due to security concerns and taking into consideration the other international officials on board, President Kaczynski wanted to fly directly to Tbilisi, and not - as was the plan - to Azerbaijan with the already arranged ground transportation to the Georgian capital.

"Well, I will have to see if we can safely fly there and land." Captain Pietruczuk told the Chancellor. [12]

Upon researching his options, the Captain found out that not much was known about what was happening in the skies over Tbilisi or at the airport. They had no diplomatic approval to fly to Georgia nor did they have any information about the weather situation at the airport, or about the state of navigation systems there. There was an armed conflict going on in the country. After all, this was the reason the dignitaries were flying there. Captain Pietruczuk did not know if he would have any radio communication. He also understood the reality that, in the territory of Georgia, Russian warplanes were operating. The Tu-154 did not have a radar warning or IFF (Identification Friend or Foe) system; they would be flying blind into a war zone vulnerable to shoot down or collision with

---

[12] "Tchórz" zabolał mnie najbardziej"
Rozmawiali Agnieszka Kublik i Wojciech Czuchnowski 29.03.2011 http://wyborcza.pl/1,76842,9337581,_Tchorz__zabolal_mnie_najbardziej.html

other aircraft in the area. It had not been reported that the runway at Tbilisi had ever been directly hit by any bullet or a bomb "but I do not know if there was an outbreak of five or ten meters from the runway," Pietruczuk later said. "The landing strip can be damaged over a very large area, and the Tupolev needs a few kilometers runway to land. For me, it was a crucial piece of information, if I have the landing strip or not. Not knowing this, I could not - with the leaders of the five countries on board - take such a risk." [13]

Pietruczuk even went so far as to attempt to contact people he knew in Tbilisi to determine the conditions there, but these people had already fled from the capital, so did not know what was happening at the airport there or if it was even still open.

Stasiak, in spite of all these problematic issues, persisted with the President's demand that the pilot take the plane directly to Tbilisi.

Meanwhile one of the flight attendants came into the cockpit to inform the pilot what was happening on board among the passengers. The situation was causing great tension. It was August and the air conditioner was not working to cool the passenger cabin. The people in the rear were outright baking in the heat while the plane sat on the tarmac.

Captain Pietruczuk's next course of action was to take the matter to his boss, the commander of the 36th Special Squadron Colonel Tomasz Pietrzak . After making this contact and explaining the situation, the squadron commander supported his pilot's decision not to risk flying into Tbilisi.

Pietruczuk also consulted with the security chiefs for the other Presidential passengers on board the aircraft. None of them were prepared for the possibility of flying directly into the Georgian capital. "And even if we flew there," Pietruczuk said, "What then? We land, we open the door, and then what? The protection problems begin—we must ensure armored cars, protection in place, etc." [14] There was no plan and no preparation for such an undertaking which was uncertain at best and dangerous at worst.

Standing fast in his refusal to follow the Polish President's order, Pietruczuk received another call. This time it was from General Krzysztof

---

[13] Ibid.
[14] Ibid.

Zaleski, Deputy Commander of the Air Force, ordering him to carry out the desires of the President. Pietruczuk relayed all of his concerns to the Air Force Commander, and asked him if there were any radar protection systems which would ensure the aircraft's safety in the war zone. The General had no answer to this question, so he proposed a possible solution. If Pietruczuk would not fly into Tbilisi, perhaps it would be possible to replace him as pilot in command with the copilot, Captain Protasiuk. But this was not a valid option since Protasiuk was not trained and qualified as an aircraft commander in the Tupolev. Even if it had been possible, Pietruczuk believed the situation would not change since Protasiuk concurred with his position not to fly into Tbilisi. "He would take the same position as I did. He would refuse." [15]

Alarmed about the conflict and the stalemate that was reached, General Zaleski sent a fax from Warsaw to the commander of the 36th Aviation Squadron ordering execution of the will of President Kaczynski. On his letterhead Zaleski wrote by hand: "Please immediately execute the command of the President and perform flight from Ganja airport to Tbilisi." By this, General Zaleski was proposing the plane fly as scheduled to Ganja, but then continue from there with a flight into Tbilisi. But this, too, was not possible since the aircraft had no permission to enter the airspace of countries whose borders it would have to cross in order to perform a flight after the modified route. There was the concomitant risk that the aircraft would be treated as a" disturber ". [16] The Tu-154M was not designed to operate in the zone of armed conflict.

Pietruczuk next received a call from his squadron commander who had received and read Zaleski's fax. The colonel reluctantly told his pilot, "Greg, listen, they have sent a written order." [17] He desperately wanted to support his pilot but his back was to the wall. The decision was over his head.

The VIP passengers now began reboarding the plane for the continuation of the flight—whatever that might entail. Once everyone was on board, President Kaczynski entered the cockpit.

---

[15] Ibid.
[16] Ibid.
[17] Ibid.

"Gentlemen," he addressed the crew, "Who is the head of the armed forces?"

Pietruczuk replied, "You, Mr. President."

"Then I suggest you follow the command and fly to Tbilisi." [18]

Without waiting for any response or explanation of the inadvisability of the order, Kaczynski turned and left the cockpit.

Pietruczuk once again analyzed the situation. He discussed it with his crew. He checked and double checked if there was anything he might have overlooked. But he could come to no other conclusion than that the risk of flying into Tbilisi was too great, and he would not do it. He had the full support and the backing of his crew, which was very important to him. He was convinced, as was his crew, of the rationality of his argument. They felt there was only a political argument in the mind of President Kaczynski that the Polish flight needed to land before President Sarkozy of France who was in the process of brokering a ceasefire in the conflict and was also flying that day into Georgia.[19]

"The ministers tried to convince me that if the President of France can fly to Tbilisi, then we can," recalled Pietruczuk, "But I could not accept such an assumption. I did not know what information the French had, what they knew about the airport, what kind of plane they were flying, and consequently, what conditions they needed to land."

The French were, in fact, flying in to Georgia from Russia, and they were accompanied by Russian fighters. [20]

President Kaczynski and his men finally were forced to concede that nothing else could be done. They would have to fly the original plan to Azerbaijan.

---

[18] "Incydent gruziński oczami pierwszego pilota" by Marcin Górka 28.04.2010 http://wyborcza.pl/1,76842,7821881,Incydent_gruzinski_oczami_pierwszego_pilota.html

[19] "Tchórz" zabolał mnie najbardziej" Rozmawiali Agnieszka Kublik i Wojciech Czuchnowski 29.03.2011 http://wyborcza.pl/1,76842,9337581,_Tchorz_zabolal_mnie_najbardziej.html

[20] "Incydent gruziński oczami pierwszego pilota" by Marcin Górka 28.04.2010 http://wyborcza.pl/1,76842,7821881,Incydent_gruzinski_oczami_pierwszego_pilota.html

The flight proceeded as originally scheduled. Upon disembarking at the completion of the flight to Azerbaijan, Kaczynski thanked the crew but was decidedly cold. As he shook the hand of Captain Pietruczuk, Kaczynski looked him in the eye and said – "I have yet to finish with this. When we return to country I will report this situation to the commander of the Air Force and the Minister of National Defense. We shall deal with this matter." [21]

The entire crew witnessed this. All were amazed at Kaczynski's attitude. [22]

The VIP contingent safely made its way to the Georgian capital by ground. After celebrating the fifth anniversary of Georgia's Rose Revolution, the country's president Mikhail Saakashvili took his guest and long-time ally, Lech Kaczynski, on a tour near the war-ravaged region of South Ossetia. Shortly afterwards their convoy was fired upon by Russian soldiers. No one was hurt. After his return to Warsaw, President Kaczynski said that nobody but him should be blamed for the incident, because it was he who asked to change the route of the convoy. It was originally planned that he would only visit Tbilisi, but the Polish leader decided that he should also inspect the refugee camp near the South Ossetian border. *"The risk was necessary. These are the obligations of the President of Poland. Everything that happened in Georgia happened under my agreement. I was not afraid,"* he said. [23]

The visit in support of Georgian President Saakashvili was considered a great diplomatic success for President Kaczynski, but no matter. Despite the incident where the convoy was fired upon, which should have served as proof to Kaczynski of the danger that would have been posed had the Tupolev tried to land there, the pilot's refusal of his order to fly the plane directly to the capital city stuck in his craw and he was not about to let it go.

---

[21] "Tchórz" zabolał mnie najbardziej" Rozmawiali Agnieszka Kublik i Wojciech Czuchnowski 29.03.2011 http://wyborcza.pl/1,76842,9337581,_Tchorz_ zabolal_mnie_najbardziej.html

[22] Ibid.

[23] 'Shots fired' near Georgian presidential motorcade
Published time: 24 Nov, 2008 10:56 Edited time: 24 Nov, 2008 13:56
https://www.rt.com/news/shots-fired-near-georgian-presidential-motorcade/

After returning to Poland, Kaczynski continued to threaten that there would be consequences for the pilot. The Polish newspaper "Dziennik" reported Kaczynski as saying, "If someone decides to become a pilot, he cannot be fearful."

"What hurt the most," Pietruczuk later recounted, "Is when I heard that the president in an interview with reporters on board called me a 'fearful' pilot. Personally, I was hurt. I have flown to Iraq, to Afghanistan; I flew during the conflict in Bosnia and Chad and never felt fear. It hurt me all the more because I was trying to carry out my duties as best as I can. My duties are to ensure maximum safety for passengers, and in this case very important passengers. Today with full determination, I can say that this attitude {refusing the President's order} required more courage." [24]

Kaczynski's dispute with the pilot had further consequences. After the delegation returned on August 25, Polish Parliament member Karol Karski submitted to the prosecutor notice of the possibility of the commission of a crime by the aircraft captain, who "refused to obey the order of the President." [25]

"The soldier has brought shame to the Polish State and its Armed Forces," Karski alleged in his complaint. "He showed cowardice, when on the same day in Tbilisi landed the plane of the president of France. He brought shame to the Polish State in the eyes of other heads of state then on board and led to mocking of the Poles in articles in the foreign press." [26]

He alleged that Pietruczuk "hindered the president in performing his constitutional duties, exposed him to danger of loss of life (because the land route ran "near the front line"). Karski asked: "Is the government going to tolerate this type of {behavior} in professional soldiers and cowardice in the presence of the Head of State?" He further warned that permitting this disobedience can lead to a situation that "on the sea Polish warships will not go (because the masters recognize that it is dangerous), Polish patrols on peacekeeping missions will refuse to leave the area (because it is not

---

[24] "Incydent gruziński oczami pierwszego pilota" by Marcin Górka 28.04.2010 http://wyborcza.pl/1,76842,7821881,Incydent_gruzinski_oczami_pierwszego_pilota.html
[25] Ibid.
[26] Ibid.

safe), and in the situation of a possible invasion of Poland the soldiers will refuse to defend it." [27]

After reviewing all the evidence and hearing all the witnesses, the prosecutor declined to press any charges against Captain Pietruczuk saying, "Taking everything into account and in view of the importance and the number of passengers, the crew commander could not do otherwise… This has been confirmed by the investigation conducted … It should be noted that he was acting under pressure in assuming the responsibility for the decision…Captain Gregory Pietruczuk demonstrated responsibility, professionalism and a very good knowledge of the regulations, which absolutely should not be regarded as a lack of discipline or cowardice. On the contrary, he acted in accordance with the highest values of ensuring the safety of the most important person in the country and the passengers and crew. The main decision-maker in an aircraft is the commander who is responsible for the safety of the ship. The decision taken by Captain Pietruczuk was correct and in accordance with the rules." [28]

The prosecutor further opined that "Although the president is the head of the army, the 'terms of flights of the armed forces' clearly say that on an airplane the pilot's decisions must supersede all, regardless of their military rank and status." [29]

After the proceedings, Defense Minister Bogdan Klich honored Captain Pietruczuk with a Silver Cross for the Defense of Homeland in recognition of his "adherence to procedures and responsibility for the safety of the four presidents on board."

Even after all was said and done in this troubling incident, the prosecutor's decision provoked a sharp reaction from the head of Poland's PiS party, Przemysław Gosiewski. In a parliamentary inquiry of September 23, 2008 Gosiewski wrote to the Defense Minister: "Does the Minister in deciding not to take action in this case, want to show that it will be weak in future cases of insubordination, cowardice and refusing to follow orders?" [30]

---

[27] Ibid.
[28] Ibid.
[29] Ibid.
[30] Ibid.

Gosiewski was to later die in the Smolensk crash.

Captain Gregory Pietruczuk was never asked to fly the Polish President again. In the wake of this incident, he would be troubled with depression in the years that followed.

CHAPTER THREE

KATYN

For the purposes of understanding the context in which the rest of this story occurs, we need to take a little side trip. We need to understand a little bit about the "Katyn Massacre".

After the German invasion of Poland in September of 1939, as part of a secret prearranged pact made with the German government, the Russians invaded Poland from the east. Polish officers and senior NCO's and other members of the Polish intelligentsia and educated and landed classes were captured by the Red Army, arrested and deported to Russia. There they were kept in three prison camps: Kozielsk, Starobielsk, and Ostashkov.

Kozielsk, contained more than just officers. It contained arrested Polish university lecturers, surgeons, physicians, barristers and lawyers. One woman prisoner was held at Kozielsk – Janina Lewandowski. Her body was found at Katyn clothed in the uniform of the Polish Air Force. A total of 5,000 Polish citizens were imprisoned at Kozielsk during WWII.

Ostashkov held officers – but it also held anybody from Poland who was considered to be 'bourgeois'. A total of 6,570 prisoners were held here.

Starobielsk held only officers from the Polish military which totaled 4,000 men.

On 5 March 1940 the chief of the NKVD (People's Commissariat for Internal Affairs—i.e, the Soviet Secret Police) Lavrentiy Beria issued an order to execute 25,700 Polish "nationalists and counterrevolutionaries" and others that the Soviets deemed to be "intelligence agents, gendarmes, landowners, saboteurs, factory owners, lawyers, officials, and priests" kept at camps and prisons in occupied western Ukraine and Belarus. Of those selected for execution, 4,421 were from Kozielsk, 3,820 from Starobielsk, 6,311 from Ostashkov, and 7,305 from Byelorussian and Ukrainian prisons. The order had been approved by the Soviet Politburo, and its leader, Joseph Stalin. [31]

Prisoners from the Kozielsk camp were executed in the Katyn Forest; those from the Starobielsk camp were murdered in the inner NKVD prison of Kharkiv and the bodies were buried near the village of Piatykhatky; and officers from the Ostashkov camp were murdered in the internal NKVD prison of Kalinin (Tver) and buried in Mednoye.

So, while the term "Katyn Massacre" originally referred to the massacre at Katyn Forest near Smolensk, Russia, of Polish military officers confined at the Kozelsk prisoner of war camp, the term subsequently came to be applied also to the execution of prisoners of war held at Starobielsk and Ostashkov camps, and political prisoners in West Belarus and West Ukraine. All were shot, on Stalin's orders, at Katyn Forest, at the NKVD Smolensk headquarters, or at a slaughterhouse in that same city, or at prisons in Kalinin (Tver), Kharkiv, Moscow, and other Soviet cities.

The executions were meticulously organized and coldly carried out in several locations but basically in the same calculated and horrific fashion.

Vasily Mikhailovich Blokhin, chief executioner for the NKVD—and quite possibly the most prolific executioner in history—is reported to have personally shot and killed 7,000 of the condemned, some as young as 18, from the Ostashkov camp at Kalinin prison, over a period of 28 days in April 1940. The killings were methodical. [32]

After the condemned individual's personal information was checked and approved, he was handcuffed and led to a cell insulated with stacks of sandbags along the walls, and a heavy, felt-lined door. The victim was told to kneel in the middle of the cell, and was then approached from behind by the executioner and immediately shot in the back of the head or neck. The body was carried out through the opposite door and laid in one of the five or six waiting trucks, whereupon the next condemned was taken inside and subjected to the same fate. In addition to muffling by the rough

---

[31] Katyn Massacre," Wikipedia, http://en.wikipedia.org/wiki/Katyn_massacre
[32] Ibid.

insulation in the execution cell, the pistol gunshots were also masked by the operation of loud machines (perhaps fans) throughout the night.

Those from the camps who were to be executed in the Katyn forest were transported two days by train without food or water to their killing field. When they arrived at their final destination, they were bundled onto coaches with windows smeared with cement to obscure their view. After a short drive, the men were directed one by one to the rear door of the vehicle. [33]

When the prisoners were led out of their transport coach, they were marched ahead to an L-shaped pit which already contained the fresh corpses of their fellow Polish officers who had gone before. Those who struggled or attempted to escape had their hands tied and a choke knot applied to his neck. Those who still tried to break free had their skulls smashed, or were repeatedly bayoneted. Eventually all were shot, usually with German-made .25 ACP Walther Model 2 pistols supplied by Moscow. The first such transport contained 390 prisoners, but the executioners had difficulty killing so many people in one night. The following transports held no more than 250. [34]

Those who died at Katyn included soldiers (an admiral, two generals, 24 colonels, 79 lieutenant colonels, 258 majors, 654 captains, 17 naval captains, 85 privates, 3,420 non-commissioned officers, and seven chaplains), 200 pilots, government representatives and royalty (a prince, 43 officials), and civilians (three landowners, 131 refugees, 20 university professors, 300 physicians; several hundred lawyers, engineers, and teachers; and more than 100 writers and journalists). In all, the NKVD executed almost half the Polish officer corps including 14 Polish Generals. [35]

The execution sites and mass graves went undiscovered until 1943 when the government of Nazi Germany announced they had uncovered mass graves containing over 4,300 Polish officers in the Katyn Forest near Smolensk in Russia. The Germans claimed that they found a ditch 28 meters long and 16 meters wide at the Hill of Goats in which were

---

[33] "Katyn Forest Massacre," Wikipedia, https://en.wikipedia.org/wiki/Katyn_Forest_Massacre

[34] Ibid.

[35] Ibid.

3,000 bodies piled up in layers of twelve. All the bodies were fully dressed in military uniform; some were bound and all had pistol shots to the back of their heads. The Germans claimed that the bodies were in good condition. The soil had done a great deal to preserve the bodies and any documentation found on them.

When the London-based Polish government-in-exile asked for an investigation by the International Red Cross, Stalin immediately severed diplomatic relations with it. The USSR claimed that the victims had been murdered by the Nazis in 1941 and continued to deny responsibility for the massacres until 1990. [36]

With the openness that followed the fall of the Soviet Union, the government of Mikhail Gorbechev, in the era of "glasnost," released a flood of previously classified documents. Though the Russians had up until that time firmly maintained that the Germans were responsible for the massacre of the Polish nationals in or near the Katyn forest, the release of the documents prompted the Soviet government to finally admit that the executions were, in fact, carried out by the Soviet Union NKVD, and that the Soviet government had deliberately covered up their crime.

An investigation conducted by the Prosecutor General's Office of the Soviet Union (1990–1991) and the Russian Federation (1991–2004) confirmed Soviet responsibility for the massacres, but refused to classify this action as a war crime or an act of genocide. The investigation was closed on the grounds that the perpetrators of the atrocity were already dead, and since the Russian government would not classify the dead as victims of Stalinist repressions, formal posthumous rehabilitation was deemed inapplicable. [37]

But the world now knew the truth. The Poles officially received confirmation of what they had already long suspected. But that did not mitigate the pain of the families who had lost loved ones, or help the Polish people to "get over" this crime without punishment.

---

[36] Ibid.

[37] "Katyn Massacre," Wikipedia, http://en.wikipedia.org/wiki/Katyn_massacre

CHAPTER FOUR

"PAMIĘTAMY" (WE REMEMBER)

On April 7, 2010, a Tu-154M from the 36th Special Regiment of Aviation Transport (SPLT) took Polish Prime Minister Donald Tusk to Smolensk for a special ceremony to commemorate the 70th anniversary of the Katyn massacre. He was accompanied by a delegation which included Former Polish President Lech Walesa, former Prime Minister Tadeusz Mazowiecki, film director Andrzej Wajda (his own father a victim of the massacre) director of the well-received film "Katyn" which highlighted the anguish of the families of the Katyn victims, and other representatives of Polish culture and clergy. There they would be joined by then Russian Prime Minister Vladimir Putin.

This historic meeting was planned the previous year during Putin's visit to Poland on the occasion of the 70th anniversary of the Second World War. At that time, Prime Minister Putin extended an invitation to his Polish counterpart, Prime Minister Donald Tusk, to join him at the Katyn memorial in Smolensk to commemorate the 70th anniversary of the forest massacre in 2010. Tusk, whose forward looking platform embraced the European Union, pushed for Poland to play a greater role at the heart of E.U. institutions, and forged greater political and economic ties with Germany called the invitation an important step in improving bilateral ties. "I accepted Prime Minister Vladimir Putin's invitation with satisfaction as I see that he has made a really important step," Tusk told members of the Polish parliament. He said the invitation "is important as a remembrance for the victims and also for promoting friendly Polish-Russian relations." [38] It would be the first time that a Russian prime minister had commemorated the victims of Katyn. This was indeed a demonstration of historical significance for the two countries who have shared mutual animosities throughout much of their respective histories. By extending this invitation to his Polish counterpart, Putin hoped it would be symbolic of both their countries forgetting their differences and moving forward.

Polish President Lech Kaczynski was not invited to the ceremony. "Moving forward" was not on the agenda of the Polish Law and Justice (PiS) party, led by Kaczynski who represented the old values of Poland –traditional, patriotic, Catholic, and some might say "euro-skeptic." Nor was it on the agenda of Poland's top generals and military officers. Kaczynski and his party held fast to the painful memories of Poland's past, taking a certain pride in the tradition of Poland's history of martyrdom. The pain many Poles felt about the Katyn massacre was as raw and oppressive 70 years later as it was on the day German troops first discovered the corpses of Polish citizens in a mass grave in the Katyn forest near Smolensk, Russia.

Kaczynski decided to arrange a memorial ceremony of his own and bring along members of his own party, sympathetic to his point of view including high ranking members of the Polish military, Polish parliament members, clergy, and some families of descendents of the Katyn killings. Kaczynski would arrange to hold this ceremony also at the Katyn memorial in Smolensk and it would take place three days after the ceremony held by Vladimir Putin and Donald Tusk. They would commemorate the Katyn massacre in their own way with their own contingent of guests.

For the Prime Minister's trip on April 7th, the Tupolev was piloted by LtCol Bartosz Stroiński, who was the current deputy commander of the 36th SPLT. His co-pilot for the flight was Captain Arkadiusz (Arek) Protasiuk. The two men were more than just colleagues—they were good friends. Arek was in very good spirits that day, joking with the crew and lending to an easy atmosphere in the cockpit as his fellow crewmembers

---

[38] "Tusk praises Russia's invitation to Katyn massacre memorial" WORLD 15:28 04.02.2010 http://sputniknews.com/world/20100204/157771784.html

always remembered him doing. Bartosz and Arek were scheduled to fly the Prime Minister to the United States the following Monday and the two men talked about that flight. Arek was looking forward to it and planned to buy a camera to document the trip. The weather was perfect that day and the flight to Smolensk a quiet and easy one. [39]

The winter snow had not yet finished thawing on the ground under the pine trees in the western Russian forest of Katyn on that day. The air was clear, but full of the moisture only a spring thaw in the woods can bring. Many of the attendees were bundled in their winter coats and scarves. Others braved the chill in just suit and tie.

To the steady thrumming of a snare drum, Polish Prime Minister Donald Tusk and Russian Prime Minister Vladimir Putin followed slowly behind the two Polish and two Russian soldiers as they marched two large wreaths forward to an altar before the red brick Katyn memorial wall. One wreath, carried by the Polish soldiers bore a ribbon in the colors of the Polish flag—red and white. The other, carried by the Russian soldiers bore the red, white, and blue of the Russian flag. The two men stood solemnly before the wreaths in the cemetery complex. Each accepted a large blue urn containing a candle to set down beside the wreaths. Donald Tusk bowed his head in tribute, then Vladimir Putin did the same.

Ecumenical prayers of Polish priests of different religions – Orthodox, Catholic, Jewish and Muslim (representatives of all the religions of those executed; Belarusians, Russians, Ukrainians and Jews are buried in Katyn) – sounded before Donald Tusk and Vladimir Putin laid their respective country's wreaths on their respective side of the memorial. On the Russian side of the memorial, where the dead Soviet citizens are buried, only an Orthodox prayer service was held. The live broadcast went out only on Polish television.

After the prayers and the wreath-laying, and after the Russian military band played both Russia's and Poland's national anthems, the two Prime Ministers gave their remarks.

Putin spoke first. – "We are gathered here in connection with shared memory and shame. We bow our heads before those who bravely accepted

---

[39] "Tupolev pilot friend: We were like a family with Arek" http://www.fakt.pl/Przyjaciel-pilota-tupolewa-Bylismy-z-Arkiem-jak-rodzina,artykuly,71923,1.html

death here, those whose struggle, hope, and talents have been trampled here. You can not erase from memory the martyrdom of innocent victims. In this land are citizens of Russia, who were destroyed during the Great Purge of the 1930s, Polish citizens who were killed on Stalin's orders, and those who died at the hands of the Nazis during the Great Patriotic War. At Katyn they are forever joined in their fate. Here, as brother and brother in a common grave they have eternal peace, but are not forgotten." [40]

In his remarks, Putin urged reconciliation between Poland and Russia. But he fell short in offering an actual apology for the Katyn tragedy. In fact, he emphasized that the Russian people, too, suffered at the hands of Stalin's regime. "A lie was told for decades, but we cannot blame the Russian people for it," he said. "In our country there has been a clear political, legal and moral judgment made of the evil acts of this totalitarian regime, and this judgment cannot be revised… in no way can this crime ever be justified… for this crime was responsible for the martyred death of both Soviet citizens and Polish officers." Putin condemned Stalin's claims that the missing officers had "fled to Manchuria" by saying "With decades of cynical lies, they tried to blot out the truth about the Katyn shootings. It would be a similar kind of falsehood to … place the blame for these crimes on the Russian people" [41]

"However hard it may be, we must try to come to terms with a common historical truth and realize that we cannot go on living in the past alone."

Prime Minister Tusk told those gathered at the memorial, "We still have a way to go on the road to reconciliation. A word of truth can mobilize two peoples looking for the road to reconciliation. Are we capable of transforming a lie into reconciliation? We must believe we can…Prime Minister Putin, the empty eye sockets of those killed here by a shot to the back of the head are looking at us today and waiting to see whether we are ready to turn this lie into reconciliation…Every name is important for us, all information, all testimony. We will always remember those killed here… We want to share this truth…make it sound forth…it is like a suit

---

[40] "President Goes to the Ceremony to Katyn" April 9, 2010 http://www.se.pl/wiadomosci/swiat/putin-poko-ni-sie-polskim-bohaterom-w-katyniu_135709.html
[41] "Russia and Poland honor Katyn massacre dead" April 7, 2010
http://www.dw.com/en/russia-and-poland-honor-katyn-massacre-dead/a-5440981

of armor for all of us, for the generations of postwar Poland. With this armor we survived… Are we able to put violence and lies behind us and turn toward reconciliation? If we do, it will be a victory for the soldiers who were killed in Katyn." [42]

After the ceremony, Tusk and Putin attended a luncheon together and met to discuss some difficult political issues between their two countries. Tusk and his contingent then returned to Poland.

---

[42] Ibid.

CHAPTER FIVE

PREPARATIONS

On April 10, 2010, Polish President Lech Kaczynski would make his own pilgrimage to the Katyn Memorial in Smolensk. The President would be accompanied by his wife, Maria, and a contingent of 86 others including members of the President's staff, representatives of the Polish Parliament, all four military service chiefs, clergy, and descendents of some of the victims of the Katyn massacre which had occurred now 70 years ago.

The subject of commemorating the 70th anniversary of the Katyn Massacre, including the possibility of the Polish President visiting the memorial, was raised on Dec 8, 2009 in a meeting of the Polish Under-Secretary of State with the Ambassador of the Russian Federation to Poland. Planning began from that point to organize this solemn and historic event. On Feb 23, 2010, the Chief of the Presidential Office confirmed the President's planned participation as well as his office's full readiness to cooperate and co-ordinate efforts to bring this undertaking to fruition. [43]

---

[43] Final Report from the examination of the aviation accident no. 192/2010/11 involving the Tu-154M airplane, tail number 101, which occurred on April 10, 2010 in the area of the Smolensk North airfield (the Polish report)

On March 9, 2010, the Polish President's Organizational Support Team placed an order with the 36th Regiment for two flights to Smolensk on April 10, 2010 to be performed by a Tu-154M and a Yak-40 aircraft. [44]

Notes were sent to the 3rd European Department of the Russian Federation on March 22, 2010 containing a request to have current airport charts and procedures accessible as well as an escort crew (a guide navigator) sent to Warsaw to lead the flight. Nine days later, the request for the guide navigator was cancelled because, it was explained, a Russian speaking crew was assigned for the flight. [45]

The Polish preparation group planned to go to the Smolensk air field on April 5 so they could oversee preparation for the visit. Officers from Poland's Government Protection Bureau (BOR) made an attempt to reconnaissance the Smolensk North airport on April 6 in order to assess the airport's preparation in terms of security. Because the preparation group did not contain any representative of the 36th Regiment no assessment of the airport's preparation in the aspect of flight safety could be made. There was no regulation that directed that such an inspection would be carried out. The Polish embassy in Moscow had not been previously notified of the intention of the BOR officials to visit the airport and they felt they could not ask the Russian side for a clearance to enter the airport area. So, the BOR officers never set foot on the airfield.

Initially, Deputy Commander of the 36th Regiment Lt. Col. Bartosz Stroiński was to captain the flight on April 10 as he did on April 7; however, he had a family conflict and requested he be replaced as pilot in command. The assignment was given to Captain Arkadiusz Protasiuk. The co-pilot would be Major Robert Grzywna; he was informed of his assignment to the flight about two weeks in advance. [46]

On Apr 9, during the morning brief in the squadron leader's room the tasks, including the final crew assignments were made for the next day's flight. Lieutenant Andrzej Michalak, was selected as the flight engineer. A navigator had yet to be assigned. In the course of the brief, the squadron leader twice changed navigators. Originally, the only full-time navigator

---

[44] Ibid.
[45] Ibid.
[46] Ibid.

in the Regiment was assigned but he was due to fly to the United States and Canada on Apr 12, and an Apr 10 flight to Smolensk would not allow him enough time to prepare for his trans-Atlantic trip. Still another airman did not have an entry visa to the Russian Federation. After checking recency of visas in terms of the flight to Smolensk, Captain Protasiuk requested Lieutenant Arthur Zietek to be his navigator for the flight and he was so assigned. At the time this decision was made, Lieutenant Zietek was on an assignment co-piloting a Yak-40 VIP flight to Gdansk. The squadron leader ordered that he be informed of his assignment ASAP. After his return from the Gdansk flight, at 6:30pm on the 9th, he went home and began preparing for the next day's flight. According to his wife, he was studying maps and reviewing weather conditions forecast for the Warsaw-Smolensk flight route. He summarized preparations by stating that he expected fog during his performance of the task, and ended his preparations about 8:00pm. [47]

On April 9 at 2:15pm, Captain Protasiuk telephoned the Warsaw-Okecie airfield weather forecaster on duty in order to check the preliminary weather forecast for the flight to Smolensk. The forecaster predicted visibility 4-5 kilometers, with medium and tall clouds, with cloud base lowering to 200-300 meters a possibility. While he did not forecast weather conditions below crew minima for the time of the aircraft landing he suggested that the worst conditions would be present during morning hours, at the time of the scheduled landing of the Yak-40 aircraft which was ferrying a group of journalists to Smolensk for the ceremony in advance of the President's plane. [48]

The rest of the pre-flight preparations took place later on that day (the 9th) in the afternoon and evening. Some were not undertaken until the actual morning of the flight.

---

[47] Ibid.
[48] Ibid.

CHAPTER SIX

THE COCKPIT CREW

The cockpit crew was now established for the mission to transport the Polish President and his contingent to Smolensk on April 10. Captain Arkadiusz Prosasiuk would fly as Pilot in Command, Major Robert Grzywna would co-pilot, the navigator was Lieutenant Arthur Zietek, and the flight engineer Warrant Officer Andrzej Michalak.

Just a few months earlier, this very same crew had worked together on a humanitarian mission to Haiti in support of earthquake relief for the beleaguered country. The island of Hispaniola had sustained a major quake on January 12. Measuring 7.0 on the Richter scale the quake had its most devastating effect on Haiti.

On January 20, 2010 Polish television cameras at the military airport in Warsaw showed the four pilots, surrounded by dozens of firefighters packing donations for victims of the earthquake. The Tu-154M took off from Warsaw Chopin Airport (Okecie) at 16:40. On board was eighteen tons of aid; three to four tons of gifts, mainly blankets, sheets, tents and canned food and rice, medicines, medical equipment and food donated by the Polish Medical Mission. The flight also included seven medical providers.

The flight was made with two stopovers – Keflavik, Iceland and the military base in Bangor, Maine, USA. Two crews flew out of Warsaw on the Tu-154M. Due to the limits on working time, one of them would perform the flight to the US while the second crew would continue the flight to Port-au-Prince. After arriving in Haiti and unloading the cargo and the humanitarian workers, the aircraft was flown to the Dominican Republic for a 24-hour rest.

The plane began its return trip January 23rd with the intention of following the same route as the Tupolev took to get there—with the two stopovers in Bangor Maine and Keflavik, Iceland. But on the way back the aircraft suffered a serious problem with a failure of the autopilot and the aileron control system on the plane and had to make an emergency landing in Puerto Rico.

The Air Traffic Controller in the tower recalled that day and his amazement that despite the tense situation, Captain Protasiuk was "neither stressed nor confused…I watched the position of the Polish Tupolev and I could not believe it. He approached at an ideal rate and perfect glide path." If he had not known otherwise, the controller remarked that he would never have known the aircraft was experiencing a problem at all, so perfect was the landing. "I was completely stunned. Landing without the control system? Such a thing I have never seen before. This guy had to be a champion of champions…."[49]

The 36th Regiment back in Warsaw set up a crisis team to help the crew repair the problem. It consisted of three sub-groups: technicians in Puerto Rico, the second regiment in Poland and professionals in Russia. After consultations with the experts and engineers from Russia the crew managed to repair the Tu-154.

There was not time to repair the autopilot; technicians repaired only the aileron control system. "As soon as they fixed the problem," the Puerto Rico air traffic controller marveled, "those boys reboarded their aircraft and flew away as if nothing had happened". [50]

For 14 hours Protasiuk and his crew flew without the benefit of autopilot, making four stop overs before finally arriving safely back in Warsaw.

---

[49] " Tu-154 ponownie leci na Haiti," 20 Jan 2010, Lotniczapolska, http://lotniczapolska.pl/Tu-154-ponownie-leci-na-Haiti,11361
[50] Ibid.

On February 4 Captain Protasiuk and his crew received an award for the mission in Haiti and for piloting the plane safely home under extremely difficult conditions.

Thirty-six year old Captain Arkadiusz Protasiuk was born 13 November 1974 in Siedlce, Poland. He had been with the 36th Special Regiment since his graduation from the Polish Air Force Academy in Deblin in 1997.

"Since he was small he wanted to fly. It was his dream," said his parents Wladyslaw and Lucyna Protasiuk. "From an early age he wanted to be a pilot. I remember when as a child he watched the sky for flying planes. Surely he was already imagining that someday he would be sitting in the cockpit at the controls of such a great machine. I was afraid that the sky would swallow him, but I was also proud that he had realized his dream as one of the best pilots, transporting the prime minister and president." [51]

Protasiuk first trained as a co-pilot for the Regiment's Yakovlev (Yak)-40 aircraft. In 2001, he trained as both navigator and co-pilot in the Tupolev (Tu)-154. In 2005, he began training to become a commander of the Yak-40. As of April 2010, he had just under 500 hours flying as Pilot in Command of the Tu-154M. Most of his flight hours (about 1800) were as co-pilot of the Tupolev. He flew over 600 hours as navigator.

In his first years of service with the 36th Regiment, Protasiuk flew the most difficult missions. While colleagues flew to Brussels or to military units in Poland, he piloted transport planes to Chad, Afghanistan and Iraq, where Polish military contingents were stationed and where regularly they had to carry supplies. If he felt discriminated against, he never complained. [52]

On duty, still developing his skills, he signed up to study political science at the School of Journalism and Political Science. In 2003 he graduated from postgraduate studies at the School of Cybernetics of the Military University of Technology in the field of European integration and national security.

---

[51] "Zamach w Smolensku," by Leszek Szymowski, Bollinari Publishing House, Warsaw, 2011
[52] Ibid.

The Final Flight

During the "Georgian Incident" in which the Pilot in Command, Gregorz Pietruczuk refused to follow the President's order to change the flight plan and fly the plane with the five heads of state directly into the war zone in Tbilisi, Protasiuk was the copilot. After this incident, when President Kaczynski refused to have Pietruczuk fly him anymore, it was Protasiuk who was asked to be the main pilot for the Polish President. He flew him to Lithuania, Slovakia, Afghanistan, Belgium, and Germany. Protasiuk flew to all corners of the world: Japan, Korea, Greece, France, Mongolia, and dozens of other places.

Protasiuk's fellow pilots and crew in the 36th Regiment described him as a pilot who was methodical and precise; he was someone who always created an easy atmosphere in the cockpit.

Lesław Powierża, a flight mechanic, and Protasiuk's neighbor had built their condos next door to each other. "During one of our flights we looked at an elegant, newly emerging housing estate in Warsaw. Arek said it would be fun to live there--the area is beautiful. Shortly thereafter we bought twin condos in this neighborhood. In one part Arek settled with his family, in the second myself. We were neighbors for five years, we knew each other for ten years. [53]

"We became friends while working together. We often flew together and regularly teamed-up together both in and outside of work. Arek was a calm man but he was also witty. He was incredibly talented, and capable of independently making difficult decisions. He often said that he loved to fly Tupolevs. He knew this aircraft very well." [54]

Arek Protasiuk left a wife, Magdalena and two children: a son Nicholas, 8 and daughter Maria, 4.

---

[53] "The Picture of the Polish Flight Crew as Expert-Flyers Emerges: The Crew Cleared of Any Wrongdoing. Written by Peter Czartoryski-Sziler for "Nasz Dziennik" ("Bez zastrzeżeń do załogi" Czwartek, 19 lipca 2012, Nr 167 (4402))Translated by Jola D. with futher editing by Jan C.
http://www.doomedsoldiers.com/Poland-pilots-and-crew-were-expert-flyers.html
[54] Ibid.

Major Robert Grzywna was born 8 February 1974 in Jelenia Goracame, Poland. He was from the area of Szklarska Poreba, in the mountains of south-western Poland. It is a popular ski resort and an important regional and national center for mountain hiking, cycling, and skiing. As such, he would say "I'm almost a mountain climber; 'almost', because at a young age I put on a uniform and moved to Deblin."

In childhood he was an active athlete, belonging to sports clubs and took part in many skiing competitions. After that, as an officer he repeatedly won competitions in the giant slalom, organized among the crew of the Air Force. He was so good that just getting close to his record became a big feat. He also played football, and together with a team from the 36th Regiment, he won several trophies and prizes. [55]

Like his colleague Arek Protasiuk, Grzywna was assigned to the 36th Special Air Transport Regiment directly upon his graduation from the Polish Air Force Academy in Deblin in 1997. In 2003 he graduated from the National Defense Academy in Warsaw.

He was qualified to fly as commander of the Yak-40, though most of his flight hours were spent as co-pilot of that aircraft. He trained as navigator for the Tu-154M in 2008 and co-pilot in 2008-2009 but accumulated less than 500 hours on the aircraft—193 as co-pilot and 281 as navigator.

His friend and fellow 36th Regiment pilot, Peter Kulich had a particularly close relationship with Grzywna. "In recent years, we spent a lot of time together with our families. He was an extremely intelligent man with a very wide range of interests and great knowledge of many fields. You might say he was erudite. And even though he had so much knowledge, everyone could speak freely with him on any subject without feeling the worse for it because Robert could lead any conversation without exalting it over those who were talking with him. Robert was known especially for his sense of humor. That was his great asset, and that would always break the ice when he was dealing with others. He was a very cheerful and witty person who was extremely well liked by all his colleagues. [56]{4}

---

[55] "Niezwyciezony w slalomie gigancie", 30 Mar 2011 http://www.radiomaryja.pl/bez-kategorii/niezwyciezony-w-slalomie-gigancie/
[56] Ibid.

"He was very much involved in family life. Daily in our mutual discussions he would refer to his daughter Martyna often telling me how much she is growing and how proud he is of her. If his daughter was ill, and he had work to do which led him away from home, he worried about her and often called his wife and asked about his baby girl. With such small gestures, you could see how much he was involved in his family life. [57]

"He also had a passion for music. Robert, during his early youth, attended music school. He played the piano, accordion and trumpet. I remember the times together with friends when they would persuade him to play something. He always did, to our great delight. He had in his repertoire a lot of military and other melodies that had formed part of the nature of our meetings. I will always recall him as a man who, thanks to his character and optimism stole the hearts of people. I could see that he also liked people very much." [58]

Robert Grzywna left a wife, Agnieska and a daughter Martyna, 7.

Lieutenant Arthur Ziętek, 31, was born October 12, 1978 in Radom, Poland. In 2001 he graduated from the Academy of Military Air Forces in Deblin . From 2001-2007 he served in the 2nd Aviation Training Center in the positions of pilot and senior pilot. Since 2007, he served as a senior pilot in the 36th Special Air Transport Regiment.

As a child in Radom, Arthur dreamed about flying airplanes, said a neighbor. "He was a very polite…a helpful, smiling boy; he was very outgoing." From childhood, his passion was airplanes. His mother was afraid of her son's passion to fly and he tried to convince her that everywhere, even on the street, something can happen and you can die. Still his mother never wanted to know where and when he was flying. [59]

His mother recalled, "At the beginning I would like to note that Arthur was born on October 12th, the day on which is celebrated the Feast of the

---

[57] Ibid.
[58] Ibid.
[59] "Kapitan pilot śp. Artur Ziętek" Opublikowano 12 Oct 2012, autor: emka http://hej-kto-polak.pl/wp/?p=62929

Polish Armed Forces. I remember how after his birth the doctors told me that 'we had our second Hermaszewski' [General Miroslaw Hermaszewski was a Polish Air Force officer and cosmonaut- -the first and only Pole to go into space when he flew aboard the Soviet Soyuz 30 spacecraft in June 1978] These words began to be realized in elementary school, when Arthur began to dream of flying. At the same time, four days after his birth, Karol Wojtyla was elected as Pope, and therefore Arthur received at baptism his second name Karol. [60]

"Of my Son, I cannot really say anything bad. Arthur was a really good kid, a great son, a loving husband and a caring father to his daughters. Arthur has always been a very humble person, and this modesty to the end remained. It was his most striking feature. He never liked to talk about his achievements." [61]

His father, Mieczyslaw Ziętek recalled of his son, "Arthur was a very ambitious child and highly valued honor. Often now I recall the words of his oath 'to serve his country, and even die for it'. This oath he fulfilled to the end". [62]

Arthur Ziętek "was an interesting man, always with a lot of questions. He always soaked up his older colleagues' knowledge. It paid off for him in his ability to rapidly grow," said Capt. Gregorz Pietruczuk of the 36th Special Air Transport Regiment.

At the funeral for Arthur Zietek in his homily Col. Janusz Radzik remarked of the navigator: "He knew well how to communicate with colleagues, superiors and friends. He was extremely ambitious…a responsible and honorable man, a good friend. A Peaceful Warrior". [63]

Arthur Zietek left a wife Magdalena and two daughters, Patricia, 5 and Martha, 2

-----

[60] Ibid.
[61] Ibid.
[62] Ibid.
[63] "W Radomiu pochowano kapitana Artura Ziętka," 24 Apr 2010, http://www.rmf24.pl/raporty/raport-lech-kaczynski-nie-zyje-2/fakty/news-w-radomiu-pochowano-kapitana-Arthura-zietka,nId,274320

Warrant Officer Andrzej Michalak, 37, was the aircraft's Flight Engineer with a little over 300 hours in the Tu-154M in this position.

Born on May 3, 1973 in Rawa Mazowiecka, Poland, he graduated from the Technical School in Rawa Mazowiecka in 1993 and in 1996 the Air Force Technical Officers School. He was a graduate of the School of Commerce and International Finance in Warsaw 2000.

He first served with the 45th Experimental Air Squadron, Modlin, and then joined the 36th Special Air Transport Regiment in 1998. He became a senior technician on board in 2008, working as a ground handler for the Tu-154M. In 2008 he gained certification to fly on the Tupolev.

"Before he started to fly the Tupolev, he dealt with the ground handling of the aircraft. It meant to us that you could feel safe in the air," said Capt. Gregorz Pietruczuk of the 36th Regiment.

"I talked to Andrzej about the flight to Smoleńsk" recalled Lieutenant Colonel Bartosz Stroiński from the 36th Special Aviation Regiment. "I was smiling and saying that he would surely fly there because the flight was scheduled on Saturday and he liked to fly on Saturdays. And so, unfortunately, he flew,"

The crew with whom Andrzej flew that day were people he really appreciated and liked. When he was asked on April 9, whether he really needed to go there {to Smolensk} he replied "It does not matter where I'm going, it's important that I'm going with a good crew and cool people." [64]

His parents were proud to have a son who was flying with the most important people in the country. But he did not brag about it and did not really want to talk about it. But when someone complained that the Tu-154M planes are old and should be replaced, he always said that it was a very good aircraft. [65]

In addition to his passion for aviation he had a passion for cars. "He could talk about cars for hours – he knew everything about them, knew each model, details of the car and trivia associated with it", said his friend

---

[64] "Pamietamy o Zalodze tupolewa—Andrzej Michalak" Joanna Racewicz http://3obieg.pl/pamietamy-o-zalodze-tupolewa-andrzej-michalak
[65] Ibid.

Stanislav Orzeszek. He was also an avid lover of Formula 1. His biggest idol was Ayrton Senna. Then he followed Felipe Masy and Fernando Alonso.[66]

Andrzej also loved photography. In his computer he left many pictures he had taken with the crew members of the presidential Tupolev, who flew to Smolensk that day.

One friend remembered "from the times of high school Andrew was a heavy metal head. He once wore hair to his waist and boots. Before the crash he bought a ticket for the May concert of AC / DC. He never got the chance to go". [67]

Andrzej Michalak left a wife Margaret and son Julian, 6 months who was to be baptized in May.

Though the Pilot in Command (PIC) of the April 10th flight, Arek Protasiuk, was undoubtedly an excellent pilot who had proved his mettle in difficult situations, there was every indication that his training, as well as that of the other pilots in the 36th Regiment was not at the level it should have been. For Protasiuk, his training was not steady, as there were breaks ranging from 3-6 months and much of it was unsupervised. During 2009 and 2010 he did not do any training flights in a Tu-154M (nor in a Yak-40 in 2010) beside regular operational tasks. He did not perform flights where he could systematically practice emergency landings with one engine inoperative or make use of various landing systems either. The last training flight which he performed involving a one engine inoperative landing was on a Tu-154M on July 29, 2008 during training as PIC . Since that day, he had not practiced this and in fact, at the time of the crash, had less than 500 hours as Pilot in Command of the Tu-154M, most of his flight time being spent as co-pilot for that aircraft. [68]

---

[66] "Samolotyniemiałyprzednimtajemnic"byPaulinaGlinska,10Apr2015http://polska-zbrojna.pl/home/articleshow/15676?t=Samoloty-nie-mialy-przed-nim-tajemnic
[67] Ibid.
[68] Final Report from the examination of the aviation accident no. 192/2010/11 involving the Tu-154M airplane, tail number 101, which occurred on April 10, 2010 in the area of the Smolensk North airfield (the Polish report)

The Polish investigation report opined that there was an insufficient level of crew training and safety standards in the functioning practice of the 36th Special Regiment primarily in the area of Crew Resource Management, Operational Risk Management, and Multi-Crew Cooperation. [69]

The report noted that aircraft commanders, co-pilots, and navigators were trained hastily, not methodically, careless about documenting the process. The flight crew had little experience in flying the Tu-154 in difficult atmospheric conditions and with the use of non-precision landing systems. [70]

The Russian investigation report on the Smolensk crash noted that Captain Protasiuk, though the Regiment's most experienced pilot on the Tu-154, had comparatively insignificant experience of unsupervised flights in his position. His crew had even less experience of unsupervised flights on the Tupolev (the co-pilot had 160 hours, navigator 26 hours and flight engineer 240 hours.) [71]

During transition training to different aircraft types, Lieutenant Zietek and Major Grzywna conducted regular flights on their previous aircraft types which could have affected the quality of their training on the new aircraft. Captain Protasiuk, after commissioning as PIC, regularly changed his piloting seat from left as PIC to right as a co-pilot instead of strengthening his skills of piloting and crew management. [72]

There were no simulators in the unit which made training and maintaining a needed professional level in Instrument Flight Rules (IFR) flights and handling emergency situations virtually impossible. No other simulator training centers for the Tu-154 were used to provide this type of training. The conduct of training not only failed to include refreshment and flight simulators, it did not include any exercises in the Terrain Awareness Warning System which might create loopholes in training with the use of such systems (especially complacency regarding warning signals). [73]

---

[69] Ibid.
[70] Ibid.
[71] Interstate Aviation Committee Air Accident Investigation Committee Final Report (Russian MAK report)
[72] Ibid.
[73] Ibid.

Troubles began for the 36th Regiment in late 2007 and 2008, when the last three experienced pilots left, including the commander of the regiment Tomasz Pietrzak (who left in August 2008). Before leaving, they had to quickly train their successors Protasiuk and Pietruczuk. After the departure of their mentors they, despite the fact that they were barely into their thirties, became the only pilots for the Tu-154. What's worse, others could not be quickly trained. For almost the entire year in 2009, one of the Regiment's Tupolev aircraft was being refitted in Russia, so, during that time period, the regiment had only one plane to carry VIPs. There was little time or equipment available to train new crew and captains.

The unit faced budget cuts from year to year and the promise of buying new aircraft was postponed indefinitely. "We were on the edge" said a retired Regiment officer. "Planes were getting older, crew getting younger, and the procedures, which we were used to in the '70s and '80s fell by the wayside." [74]

Said another former pilot, "In the regiment we were understaffed, so we had to be in a constant state of readiness. I went once with my family for a weekend outside of Warsaw. Suddenly the phone rings; it's the squadron commander: 'Sikorski wants to fly to Bydgoszcz'. I dropped everything and flew to him to Bydgoszcz, even though it was my day off." Another former pilot remarked that politicians treated planes as taxis. A colleague once waited for Prime Minister Tusk for fourteen hours. "They thought us errand boys. We were at their every beck and call." [75]

In 2009 there was a glimmer of hope that the fate of the Regiment could be reversed. The Defense Ministry adopted a proposal to lease Embraer aircraft and sent twelve pilots to Swiss Aviation Training School in Zurich to train on the new aircraft for five weeks. When they returned trained and ready, there was no money to lease the planes.

By 2010, the 36th regiment was down to two and a half crews trained to fly on the Tu-154M. Protasiuk, though he had hardly spent 500 hours as the commander of the Tu-154M, was the most experienced pilot of

---

[74] "Twarde lądowanie Specjalnego Pułku," by Michal Krzymowski, Dziennikarz działu Polska
09-11-2012   http://polska.newsweek.pl/twarde-ladowanie-specjalnego-pulku, 97938,1,1.html
[75] Ibid.

the aircraft in the whole regiment. Lieutenant Colonel Bartosz Stroiński, trained in 2009, was the least experienced. The only other experienced Tupolev pilot in the Regiment was Grzegorz Pietruczuk who had passed his exams in 2008.

It was the opinion of the Polish crash investigation committee that, in the aftermath of personnel shuffling in 2008 after many experienced pilots and instructors had left, the large number of orders for transportation, the prestige of flying the Tu-154M with VIPs, and the perks that these missions carried with them, created a situation where the squadron leaders were interested solely in clocking in flight time in foreign sorties, neglecting recurrent training. [76]

---

[76] Final Report from the examination of the aviation accident no. 192/2010/11 involving the Tu-154M airplane, tail number 101, which occurred on April 10, 2010 in the area of the Smolensk North airfield (the Polish report)

CHAPTER SEVEN

BEFORE THE FLIGHT

Direct preparations for the flight to Smolensk began on April 10 at 4am when the flight engineer, Warrant Officer Andrzej Michalak arrived at the military air field at Warsaw-Okecie Airport. It was his duty to participate in the direct preparation of the aircraft for the VIP flight and at 4:20 am he took the aircraft over from flight engineering services. At 5:05 on the tarmac, the engines were started to check for any abnormal indicators. The engine test was completed around 5:20 am and after the flight engineering services specialists finished maintenance, the aircraft was declared technically fit for the VIP status flight. Michalak remained in the aircraft awaiting other members of the crew.

By 5:30 am, the three flight attendants--Natalia Januszko, Barbara Maciejczyk, and Justyna Moniuszko were on board.

Captain Protasiuk, Major Grzywna, and Lieutenant Zietek arrived at their unit between 5:15 and 5:25. First, they went to the briefing room, then to the flight personnel preparation room. There, Captain Protasiuk confirmed his crew's readiness for the task by signing in the task log.

At about 5:45 am the Warsaw-Okecie airport controller received a phone call from one of the crew of the Yak-40 aircraft that was flying a group of journalists to Smolensk that morning for the ceremony. The Yak-40 reported that weather conditions for landing in Smolensk north were: ceiling of 60 meters and visibility around 2 kilometers. This information was passed at 6:32 to the meteorologist-on-duty and to the senior

Operations officer. Additionally, information from the hydrometerological center reached the senior operations officer that on the basis of a report from the Smolensk South airport, weather at Smolensk North had worsened. The senior operations officer asked the airport's controller to pass this information about the worsening conditions to the crew of the Tu-154M and to establish which alternate landing possibilities were the closest. Judging by the transcript of voices in the cockpit of Tu-154M this information never reached them.

At 6:02, the Deputy Commander of the 36th Regiment, whose crew was flying the VIP mission this morning went to the airport Meteorology Office to obtain the most recent information on predicted weather conditions for the time of Tu-154M landing in Smolensk. He received a report that the Smolensk air field was forecast to be "in mist; visibility 3-5 kilometers with a ceiling of 200-300 meters". The Deputy Commander then made his way to the military airport and reported to the Air Force Commander, General Andrzej Blasik on crew preparations for the flight. In the talk, the Air Force Commander, who would also be a passenger on the morning's flight, told the Deputy of his wish to make a report to the President himself in the presence of the aircraft's commander

At 6:06, a bus pulled up, bringing Protasiuk and Grzywna to the aircraft. At 6:11, the two men disembarked and went to the crew dispatch room where they both obtained weather information from the meteorologist at about 6:20 am. The meteorologist-on-duty informed the aircraft commander that according to information from 5:00am, the weather in the area of Smolensk airport was cloudless, with visibility 4000 meters in mist, winds southeast about five knots. At 6:21 the aircraft commander, co-pilot, and the two flight attendants came back on board the aircraft.

The first group of passengers embarked the aircraft at 6:41.

Protasiuk then got out of the aircraft and went to the bottom of the passenger steps to await more passengers. General Blasik arrived at the steps and Protasiuk reported. A moment later, the Deputy Commander of the Regiment joined them to report the crew's readiness, and then he departed to the crew briefing room to await the arrival of the President.

The flight was scheduled to take off at 7:00am, but the President and First Lady arrived late, at 7:07 accompanied by officers of the Government

Security Office (BOR). General Blasik reported to the President the aircraft crew's readiness for the flight and presented Captain Protasiuk as the aircraft commander.

The last of the passengers embarked at 7:08.

At an Easter service on April 4th, at St Trinity in Hajnowka, in the northeastern part of Poland bordering Belarus, crowds listened to a sermon given by Archbishop Miron Chodakowski, Orthodox Ordinary of the Polish Army and Bishop of Hajnowka. In his sermon, he talked about death and resurrection. "In the Bible, one finds the essence and meaning of life, as well as the image of the human soul, which often through repentance rises from the fall to the heights of heaven". [77]

"Usually, he was always rushing somewhere or other always in a hurry," later recalled Michael Niegierewicz, Pastor of St Trinity. Usually after the Easter services in Hajnowka, Archbishop Chodakowski would be heading to Warsaw. But this year, it was different. He was muted, quiet. Although he never did it before that morning, this Easter morning he walked around the church. He prayed, he thought. It appeared to the Pastor that he did not want to leave. [78] Six days later, Archbishop Chodakowski boarded the Tupolev with the President's contingent for the flight to Smolensk from which he would never return.

Thirty-five year old Agnieszka Pogródka-Węcławek, as a female agent of the Polish Government Protection Bureau (BOR) was the favorite BOR officer of First Lady Maria Kaczynski. Though she never bragged about it, her closest friend revealed that Agnieszka, like no one else, had access to the First Lady. It was a close relationship. [79]

---

[77] "Arcybiskup Miron Chodakowski, Prawosławny Ordynariusz WP nie żyje" 10.04.2010 wyborcza.pl Gazeta Wyborcza Fakty SmoleńskieRegiony po stracie swoich liderówWspomnienia

[78] Ibid.

[79] "She smiles she could win a first lady" by Anita Czypryn 2010-04-13 http://www.polskatimes.pl/tag/agnieszka-pogrodka-weclawek-maz/

Though media photographs always depicted the BOR agent with a serious or even dour expression, those who knew her pointed out that this portrait defied her real countenance of one who was always smiling. They all speculated that it was her smile which endeared her to the First Lady. She was dubbed "Cleopatra" because she combed her hair a little up and down, giving her the appearance of the Egyptian queen. And so happy. And so in love with her husband of five years who was also a BOR officer. They had just moved to a new apartment and were planning to have a baby.[80]

Agnieszka's husband knew his wife did not like flying with President Kaczynski. "The main problem was his eternally being late. In general, it did not happen that the president was on time. The president could be delayed three hours." So on the morning of April 10, "my wife got up at 3 am, put on her uniform and, though reluctant, went to the airport."[81]

Just the day before, she boasted to colleagues that she was in this new jewelry store at ul. Mokotowskiej and she managed to find a four leaf clover charm for her bracelet and had the name of her husband, Albert, engraved on it. And this bracelet with the name of her beloved husband Agnieszka took with her on Saturday on board the presidential plane, on her last service to the President and First Lady.[82]

Stanisław Mikke, vice-chairman of Poland's Institute of Military History, set and checked his alarm clock five times on the evening before the flight. He woke up at 3:40 am on April 10. He was concerned about making the flight on time and wasn't confident he had been given the correct information about the departure time. He called around until he got the phone number for the military airfield at Warsaw Airport. Reaching the air field, he asked the dispatcher what time the presidential plane was flying to Smolensk for the ceremony: was it at six or seven

---

[80] Ibid.
[81] "Testimony husband sp. Agnieszka Pogródka-Węcławek" http://mmariola.salon24.pl/255295,z-kim-i-czym-miala-leciec-sp-agnieszka
[82] "She smiles she could win a first lady" by Anita Czypryn 2010-04-13 http://www.polskatimes.pl/tag/agnieszka-pogrodka-weclawek-maz/

o'clock? He doubted he had been given the correct time because every April he flew to Smolensk for the ceremony at the Katyn cemetery, and always the plane departed at 6:00 am. But this year was the first time he would be flying with the Polish President, and so the flight would not be leaving until 7:00am. [83]

Stanislaw left the house at about 5:30 am, driving his own car to the airport. With him he carried a memorial wreath and 120 copies of the second edition of his book, to distribute to the passengers.

His book, "Sleep, Courageous" is a diary of the Katyn exhumation in which he participated; the unique record of his fight with the Soviet authorities to find the place of the murders and force them to a final place of honor. Discovering the truth about Katyn was his mission and passion. His uncle, Stanislaw Mikke, died of exhaustion in Arkhangelsk, where he had been exiled with his family - his wife and five children. And that is where his grave now lies. Stanislaw Mikke was named for his martyred uncle.

Mikke had had a choice: to fly on April 7 with the Prime Minister or April 10 with the president. Andrew Przewoźnik, with whom he had worked for years asked him "Just tell me when {you would like to go}." [84] Stanislaw made his decision at the last minute to go on the 10th. He wanted to take the copies of his book with him and the book did not leave the printing house until the 9th—a coincidence of fate which might later cause some to say that it was his book that killed him.

Fleet Admiral Andrzej Karweta, Commander in Chief of Polish Naval Forces boarded the plane for Smolensk on the morning of April 10th with thoughts of his garden at home. He loved to create compositions of flowers and couldn't wait to start on the garden in their new home in Banino, which he had just purchased the year before. He had already planted some trees and shrubs and a few flowers. Yesterday, he bought some plants and seeds, and dug into the clay, raking the beds into a vegetable patch. There

---

[83] "Torańskiej wywiad o Smoleńsku" *by Teresa Torańska* 03102012 http://polska.newsweek.pl/toranskiej-wywiad-o-smolensku,96584,1,1.html
[84] Ibid.

he planned to grow carrots and lettuce--something he had always wanted to do. The weather was beautiful as the weekend approached and he wanted to take advantage of every minute. But he could not do everything. He had to fly to Warsaw and then to Smolensk for the Katyn ceremony. "I'll finish up when I return from Katyn, maybe even Saturday evening," he told his wife. After all, it was to be a short trip. And he couldn't deny General Gagor, the Chief of the Armed Forces, who invited him to come along on the flight and announced that he also would be there. [85]

The seeds never got planted.

Fifty-eight year old General Franciszek Gągor, as Chief of the General Staff of the Polish Armed Forces, may have held the highest post in the Polish military and some thought, a sure candidate for Commander of NATO forces, but he was also the beloved father of Catherine and Michael, and devoted husband to his wife Lucyna.

He came from a small town from a large family. In Polish society there is a stereotype that if you're from a small town, there is no chance of a career, to develop your greatest passion. Franciszek Gagor broke all the stereotypes. He studied not only in Poland; he was a graduate of, among others, the NATO Defense College in Rome and the National War College of the National Defense University in Washington, DC. His colleagues say that he was in his office at the earliest dawning light until the last of daylight faded. He wanted to be as perfect in what he was doing as he could. Despite his demanding schedule, he always made time for his family. [86]

On the morning of the impending flight to Smolensk for the 70th anniversary Katyn ceremony, though he didn't want to eat anything, Lucyna persuaded him to have something. He drank a cup of tea. He put on a white shirt. He had a full dress uniform ready. And the last

---

[85] "Mariola Karweta: Bardzo lubiłam być Twoją żoną" by Irena Łaszyn 8 APR 2011 http"//www.dziennikbaltycki.pl/artykul/389523,mariola-karweta-bardzo-lubilam-byc-twoja-,7,id,t,sa.html

[86] "General Franciszek Gagor (1951 - 2010)" 2013-04-12 http://www.miastons.pl/59,Ludzie.htm?id=7163

moment he stood in the doorway, and said goodbye. General Gągor had to fly quite often in his capacity as a military representative to NATO and Lucyna always worried about him. She recalled: "He said: 'Bye, my darling', and I said 'Take care of yourself, dumpling!' This is what I used to say to him" He would answer "Let the pilot do his best". She always would gently make the sign of the cross in the air when sending him off. That morning she didn't. And when the Secret Service car arrived, she said to the officers "Look after my husband". [87] Those were the last words and the last moments she saw husband alive.

The eighty-nine passengers and seven crew members of the Tu-154M took off from Warsaw-Okecie airport at 7:27 am--- already almost a half hour behind schedule.

---

[87] "Lucyna Gągor: I have more and more doubts.Until the end I do not know what happened to the plane" Wednesday, 10 April 2013 http://www.rmf24.pl/raporty/raport-lech-kaczynski-nie-zyje-2/wywiady/news-lucyna-gagor-mam-coraz-wiecej-watpliwosci-do-konca-nie-wiem-,nId,953693

CHAPTER EIGHT

THE PRECURSER FLIGHTS[88]

{All times in this chapter are local Smolensk time unless otherwise indicated}

S molensk North or "Severny" at one time was a military airfield with navigational equipment typical of most military airfields. The field was in operation until the disbandment of the 103rd Novosielsk Krasnoselsky Guard Transport Regiment in 2009. Since 2009 there have been no active units at the base except for a small airbase command post. The airfield had been functioning in part as a civilian airport since October 2009. On Oct 15, 2009, a Notice to Airmen (NOTAM) was issued which phased out the Outer Nondirectional Beacons (NDB), Inner NDB, and the navigation lighting system to Runway 08 approaches. On April 10, 2010, the navigational aids at Smolensk North were providing only the approach to Runway 26 which consisted of two NDB with markers. The air field no longer had an Instrument Landing System (ILS) which would

---

[88] Information and ATC transcript quotes in this chapter are from:
Interstate Aviation Committee Air Accident Investigation Committee Final Report (Russian MAK report) and Final Report from the examination of the aviation accident no. 192/2010/11 involving the Tu-154M airplane, tail number 101, which occurred on April 10, 2010 in the area of the Smolensk North airfield (the Polish report)

have enabled aircraft to land if the pilots are unable to establish visual contact with the runway.

At about 5:30 am, local Warsaw time on April 10, a Yakovlev(Yak)-40 aircraft departed the Warsaw-Okecie airport for its ultimate destination—the Smolensk North air field. The plane was one of the two aircraft the Polish President's staff had requested from the 36th Special Regiment in conjunction with the planning for the 70th anniversary commemoration. The Yak-40 was carrying a contingent of 14 journalists and members of the Presidential press office who were travelling to cover the ceremony of the 70th anniversary of the Katyn Massacre. The plane was piloted by Lieutenants Artur Wosztyl and Rafał Kowaleczko. The flight engineer was Remigiusz Mus. Two years later, in 2012, Mus was scheduled to give testimony in conjunction with the Smolensk crash which would implicate the Russian flight controllers but he committed suicide in October of that year by hanging himself in his basement. (His suicide, of course, did much to fuel the conspiracy theorists who speculated that Mus was actually murdered to prevent his testimony against the Russians).

At the same time the Yak-40 was approaching Smolensk North, a Russian Ilyushin (IL)-76 was also heading for the Smolensk air field. This aircraft had departed from Vnukovo, Russia carrying a contingent of Russian soldiers who were to serve as guards for the Katyn ceremony. The Smolensk air traffic controller (ATC)--LtCol Pawel Plusnin-- was informed that the expected landing time for the IL-76 and the Yak-40 was identical (9:20 local-Smolensk- time). He made the decision to queue the Yak-40 first for landing, straight downwind (accelerated approach procedure); the IL-76 was to land second.

The Military Unit Deputy Commander (MUDC), Col Nikolai Krasnokutski at some point joined Plusnin in the air traffic control room and throughout was heavily involved in directing the landings, despite the fact that it was not his job to do so and that his presence in the ATC room had at least the potential of adding extra stress to the controller or interfering with the controller's work flow and decision making.

Plusnin briefed his boss: "So, it's the Yak-40 first, and then ours."

"What about the distance…the separation", the Colonel asked him.

"Forty-eight…I'm leading him downwind and then the landing."

Plusnin, noting the fog that was beginning to develop over the airfield, made the decision that, due to the limited visibility, he would order the set up of the Airfield Projector Station (APS). Colonel Krasnokutski, not realizing the decision had been made already, and demonstrating his concern about the landing conditions told Plusnin, "We should be setting up the projectors".

Plusnin informed his boss "I've already given the order to set it up."

"I know, but most likely, they will not manage to do it right".

"But they follow orders. I am checking on the situation."

In reality, personnel setting up the APS were not managing very well at all, which upset Plusnin as suggested by the high number of vulgar expressions in his comments to the APS setup team and by repeated orders to accelerate the process.

"Come on….are you ready? Are you ready or not?" he barked at the APS crew leader. "Damn all of you! Faster….faster…don't you understand, damn it?!"

The hurried setting up of the APS and related issues led to the controller's excessive concentration on that particular evolution. He was operating on an ever-increasing time shortage—the Yak-40 was approaching the landing pattern, followed by the IL-76, with communication distorted by the Yak-40 commander's poor command of the Russian language, and the ATC's poor command of English. The tower microphones recorded the following conversation between the ATC (who could not see the incoming aircraft due to the developing fog) and the Yak-40:

9:02:46 ATC – Papa Lima Foxtrot 031.
9:02:50 Yak-40 - Go ahead.
9:02:52 ATC – Course 10
9:02:56 Yak-40 - Course 10, Papa Lima Foxtrot 0-3-1.
9:03:40 ATC - Papa Lima Foxtrot zero three one aah..say altitude?
9:03:50 Yak-40 - (unintelligible) of 1500 meters.
9:03:54 ATC - One five zero zero?
9:03:57 Yak-40 - Affirm
9:03:58 – ATC-What? How much did he say?
9:04:03 ATC - Papa Lima Foxtrot, one three one…Pressure 7-45, seven four five, descend to five zero zero.

9:04:22 Yak-40 - will descend to 500 meters. Confirm pressure of 7-45.
9:04:29 ATC - Roger that.
9:04:30 ATC - Where are you?
9:04:33 ATC - Fuck, who knows?!
9:04:36 MUDC - ... Can't you see him?

By 9:09, the Yak-40 was on its final approach but the visibility on the landing field was still of concern to the controllers and they still could not see the plane.

9:09:20 MUDC We have the first one?
9:09:23 ATC - Yes.
9:09:25 MUDC. – How's the visibility ...?
9:09:27 ATC – Well, I can see the outer one at about 1200, 1300, let's say.
9:09:33 MUDC - The projectors are turned on, or not?
9:09:34 ATC - Yes, everything is on.

At this point, Plusnin was once again distracted—this time by soldiers on the runway at the edge of the airfield.

9:10:18 ATC – Fuck! Soldiers, damn it!.
9:10:51 ATC - Sierioga, I'll fucking kill you! These soldiers are on the runway again, damn it! You…at the {runway} threshold, do we have radio contact with them?

Meanwhile the Yak-40 continued its approach.

9:11:25 Yak-40 - Papa Lima Foxtrot 0-3-1, request permission to approach.
9:11:30 ATC- 0-3-1 Come right on landing (unintelligible)

Colonel Krasnokutski once more interjected his concern about the visibility and the need to notify the Operations Officer in Moscow.

9:12:41 MUDC. - ... but the meteo, Marchenko said, they didn't expect this fog.

The Final Flight

9:12:53 ATC - Come on, come on, tell him, tell him anyway.

During the final approach of the Yak-40 for landing, Krasnokutski apparently noticed that Plusnin was not managing the situation as well as he thought he should be. Now the IL-76 was also approaching the airport and needed to be guided into position to follow the Yak-40. Krasnokutski once again interjected with instructions for the controller who was still agitated that the projectors were not being set up fast enough:

9:13:34 MUDC - Don't take him lower just yet.
9:13:42 ATC –Projectors, damn it. Switch the projectors on.
9:13:45: MUDC: Do something!
9:13:46 ATC – Come on, come on, come on

During the final approach of the Yak-40 for landing, the Moscow Command Center called Krasnokutski on his cell phone. The MUDC for the first time told Moscow Command about the rapid deterioration of meteorological conditions. "Vladimir Ivanovich, good morning. The first one is approaching now…We are covered with fog, right now. Have been over the past ten minutes. I'll call you back."

The impending landing of the Yak-40 aircraft caused major upset at the Inner ATC Post. The controller spotted the aircraft very late, and in a position he believed to preclude a safe landing. Now obviously more agitated, both he and the MUDC tried to wave off the aircraft, and direct it to go around.

9:14:35 ATC –Do you see the runway? Higher!
9:14:41 ATC – Initiate go-around.
9:14:44 MUDC –Fuck! Initiate go-around
9:14:45 MUDC - Fuck! You need to go around!
9:14:46 ATC - Initiate go-around!

There was no response from the Yak-40.

For whatever reason—either his inability to hear or understand the controller who was giving direction in Russian, or because he had sight of the runway and thought could make it safely, the Yak-40 pilots ignored the controller's direction to initiate a go around and landed anyway.

9:15:06 ATC - He landed. Papa Lima Foxtrot 031 after a stop, turn 180.
9:15:17 ATC (probably to MUDC) - The Yak-40 landed. Did you see how he passed the threshold?

Now the controllers had to direct the aircraft to taxi to a location which would adequately clear the runway for the approaching IL-76. Much confusion was caused by the erratic reaction of the Yak-40 aircraft crew to Plusnin's taxiing orders.

9:16:35 ATC – Well, what's this? Where is he taxiing to?
9:16:42 ATC – Watch him, if he goes left … let him go left so that….
9:16:48 ATC – Who the fuck knows! Hell, you tell him to go right, he'll go left, fuck, I've told him ten times
9:16:58 ATC - I did not get from him a single confirmation.
9:17:00 MUDC – Is he speaking in Polish?
9:17:02 ATC -He said nothing at all
9:17:03 {unknown person} - No, he speaks Russian, right?
9:17:04 ATC – Well, in Russian …prompt him to go straight on the roadway.
9:17:29 MUDC - He turned the other way?

Despite the risky landing and the Yak-40's failure to follow any of the ATC's orders the controllers now began to express admiration for the plane and the pilot's skills. Oddly, they did not ask the Yak-40 pilot why he ignored their order to go around, but instead, praised him for a job well done.

9:17:31 ATC - Papa Lima Foxtrot zero three one. Backtrack after landing. Good job
9:17: 33 MUDC - Well, he actually landed. I think he's got proper equipment, the plane isn't bad. Basically he landed without a problem, they did a good job. Frankly, I thought we would have a go around.

Turning his concern back to the weather conditions and the impending arrival of the Tu-154, Colonel Krasnokutski expressed optimism by suggesting that the deterioration of weather conditions was temporary, and that conditions would definitely improve for the Tu-154M approach. "Listen, he's landing at ten fifty. Visibility is improving now. But Marchenko (the meteorologist) said that yesterday, no one predicted fog, and everything was fine in the morning. And now at 9 o'clock, fog. Visibility about 1200. So actually I believe that's all, and I think that temperatures will rise at 10:30 already. Whatever happens, shouldn't be worse than one and a half thousand."

Now it was time for the Il-76 carrying the Russian soldiers to attempt to land. The plane made two attempts to approach, each time receiving communication from the controller as to their position with relation to the glide path and the runway centerline. At the first landing attempt, the controller only established visual with the aircraft when it was just before the runway threshold, left of the center line, and at very low altitude in relation to the airfield plane. The crew of the IL-76 made a failed attempt at bringing the aircraft to the runway center line in order to land and since they were not lined up on the correct path, Plusnin waved off the landing. But he should have given this order sooner than he did. The reaction of Inner ATC Post personnel to the faulty approach of the IL-76, the pitch of their voices, and the heavy use of expletives, suggest that both Plusnin and Krasnokutski were aware of the threat. According to witnesses, the aircraft, while going around after the failed approach, made an abrupt maneuver of banking right, with the right wing tip about 3-5 meters above ground. The delayed go-around order and actions of the IL-76 crew resulted in a maneuver threatening flight safety.

After the IL-76 went around the first time, Krasnokutski calmed down and ordered Plusnin to obtain information from the pilots.

9:28:16 MUDC- How much remaining fuel do they have?
9:28:20 MUDC-Just a minute, how much fuel do they have?
9:28:33 MUDC - Ask him if he saw the projectors

Now, once again, Plusnin was distracted by soldiers on the runway. Whether the soldiers were part of the team setting up the projectors or part of a security team, is uncertain, but clearly, they were not where they were supposed to be and this once again agitated the air traffic controller.

9:33:43 ATC- Fuck! I said ten times already, I explained, left, or right of the runway. Fuck! So just move it to the runway threshold yourself, and get them out of there, damn it, and they all can write explanations why they are running around here and there damn it!!!
9:33:47 MUDC- Have you explained it to them?
9:33:48 ATC- Ten times already, fuck! I called them here, I showed them, right here, damn it! Fuck!
9:33:55 ? ...everything's alright
9:33:57 ATC- ...don't run on the runway, damn it, get the security guys out of there, off the threshold
9:34:04 ATC- They're leaving, wave them off!
9:34:13 MUDC- Well, let him approach. It's all the same...What's this, what are you doing? Another approach....

The MUDC's last comment may suggest that Plusnin wanted to abort further Inner ATC Post operations, seeing no option of performing a safe landing, given the weather conditions, but Krasnokutski vigorously reacted to the abort attempt decision. On the second landing attempt, the controller again permitted the IL-76 crew to approach despite the fact that weather conditions were below approach minima.

During the second approach, Plusnin again became extremely agitated and Krasnokutski repeatedly tried to get him to calm down. The controller's agitation was most likely due to his conviction that the IL-76 aircraft was being guided to landing in weather conditions below airfield minima. Krasnokutski told the controller to order the crew of the IL-76 aircraft to go around.

9:41:29 Landing Zone Controller- One on approach, on flight path
9:42:36 ATC- Fuck!
9:42:38 MUDC- Stop fussing!
9:42:42 MUDC- Get him out...
9:42:46 IL-76- Going around
9:42:50 MUDC- Stop fussing!

The Final Flight

During the two approaches of the Russian IL-76 aircraft (from 9:20 to 9:39) the weather conditions at Smolensk air field were getting still worse. On its second attempt, the IL-76 decided to abandon any further landing attempts and proceeded to an alternate airfield in Moscow.

This left only the Tu-154M carrying the Polish President and his contingent.

CHAPTER NINE

THE FINAL FLIGHT[89]

All we know, and could possibly know, about what transpired on the flight of the Tu-154M to Smolensk on that morning of April 10, 2010 comes from the cockpit voice recorder and the flight data recorders recovered from the crash. There were few direct eye witnesses, and no one on the plane survived to give any evidence as to what actually happened.

The cockpit voice recorder and both flight data recorders (one Russian made and one Polish made) were recovered from the crash site. The quality of the cockpit voice recorder proved problematic for investigators. They speculated the poor quality was due to microphones not being located close enough to the crew, ambient noise which some believed to be a result of the cockpit door being left open during the flight, therefore allowing the noise and voices from the plane's cabin to enter the cockpit, and multiple conversations among the crew members overlapping each other and making it very difficult to decipher one from the other.

---

[89] Information and ATC transcript quotes in this chapter are from:
Interstate Aviation Committee Air Accident Investigation Committee Final Report (Russian MAK report) and Final Report from the examination of the aviation accident no. 192/2010/11 involving the Tu-154M airplane, tail number 101, which occurred on April 10, 2010 in the area of the Smolensk North airfield (the Polish report)

Both Russian and Polish investigating teams applied their own resources to interpret the recordings. Several years later, using newer technology, the cockpit voice recorders were once again subjected to analysis, disputing some of the original interpretations and in some cases providing new ones. Even with all the analyses that have been done over the years, controversy still remains to this day over certain particular factors—none of which really had any significant bearing on the crash, but that caused enough anguish for family members of certain passengers and crew that they persisted over the years, taking on a life of their own

(All times given hereafter, unless otherwise stated, are in local Smolensk time; subtract 2 hours to convert to Warsaw Poland local time)

The Tu-154M took off from Warsaw-Okecie airport at 7:27am local time (9:27 Smolensk time) with 96 persons on board, including four crew members, three flight attendants, and 89 passengers.

Even at this early juncture, the Smolensk Deputy ATC Commander (MUDC), Colonel Krasnokutski was heard on the tower microphones discussing the impending Tupolev flight with the Operations Officer saying, "We should tell the Poles that it makes no sense to take off. We have to tell them, damn it. Look, this one already….{referring to the IL-76 failure to land}

9:44:03 MUDC - I have the following question: My data tells me that the Tu, aaah, the Poles, are taking off, damn it. They have not announced their arrival; I mean they are flying in by themselves. They have to be told that we have fog cover.

9:44:12 Operations Officer - Well, I will let the Main Center know…

9:44:13 MUDC - Do tell them, yes, because the weather forecast didn't show this. Humidity 80%. Where did it come from at 9 o clock? But we have total cover, visibility now around 400 meters, max

9:44:22 Operations Officer - Yes, you checked the weather radar?

9:44:23 MUDC - All was clear

9:44:24 Operations Officer - All was clear, yes?

9:44:25 MUDC- Yes, nil clouds. Visibility over ten. And we had given clearance already, the forecast showed nothing.

9:44:30 Operations Officer - Aha

9:44:30 MUDC - And, all of a sudden, everything got flummoxed.

The Moscow Operations Center officer on duty notified the MUDC that Tu-154M had taken off 15 minutes before. Despite his astonishment, Krasnokutski suggested that action be taken to immediately redirect the aircraft to an alternate airfield albeit expecting that the crew would attempt to perform a trial approach to minimum height. The Operations Center's officer on duty assured Krasnokutski that he would duly notify the Main Air Traffic Management Center.

9:44:33 Operations—Yes, I copy. The large Tu took off for SMOLENSK NORTH at twenty-seven past

9:44:37 MUDC—Tu took off at twenty-seven past?

9:44:38 Operations-Yes, at 7:27

9:44:39 MUDC- Well, given the circumstances, we have to find him an alternate, that's the first thing, if he's ready. Vnukovo, or something

9:44:44 Operations- yeah, Vnukovo

9:44:44 MUDC- He will probably perform a trial approach, no problem, to his minimum…But our data shows that there is no minimum, there is nothing.

9:44:51: Operations—I copy. But anyway, it's below the airfield's minima.

9:44:54: MUDC---Sure. No, what I mean is, how low do we bring him, to what altitude?

9:44:59 Operations—Ah, well, a good minimum, a civilian airfield minimum

9:45:00 ATC—One hundred meters

9:45:01 MUDC—Yes, and according to the airfield it's one hundred--can't do any lower

9:45:04 Operations—Well, this is what I'm saying, the airfield minimum, anyway.

9:45:06 MUDC—Certainly

9:45:07 Operations—He won't get any lower

9:45:07 MUDC—Alright, if he's planning a trial approach, he will perform it. I have one question concerning fuel: if he doesn't make it after the first approach, where do I direct him?

Plusnin twice made sure that the Operations Center had notified the Main Air Traffic Management Center that a decision had been made to redirect the aircraft to an alternate airfield.

9:54:51 ATC - We have to agree on an alternate for the Poles because we just don't have the weather, and I see no improvement.
9:54:57 Operations - I contacted the Main Center, they will take him to Vnukovo

Even though this conversation would seem to suggest that the decision had already been made to redirect the Tu-154M to an alternate airfield, further conversation a minute or two later only hinted that such a decision had been made.

9:55:02 ATC—We have to contact the Main Center somehow so that the main Pole...is told, firstly, to prepare for a go around to an alternate. Oh, and find out how much remaining fuel he's carrying because he understands virtually no Russian.
9:55:20 Operations—I think that the Main Center will decide. I said that the weather in Smolensk is unsuitable.

Despite the Operation Center's assurances that the Tu-154M would be redirected to an alternate airfield, in Smolensk Plusnin and Krasnokutski were preparing to receive the aircraft. Perhaps they had a lack of confidence that the higher levels (Operations) would actually carry through with their decision to divert the aircraft. Plusnin, attempted to get more information from the airfield's meteorologist ("Meteo") without much success. In fact, the conversation just served to reduce his confidence and to further agitate him.

10:04:59 Meteo - Meteo, Sergeant Radgowskij.
10:05:00 ATC - What are you forecasting now?
10:05:01 Meteo - Now I am forecasting 80 over 800 ... storm weather.

10:05:07 ATC - Well, have you issued a STORM WARNING?

10:05:09 Meteo - Aaah, I notified Tver, well, but it is not forecast as a storm.

10:05:13 ATC - What, what, what?

10:05:14 Meteo - As a forecast…well, as, aaah, it is there. But I did not issue a storm warning.

10:05:19 ATC - And what's going on now, there is no storm?

10:05:22 Meteo - Now it's stormy weather.

10:05:24 ATC - Damn, what the humidity?

10:05:25 Meteo - 96% humidity.

10:05:40 ATC - Damn it with this meteo of ours…

10:05:54 ATC - They are fucking absolutely useless, damn it! Just give me someone who knows how to measure fucking pressure, fucking temperature, and that's it. And fuck knows why we keep them here?! What the fuck for?

Worried that the crew of the Tu-154M would not be able to speak Russian, Plusnin asked an individual over the tower microphone to provide him with a number of aviation phrases in English language to facilitate communication. The discourse would be almost comical if we did not know of the tragedy that was looming.

10:06:34 A1—"Down" *(English)*
10:06:37 ATC—"Down?" *(English)*
10:06:38 A1—"Go" *(English)*
10:06:39 ATC—What?
10:06:40 A1—"Go" *(English)*
10:06:42 ATC—"Call again?" *(English)*
10:06:44 A1—"Go around" *(English)*
10:06:47 ATC—"Call around?" *(English)*
10:06:48 A1—"Go! Go!" *(English)*
10:06:49 ATC—"Go…Go around" *(English)* Yes?
10:06:52 A1—Yes, yes. "Go around again" *(English)*
10:06:59 ATC—"Go around again" *(English)*
10:07:02 A1—This means go around?
10:07:03: ATC—Aha

10:07:05 A1—Go around to an alternate airfield?
10:07:11 ATC—Yes
10:07:12 A1—"Go to" *(English)*
10:07:14 ATC—"….to?" *(English)*
10:07:16 A1—No, another word, "Go"

Meanwhile between 9:44 and 10:10, the Tupolev was flying at an altitude of 10000 meters (approximately 33000 feet). Flight along the route was made with autopilot active. There was casual, lighthearted conversation in the cockpit, regarding the impending flight to the United States that Captain Protasiuk was to make the next Monday, discussion of flight hours, and the food in different countries they had traveled (i.e., "China—now there is where they have good food")

At around 9:44, the area controller instructed the crew to change frequency and to establish communication with MINSK CONTROL at 133.50 MHz. Lieutenant Zietek, the navigator replied "Polish Air Force 101, thank you, good day". The co-pilot, Major Gryzwna, joked to the navigator "You're supposed to say 'Do swidanija'"

"Well, I'm not sure if it's 'do swidanija' or…"

"So how about 'Dobroje ranieco'"

"Well, no, I don't agree"

"Say it and see if he gets it" Grzywna laughed.

At 10:07, the controller asked the crew about the flight level expected above navigation waypoint ASKIL. The navigator answered: "3900 meters" (approximately 13000 feet). The controller confirmed and asked the crew to notify him when they were ready to descend.

At 10:09, Zietek notified MINSK control that the plane was ready for descent. The controller issued permission to descend to 3900 meters. Captain Protasiuk issued the order to "throttle down". Flight engineer Michalak confirmed and executed the order.

At this point, the crew looked out the window to see if they could make any visual contact with the ground through the mist and fog. They had become aware that fog was enveloping the landing area but were not sure of the extent and magnitude of the conditions. At 10:11 Grzywna remarked, "I can see the ground…I can see something…maybe it won't be so bad."

At 10:10, the crew of a Transaero 331 aircraft contacted the Smolensk ATC requesting a weather condition update for purposes of forwarding it to the crew of the Polish Tu-154M aircraft, which was then flying in the Belarussian Republic airspace. Plusnin reported the fog and the reduced visibility and asked them "Are you working for the Polish aircraft?" "No," they replied, "we're simply in transit, Moscow asked us".

After this, Plusnin commented "Good, damnit. Someone got worried over there…" in hopes that the news that Moscow had asked the Transaero to obtain the Smolensk weather information on behalf of the Polish aircraft meant that someone higher up had actually become appropriately concerned about the weather conditions in Smolensk.

Between 10:12 and 10:16, the MUDC kept asking Plusnin for any news concerning the decision to redirect the Tu-154M to an alternate airfield. Plusnin repeatedly attempted to obtain such information from the Operations Center to no avail.

At 10:14, the controller transmitted the following information to the crew: "Polish one zero one, for information at zero six one one Smolensk visibility: four zero zero meters, fog". Zietek confirmed the message as received. The crew began a discussion giving an unfavorable opinion on the work of the Warsaw-Okecie airfield meteorologist, who had reported better weather conditions.

"Fuck! How do you like that Meteo {meteorologist} of ours?!"

"Yeh, our Meteo is fucking great…"

The crew expressed their disbelief that fog was present at this time. Their meteorologist at Warsaw-Okecie had not forecast this weather. Now that Protasiuk, the pilot in command, was aware of the bad weather and the inaccurate forecast, there should have taken place a discussion among the crew as to their options and plans for landing should the weather conditions prove to be too severe, but this did not occur. All they did together was complain about their meteorologist.

The Russian investigators' report attributes Protasiuk to saying at 10:16 "I'm not sure, but if we don't land here, he'll give me trouble." {presumably referring to Kaczynski.} It would be entirely natural at this time for Protasiuk, and in fact the entire crew, to be thinking about the Georgian incident in which the pilot refused to execute the order of the President to land at an unsafe airfield in Tbilisi. Kaczynski's actions following this incident had proven devastating for the pilot of that flight.

Upon learning that the aircraft was approaching waypoint ASKIL and still tracking to Smolensk, LtCol Plusnin contacted his counterpart at the Smolensk South airfield and learned the Tu-154M had just been directed to Smolensk North. During that exchange, he made a final attempt to prove the unjustifiability of directing the aircraft to the Smolensk North airfield.

10:23:00 ATC - Hello, good morning, I'm calling from North. Who is now controlling the Polish plane flight?
10:23:08 SMOLENSK SOUTH - Moscow is the controller.
10:23:09 ATC - What?
10:23:10 SMOLENSK SOUTH - Moscow is the controller
10:23:14 ATC - Well, they need to be told somehow, as long as they are fully operational, damn it, that we have fog and visibility below 400 meters. Why push him this way now?
10:23:25 ATC - And tell Moscow also, you have radio contact with them, we don't---it will be occurring soon. And if he doesn't speak Russian either, damn it, there's going to be a real mess.

Meanwhile at 10:22, the Tu-154 crew was notified that they were passing waypoint ASKIL, and were instructed to change to frequency 128.8 Mhz Moscow Control. They were granted clearance to descend to 3600 meters (approximately 12000 feet). Shortly thereafter, the crew was passed off to Smolensk North (code name "Korsazh") on frequency 124.0 MHz.

Any further attempts by Plusnin to convince Operations Center or the Main Traffic Management Center to redirect the Tu-154M to an alternate airfield were terminated when contact was established by the crew of the Tu-154M. Colonel Krasnokutski ordered Plusnin to ask the crew for information concerning remaining fuel and alternate airfields.

10:24:14 ATC - We have to chase him away, damn it
10:24:15 MUDC – So, you're telling them, we have unsuitable conditions?

Changing the frequency to Smolensk North airfield's air traffic control, someone on the crew asked Protasiuk, "Are we going to speak Russian?" to which Protasiuk replied "Yes". From that point on, communication with the Air Traffic Controller at Smolensk North was conducted by Protasiuk in Russian. Normally communication with air traffic control is handled by the flight's navigator and conducted in English but the Smolensk controllers did not speak English, and Captain Protasiuk was the only member of the Tupolev's flight crew who could speak Russian.

At 10:23, Protasiuk established communication, in Russian, with the Smolensk North air traffic controller: "KORSAZH, Polish 101, good morning. For outer NDB, we are descending to 3600 meters." In response Plusnin asked about fuel remaining and alternate airfields. Protasiuk responded that they had eleven tons fuel remaining and alternate airfields were Vitebsk and Minsk. The flight plans that had been drawn up for the current flight were actually duplicates of the plans for the April 7th flight and, so, the current flight included the listing of Minsk and Vitebsk as alternate airfields as they had been on the 7th. While the Vitebsk airfield was in operation on the 7th, it was closed on the 10th and so was not in fact even available as an alternate destination.

At 10:24, Plusnin communicated: "PLF 101, fog on KORSAZH, visibility 400 meters" Protasiuk requested further information: "Please provide temperature and pressure"

"I'll tell you what the temperature is….coooold," Grzywna joked.

Plusnin responded: "Temperature plus two, pressure seven four five. Unsuitable landing conditions"

At 10:25 Protasiuk responded: "Thank you. If possible, we shall attempt approach, and if the weather is too bad, we will go around." Protasiuk told the crew that the go around would be performed on autopilot. The Tu-154 manual indicates that a go-around using autopilot must be initiated at 200 meters if the engines are running at or below 75%. This is because jet engines have to "spool up" in order to produce more thrust. At power settings higher than 78%, this response is almost instantaneous; at idle power, it can take a full 8 seconds for a jet engine to "spool up" to full power. In the case of the Tu-154, the engines were well below the 75% minimum reading, and the crew should initiate a go-around at 200 meters even though it was above their Minimum Decision Altitude (MDA). It appeared as if Protasiuk was either not aware of or did not consider this factor. If anyone else on the crew knew this, they did not speak up.

The controller asked: "101, have you got enough fuel for getting to alternate airfield after trial approach?" Protasiuk confirmed "Enough" and requested clearance for further descent.

Meanwhile, at 10:24, the Yak-40 pilot who had already landed in Smolensk, contacted the Tu-154 on another frequency and conducted a conversation with the co-pilot and relayed his assessment of the weather conditions: "Visibility 400 meters with cloud base below 50 meters and thick." He said that he had landed, that the crew of the Tu-154M could try landing, and that a double APS gate had been set up at the airfield. "You know, generally, it's absolutely shit here…we were lucky to land at the last moment. But frankly speaking you could try of course, there are two APS, they've made a gate. ..If you will not be able to make it the second time then I suggest you fly to Moscow for example or somewhere else."

Protasiuk and Grzywna discussed the Yak-40 landing.

Grzywna: "Artur is saying that in their opinion there is around 400(meters) visibility; 50 meters base"

Protasiuk: "How much?"

Grzywna: "400(meters) visible; 50 meters base"

Protasiuk: "But he landed. What is he saying?"

Grzywna: "Yes, they made it"

The Yak-40 pilots also told the crew of the Tupolev that a Russian Ilyushin 76 had gone around due to the visibility issue, then five minutes later radioed the Tupolev reporting the Russian Ilyushin had gone around a second time and diverted. Seven minutes later, the Yak-40 crew radioed the Tupolev crew again reporting they estimated the visibility was now only 200 meters.

In the radio exchanges with the Tu-154M the Yak-40 Commander passed his assessment of the atmospheric conditions in a very undecided way. He did not say that clouds were merging with the fog and it was not possible to see the runway from the height of 100 meters when on final approach. And yet, he suggested the Tupolev might try a landing.

At 10:25, the controller provided clearance for descent: "101, on heading 40 degrees, descend 1500". Protasiuk confirmed.

At 10:26 the MUDC, Colonel Krasnokutski said to Plusnin, " …so, he will perform a trial approach, that's the commander's decision, he will perform a trial approach to an altitude of one hundred meters, then he goes around, so they should ask if Minsk or Vitebsk are ready as alternates…You bring him down to 100 meters. Not a meter more, damn it!"

Protasiuk asked his co-pilot to contact the Yak-40 again and "ask Artur if these clouds are thick." The Yak-40 pilot replied "As far as we can remember, at 500 meters we were still above the clouds" He also informed the Tu-154 crew that the airfield had APMs set up 200 meters from the edge of the runway. The Captain asked the co-pilot to inquire if the Russians (the IL-76) had made it. The Yak-40 pilot informed that they went around and landed somewhere else.

At some point around this time, the Director of Diplomatic Protocol, Mariusz Kazana, entered the Tupolev's cockpit.

At 10:26 Protasiuk is heard on the cockpit voice recorder addressing Kazana : "Mr. Director—fog has come out now and under present conditions we will not be able to land. So, please start thinking about your decision as to what we are going to do." To this the Director replied, "So, we have a problem." Protasiuk explained: "We may hang around for a half an hour, {to see if conditions improve} then we must depart for an alternate airfield." When asked about alternates, he answered: "Minsk, also Vitebsk". The Director then left the cockpit, presumably to report the situation and obtain guidance from the President.

One of the pilots is heard to say "Before he decides, maybe we should go over the checklist in the meantime. It doesn't matter if it will be Minsk or Vitebsk." Protasiuk agreed.

At 10:30, Plusnin gave the Tupolev clearance to descend to 500 meters and then ordered a heading change to 079. Protasiuk confirmed.

Kazana once again appeared in the cockpit. "No decision as yet from the President as to what we are doing next," he told the crew before turning and leaving the cockpit.

10:30:35 MUDC - What? He intends to approach?
10:30:36 ATC - Damn, he is approaching us at the moment, yes…Well, yes that's what they said, damn it. I'll bring him down for the time being
10:30:52 MUDC - Well, okay

The Final Flight

After having confirmed the crew's intentions, Krasnokutski ordered Plusnin to communicate the minimum descent altitude.

10:31:45 MUDC - No, we're going to do our duty
10:31:51 MUDC - Tell him that it's 100 meters here, communicate the decision at 100 meters. That's it!

Plusnin asked the pilot if he had reached 500 meters yet. "No," Protasiuk replied, "Not yet. We're at 1000 and descending". It was apparent from this exchange, and a few subsequent similar exchanges asking about their altitude, that the Smolensk controller was having difficulty tracking the Tupolev's position. Plusnin later told a Moscow news agency that he had had difficulties understanding the crew, who he claimed had spoken poor Russian. "Numbers were hard for them, so I could not determine their altitude," he said. [90]

At about 10:33, Protasiuk informed his crew "We will approach for landing...in case of unsuccessful approach, we will go around on autopilot." Grzywna confirmed.

Plusnin made an attempt to get an update of the weather conditions to see if there had been any improvement, but the information he got, he and Krasnokutski did not deem to be credible.

10:33:20 ATC - Is this Meteo crazy or what? He is showing 800 meters now.
10:33:22 MUDC - What do you mean, 800?!
10:33:29 MUDC - That's it, now he's showing 800 meters, and there's nil there. Look, it's something like 200 or 300 meters there and 200 max over here.

Between 10:33 and 10:34 an unidentified general called Krasnokutski's cell phone, and the MUDC—inexplicably--communicated the airfield's full readiness to receive the Tu-154M.

The Tu-154M was now performing the base leg approach.

---

[90] "Kontroler: Zrobiłem wszystko, by do tego nie doszło" http://www.fakt.pl/wydarzenia/polityka/kontroler-zrobilem-wszystko-by-do-tego-nie-doszlo/cqh1wxp

At 10:35 Plusnin asked the pilot, "Have you performed landings at military airfields?" To which Protasiuk replied "Yes, of course".

Plusnin informed the Tu-154M that projectors in day mode were on the left hand side at the beginning of the runway.

At 10:35 flight attendant Barbara Maciejczyk reported to Protasiuk: "Commander. Deck is ready for landing."

At 10:35:24, Plusnin communicated to the crew they should be ready for a go-around. "Ah, Polish one zero one, prepare for a go-around from one hundred meters." Protasiuk confirmed.

At 10:36:48, Air Force Commander in Chief (Andrzej Blasik) appeared in the cockpit, probably after a discussion with the Director of Protocol.

Upon the aircraft's final approach, ATC expressed doubt as to the landing's success for the last time

10:37:36 ATC - He will not be able to approach.

10:37:44 MUDC - The main thing is, prepare him for a go-around…a go-around, that's it. And then let him hang there. It is his call, let them continue by themselves.

At this critical point Plusnin and Krasnokutski abandoned any further attempts to prevent the landing approach of the aircraft in weather conditions well below the airfield's minima, shifting liability for any further action to the aircraft commander. These, in fact, were the rules for international flights landing at foreign airports.

At 10:38, the Russian interpretation of the cockpit voice recorder reports hearing a person, most probably the navigator, say "He'll go crazy if…" (presumably referring to the anticipated reaction from President Kaczynski if he learns they will not be landing at Smolensk.)

The Polish report noted that though the Landing Zone Controller, ATC, and MUDC were monitoring the readings of the final approach of the Tu-154M, no one at Inner ATC Post reacted to the aircraft's incorrect position in relation to the approach path or the runway axis. In fact the Landing Zone Controller notified the crew that their position was correct: "on course and on glide path". This could only have acted as assurance to the crew that they were performing a correct approach and carried no warning of the necessity of performing an immediate go-around.

The Final Flight

At 10:39:45, the Tupolev commenced the final leg of approach at a distance of 1.54 meters before the outer beacon.

At 10:40:09 at a radio altimeter altitude of 356 meters at a speed of 306 km/h, the Terrain Awareness Warning System (TAWS) alarm sounded for the first time: "TERRAIN AHEAD. TERRAIN AHEAD"

Grzywna remarked, "There is a lowering of the terrain, Arek."

Protasiuk replied, "I know. It will be a moment…"

At 10:40:15 at a radio altimeter reading of 366 meters, at a speed of 309 km/h, the barometric pressure altimeter was switched to the default setting, causing the altimeter readings of the aircraft to increase by 168 meters. This fed incorrect information to the system, as a result of which it assumed the aircraft to be at a higher than actual altitude, and failed to generate warnings. Immediately afterward, at 10:40:15, TAWS stopped generating the TERRAIN AHEAD message.

Investigators found that since most military airports, including the one at Smolensk North, were not programmed into the TAWS database, it was common practice for pilots to reset their barometric altimeters to prevent the TAWS warning from going off during landing. They did this to silence what they came to consider a "nuisance alarm". Because of the location of the altimeter reset button, only the navigator and the pilot were in a position to have been able to do this. From this point on, the navigator was reading from the plane's radio altimeter.

A radio altimeter measures altitude above the terrain presently beneath an aircraft by timing how long it takes a beam of radio waves to reflect from the ground and return to the plane. This type of altimeter provides the distance between the antenna and the ground directly below it, in contrast to a barometric altimeter which provides the distance above a defined data point, usually mean sea level. Radio altimeter readings provide a 'snapshot' height above ground and can give a false impression of clearance margins in regions where terrain rises sharply ahead of the aircraft. The approach to Smolensk taken by the Tu-154 featured a valley followed by a rising valley wall about one kilometer from the runway threshold. The radio altimeter was reading the distance of the aircraft from the bottom of the valley, not the distance from the airfield plane.

At some point after passing the outer runway marker the crew, obviously realizing they were above the glide path, increased their vertical speed of descent to 8 m/sec. To correct this error the vertical speed should not have exceeded 5-6m/sec. This excessive speed of descent was retained until the crew began to take actions to avoid collision with obstacles. No attempts were made to decrease the vertical speed even when reaching the altitude of the airfield minima of 100 meters. The Russian investigators concluded from this that the pilot in command was not monitoring the aircraft's vertical speed at the final stage of descent (below 100 meters). Air accident investigation experience shows that such situations occur when the pilot distracts his attention from the instruments "turning his eyes and attention to the space outside the cockpit in order to search for the runway or ground reference (mainly lights: threshold or approach lights), while the other crew members such as the co-pilot are not monitoring the instruments.

Around 10:40:21, it is believed General Blasik, who was still in the cockpit, told the crew "You'll make it easily…be bolder"

At 10:40:26 Blasik read out the radio altimeter reading: "Two hundred and fifty meters"

At 10:40:28 the navigator echoed the reading: "Two hundred and fifty"

> 10:40:30 Landing Zone Controller - Three on course, on glide path
> 10:40:31 TAWS - TERRAIN AHEAD
> 10:40:32 MUDC - Tell him to switch his landing lights on
> At 10:40:34.5 TAWS system warnings activated again (which continued until the aircraft crashed)
> 10:40:35 ATC - Switch landing lights on

At 10:40:36, the navigator communicated altitude "200".

> 10:40:37 Tupolev - Landing lights on

The aircraft reached the visual assessment altitude of 130 meters. At that stage the navigator or co-pilot should have called out "Decision", after which the pilot in command would start establishing visual contact with the ground references. At that time the co-pilot should have been controlling the aircraft and monitoring the flight instruments. No crew member called out "Decision" and it seems no one was monitoring the instruments.

10:40:38 TAWS - TERRAIN AHEAD

At 10:40:40, the navigator reported radio altitude: "150".

10:40:41 TAWS - PULL UP. PULL UP
10:40:42 Landing Zone Controller - Two on course, on glide path
10:40:42 TAWS - TERRAIN AHEAD. TERRAIN AHEAD
10:40:43 TAWS - TERRAIN AHEAD. TERRAIN AHEAD

At 10:40:44 at 98 meters above the airfield, General Blasik, still in the cockpit, read out the radio altimeter reading: "100 meters"

10:40:45 TAWS: PULL UP. PULL UP
10:40:46 TAWS: PULL UP. PULL UP
10:40:47 TAWS: PULL UP. PULL UP
10:40:48 TAWS: PULL UP. PULL UP

At 10:40:49 at radio altimeter altitude of 103 meters, at a speed of 280km/h the autopilot control began to increase engine thrust from low throttle range. This was due to airspeed decreasing below 280 km/h which was set for automatic engine thrust control.

10:40:49 TAWS: TERRAIN AHEAD. TERRAIN AHEAD
10:40:51 TAWS: TERRAIN AHEAD. TERRAIN AHEAD

At 10:40:51 at 49 meters above airfield level, the navigator again read out "100" as their altitude.

Three consecutive references to 100 meters radio altimeter altitude even though the actual flight altitude was decreasing resulted from the shape of terrain on approach and should have been an indication to the crew that the readings were inaccurate in reference to the airfield. But no one noticed.

At 10:40:52 when the aircraft reached radio altitude of 91 meters (39 meters above actual airfield level) Protasiuk announced to the crew:

"Going around". At 10:40:53, the co-pilot confirmed "Going around". At 10:40:54 at 66 meters (23 meters above actual airfield level) at a speed of 277km/h warning of hazardous altitude as set on the radio altimeter occurred.

>10:40:53 TAWS: PULL UP. PULL UP
>10:40:54 TAWS: PULL UP. PULL UP

At 10:40:55 Landing Zone Controler transmitted the message: "Horizon, 101" which was an indication that the aircraft should stop descent and level off.

>10:40:55 TAWS: PULL UP. PULL UP
>10:40:56 TAWS: PULL UP. PULL UP

At 10:40:57 the ATC transmitted "Altitude control and horizon." At the same time onboard the aircraft flying at 277km/h, the autopilot's pitch channel was deactivated. This resulted from the aircraft commander pulling the control column toward him. Evidently, Protasiuk could, at that moment, see the ground and obstacles (trees), assess the height visually, and realize he was too low. In this situation, his actions were instinctive. He pulled back on the control column, trying to get the plane to climb.

>10:40:58 ATC - Altitude control, horizon
>10:40:58 TAWS -PULL UP. PULL UP
>10:40:59 TAWS -PULL UP. PULL UP
>10:40:59 Co-pilot: Fuck!
>10:41:00 TAWS: PULL UP. PULL UP

The Tu-154M crew ceased responding.

>10:41:01 TAWS- PULL UP. PULL UP
>10:41:01 ? Fuck
>10:41:02 ATC - How long have we waited?

At about 1000 meters from the runway threshold and in the proximity of the inner NDB, the Tupolev collided with the first tree. The right wing sheared the tip of a birch tree with no ensuing damage to the plane which would affect its airworthiness. At that moment, the plane was about 10 meters above the ground. About 200 meters away from the first collision with the birch tree, the aircraft impacted with more trees and bushes. These were clusters of young birch trees, which were sheared at about four meters above ground by the aircraft's left wing. The plane had started climbing slowly but, its altitude above ground continued to drop.

Upon travelling 18 meters further, the fuselage and wings collided with trees whose trunk diameter was about 10 cm. Despite the sustained damage, the plane maintained its air worthiness and continued to climb.

At 10:41:02 at 1.1 meters above airfield level, at a distance of 855 meters from the Runway 26 threshold the aircraft's left wing hit a birch with a trunk 30-40cm in diameter, which sheared off 6.1 meters of the left wing, including the aileron. The aircraft rolled to the left uncontrollably, which the crew tried to counteract by turning the control column in the opposite direction. The aircraft continued to collide with trees of limb diameters up to 15 cm over a distance of 20 meters.

Turning the steering wheel and applying rudder pedals did not stop the leftward roll of the airplane. With a roll of about negative 35 degrees, having travelled 80 meters since the loss of the left wing section, the plane passed over a medium voltage power line, damaging it.

Fifty meters later the airplane's roll increased to negative 50 degrees. Thereafter, at a distance of about 40 meters the plane collided with several thicker trees, such as firs and birches, causing their limbs to break and increasing roll to about negative 90 degrees. Those impacts caused extensive damage to the leading edges and numerous damages to the elevators and rudder surfaces of the plane.

The plane's roll further increased to negative 120 degrees as the fuselage, wings, and tail impacted with two tall trees causing their limbs and branches to break. At this moment, the left elevator separated. With a roll reaching negative 130 degrees, the plane was upside down when it collided with the last group of trees.

10:41:03 ?(ATC?) But he's not there…everything…
10:41:03 TAWS - PULL UP. PULL UP
10:41:03 (unidentified crew member) Fuck!

10:41:04 TAWS - PULL UP. PULL UP

At 10:41:05 ATC issued the command "Go around!" The aircraft was at a distance of 698 meters from the runway threshold in uncontrolled rotation, with the crew unable to steer the aircraft.

At 10:41:05, a prolonged, high-pitch scream can be heard on the cockpit voice recorder. At 10:41:07.5, the aircraft impacted the ground.

At 10:41:09 the ATC issued one more command to "Go Around" but there was no response from the Tupolev.

On impact with the ground, the airplane's structure was completely destroyed-- airplane and body parts scattered over an area of 30 by 60 meters.

CHAPTER TEN

AFTERMATH

A delegation including the Polish Ambassador, Jerzy Bahr and BOR agent Gerard Kwasniewski, were at the Smolensk air field to meet the Presidential plane. That morning at breakfast, they were already discussing the weather conditions. The fog was so thick they could see only the outline of the control tower a hundred meters away. The fog had rolled in and thickened very quickly until the visibility had dropped to about 50-60 meters.

The Ambassador waited with Kwasniewski on the tarmac at the Smolensk airfield for the President's plane to land. Also on the tarmac was a column of cars waiting to receive and provide security for the dignitaries soon to be arriving. As they waited, a man came out of the air control tower and informed the ambassador that the weather was getting worse and it was unlikely that the President's plane would land. He came out a second time to inform the ambassador that the pilot had decided to descend and try to see if he could see the runway. If he couldn't, he would divert to an alternate airfield and wait for the weather to clear. Kwasniewski later said, "I was surprised. For if we could see only at a distance of 60 meters, it was hard to believe that the pilot could see more. We were waiting, but only theoretically, because we believed the Tupolev would certainly fly away. The weather was not in favor of a landing." [91]

---

[91] "Wykasowano polaczenia oficerow BOR" nwonews.pl/getpdf2,11118 http://arturb.salon24.pl/ arturb.salon24.pl/250027, bo-tu-juz-jest-delegacja

The weather was cold—two degrees C (about 36 degrees F) and the men sat in their car with the heater on. Suddenly, Kwasniewski noticed that the government cars from the Presidential column were moving, and then suddenly stopped. The agents of the Russian Federal Security Service got out of the cars and appeared to be listening to something. Something unusual was going on. Kwasniewski got out of his car and walked up to the Russians. He asked them "What do you hear? Did the plane land or not?" One of the men told Kwasniewski that they had heard the howl of an engine, a powerful bang, and then silence. [92]

"Sometimes fog is such that it suppresses sounds," Kwasniewski said. "We did not hear, but they were behaving strangely, so quickly I went back to the car and said 'Mr. Ambassador, something is wrong.'" When Kwasniewski turned to go back to the Russians, they were already driving away. "What is it?!" - Kwasniewski shouted after them. Getting back into the car with the ambassador, they drove rapidly to the runway. [93]

When they arrived at the runway, they saw nothing, so they drove off onto the grass about 50 meters. Still seeing nothing, they turned to leave and then they noticed the ground scattered with scrap wood. The entire road was strewn with it. "We saw some Russians standing there motionless. They stood stunned and staring at the sky. Then we learned that earlier the plane flew right over their heads above the roadway." [94]

From a small hill on the airfield they could see the earth with a freshly ploughed furrow, about 30 centimetres deep. Russian police officers who had been on the roadway waiting to direct the passing of the Presidential contingent as they travelled to Katyn from the air field came running up to the scene. They said they believed no one survived.

"And we still did not know what happened" said Kwasniewski "I thought, 'well, the aircraft reached the airfield. So certainly he made a belly landing. Surely someone survived.' We expected the men would need help." [95]

---

[92] Ibid.
[93] Ibid.
[94] Ibid.
[95] Ibid.

Meanwhile, cars were rushing around the area in all different directions. Kwasniewski and the ambassador went off in one direction and saw nothing. Others in the area pointed them in another direction. "We were surprised because the place they were showing us was not on the flight path. Continuing we saw two or three pieces of metal. And suddenly –the tail, twenty meters from us. Next we saw the chassis, protruding wheels, and a piece of the wing. And then it occurred to us that there was no chance."

OMON police agents (Russian Special Purpose Mobility Unit) arrived at the scene and took up their task of securing the area. Kwasniewski and the ambassador stood by the dying remains of their plane, the strong odor of fuel permeating the air. They were approached by five OMON officers, shouting that they needed to leave the area. Kwasniewski was torn. As a member of the Government Protection Bureau, it was his responsibility to protect. He understood that the Russian officers had been ordered to remove everyone from the crash site in order to secure it, but still, it was difficult to leave. Kwasniewski began to protest: "It's *our* plane that fell, not *yours*!" The Russians just continued to shout at them to leave. Finally a higher ranking Russian officer arrived and calmed everyone down. Only then did Kwasniewski and the ambassador leave the crash scene and return to the airport. [96]

Once back at the airport, Kwasniewski began trying to get in contact with his fellow BOR agents who were in Katyn providing protection for the ceremony. But there was no answer on any of their cell phones. He was able to reach his wife, Grazyna who was also in Katyn, and keeping warm in the car of Polish television. "Do not let anyone know this—but the Tupolev has crashed and probably no one survived. Find me someone from BOR, because I can't get through." When Grazyna left the car to seek out one of the other BOR agents, the journalists asked her, "Has it landed?" "Yes, I think so," she told them, not wanting to reveal the truth. She located a BOR officer and handed him the phone where her husband was still holding on. Kwasniewski told his fellow agent, "Listen,

---

[96] Ibid.

the Tupolev crashed. We were standing with the plane and it did not look like anyone survived. The Russians say they certainly do not think so." [97]

Shortly thereafter, the Polish ambassador was approached by the governor of Smolensk, apparently still muddy and dirty from the crash scene. He asked the ambassador for a list of passengers. Calling Warsaw, the ambassador received verification of who was and who was not on the plane. That is when Kwasniewski learned that on the passenger list was his wife's good friend, Agnieska Weclawek. She was scheduled to fly on the Yak that morning, but switched with a friend at the last minute to fly on the doomed Tupolev.

Lieutenant Artur Wosztyl was the pilot of the Yak-40 which had ferried the journalists to Smolensk early on the morning of April 10. He was able to safely land his aircraft despite the fog becoming more and more dense and the admonitions of the Smolensk air traffic controllers that the landing conditions were not suitable.

After landing, he and his crew deplaned and at about 10:30 local Smolensk time they began listening to see if they could hear the Tupolev approaching. With the dense fog, they could only listen for it for it would have been impossible to see it. Standing by their plane they heard the characteristic sound of the Tu-154 engines approaching for landing. Suddenly they heard an increase in the engine thrust, as if the pilot wanted to increase engine speed and thus level out or climb. Wosztyl wondered what would induce the pilot to do this. Only a few seconds passed before Wosztyl heard from the direction of the runway approach loud cracking sounds, several bangs, then an explosion. Then there was only silence. Wosztyl later said, "For me, these were frightening sounds which I hope never to hear again in my life." [98]

A Russian came out of the air traffic control tower and Wosztyl asked him what had happened. The Russian replied that the plane had flown off (i.e, aborted the landing and departed for an alternate airport). This

---

[97] Ibid.
[98] Testimony of Artur Wosztyl: Protokol Przesluchania Swiadka, Warszawa 10 Apr 2010

immediately struck Wosztyl as being impossible. If the Tupolev had indeed departed, he would have heard the sound of the departing aircraft engines. This was not the sound that he had heard. Shortly thereafter, another uniformed Russian came up to where the Yak-40 crew was standing. The man was terrified, shaking and muttering to himself. He then told them that the Tu-154 had crashed 1500 meters in front of the runway. [99]

After talking to the Russian from the control tower, Wosztyl noticed fire engines, ambulances, and a number of other cars speeding away from the airport, all racing toward the runway approach from which the terrible sounds had come. It was becoming more and more clear to him that the Tupolev had crashed. Wosztyl quickly used his cell phone to contact the 36th Special Regiment's unit commander and the duty manager of operational missions in Warsaw and informed them of what he could only surmise was the crash of the Presidential plane.

Soon confirmation came from Moscow that the plane had indeed crashed just short of the runway and it appeared that there were no survivors.

By this time, the fog had dissipated completely and the visibility at the airport had significantly improved. About two hours after the crash Wosztyl and his crew decided to go see the remains of the aircraft and find out for themselves if anyone survived. During those two hours Wosztyl fought with his thoughts---did he really want to see? But he went. [100]

Upon reaching the end of the runway, he noticed that there was a concrete fence, which prevented access to the remains of the aircraft. For this reason, the rescue vehicles had to go back to the exit gate of the airport and go to the crash site from the outside. Two of the concrete plates of the fence were eventually broken out and Wosztyl was able to enter into the crash site from there. There they saw the remains of the aircraft at a distance of about 40 meters from the fence around the airport and 500 meters from the runway threshold slightly to the left scattered over an area about 30 by 60 meters.

Among the wreckage were broken metal fragments, the main landing gear with its shank, and part of the hull. In addition, throughout this area

---

[99] Ibid.
[100] Ibid.

Wosztyl could see visible fragments of human bodies, hands, and feet; large parts of bodies which were unclothed. No one had as of yet taken an interest in even covering them. Wosztyl asked responders on the scene if anyone had survived and they shook their heads, resignedly not.

Wosztyl soon received a telephone call from his unit, telling him that, if they were able, they should return to country as soon as possible. But Wosztyl was informed by the Russians that the tower had stopped all outgoing air traffic and the state borders of Russia were closed. As a result Wosztyl and his crew were not able to leave until about 5:30 pm local Smolensk time. They arrived back at their base in Warsaw two hours later.

Deputy Chief of the Chancellery, Marcin Wierzchowski was one of the first three Polish officials to rush to the crash scene. Even seeing the foggy conditions, he had had no thought that the President's plane would not be able to land. He had flown with the President on many occasions in different weather conditions and there had never before been a problem. At 10:40 Smolensk time, Wierzchowski heard the Tupolev's engines approaching, a loud crashing sound, then silence. He saw the Russian protection officials assigned to protect the president rush across the tarmac. Wierzchowski got into the car with ambassador Jerzy Bahr and his driver, the BOR agent Gerard Kwasniewski. When they got to a place on the side of the runway, Wierzchowski got out and saw three or four people rushing into the forest. His adrenaline began pumping, as he ran after them and saw the devastation.

"The first thought that came to my mind was, 'God, it is impossible that the president and all the people on board were killed. It was not this plane.' But after a few seconds, I saw that on the scattered remains of the plane, was red and white paint. I then knew that this is the Polish plane....The enormity of the destruction which I found on the spot, it was something amazing. I already knew that no one survived." [101]

---

[101] "Wierzchowski: I saw red and white paint, I knew that no one survived..."Saturday, April 2, 2011 http://www.rmf24.pl/tylko-wrmf24/wywiady/przesluchanie/news-wierzchowski-zobaczylem-bialo-czerwone-malowania-wiedzialem-,nId,332633

The next thought that came to Wierzchowski's mind was to call his immediate superior, Minister Jacek Sasin, who was at the cemetery for the ceremony. With great pain, he called him and informed him what had happened. "He told me to calm down. That what I was saying was impossible. That even if something happened to the plane maybe it just went off the runway somewhere on the road...It was only after {he came to the crash site and} he came out of the woods, white as a sheet with tears in his eyes, {that he believed what had happened}" [102]

The four men, Ambassador Bahr, Minister Sasin, Wierzchowski, and the BOR agent Kwasniewski began to search the site of the tragedy, searching for the body of the president taking care not to disturb the wreckage of the plane. Wierzchowski was standing next to the crash site, when one of the Polish consuls came to him to ask him, as someone who sees the President every day, if he could please come and identify his remains. He agreed. He was not able to say with 100 percent assurance that it was the body of the President, but he was 75 percent sure.

"At that time, I was devastated. I was aware that all these people died - that Kasia Doraczyńska died, Pawel Wypych was killed, colleagues from the BOR, flight attendants, with whom I worked every day, that all those generals were killed, Katyn families, Mr. Stefan Melak who all the time fought for the restoration of the memory of Katyn. This may sound quite awkward, but immediately I wanted to find the greatest number of people, so we could identify them." [103]

At 10:42 local time, the Head of the Smolensk Regional Search and Rescue Service (RSRS) declared an emergency and ordered the shift on duty to depart for the scene of the accident. A fire truck and 40 emergency service workers were dispatched to the scene at 10:51. There was a small brush fire which ignited in the field and this fire was quickly extinguished within five minutes. At 11:10 seven ambulances arrived; within 30 minutes

---

[102] Ibid.
[103] Ibid.

of their arrival, the determination was made that there were no survivors, and the seven ambulances left the scene.

At the site of the Katyn cemetery, a large crowd was gathered amid flapping white and red flags awaiting the arrival of the Polish President and the contingent of dignitaries travelling with him. They were scheduled to arrive at 11:20 local time and the ceremony was to begin at 11:30.

Most of the guests had arrived very early that morning by train; some by car or bus after a long trip. Some strolled and took pictures. Others, family members of the victims of the Katyn massacre, laid flowers or small tokens of remembrance beside the plaques of their loved ones before the memorial wall. Some of the guests had already taken their seats. On each chair had been placed a small replica of the Polish flag. Several rows of empty chairs sat facing the altar awaiting the Presidential group.

Shortly after 11:00 am cells phones began ringing. Faces of those with phones pressed to their ears turned pale. A group of journalists with cameramen in tow were seen jumping up and rushing out the gate of the cemetery. Ministers and officials began to disappear from the crowd. People noticed anxiety and tension on the faces of the BOR agents present, each intently listening through their ear pieces. Someone overheard one of the BOR agents say to his colleague "The President's plane has crashed." A murmuring began to spread throughout the crowd. Here and there, sobbing could be heard. Priests began reciting prayers and saying the rosary.

Back in Poland, TV screens, computers, tablets, and cell phones began lighting up with the news that the Presidential plane had crashed. Shortly thereafter, families and friends started calling and texting their loved ones who they knew were attending the Katyn ceremony.

The Katyn cemetery was a scene of confusion, nervousness, uncertainly, and fear. At first, only pieces of unreliable and unconfirmed information began leaking through. Some people heard that there was a problem with the landing; then that there had been an accident and that 30 people were in very serious condition, while the others were dead. But hope quickly dissolved into despair. Finally, they began to hear the dire news that no one had survived the crash. But no one could yet tell them what had really happened. [104]

Minister Jacek Sasin, Deputy Chief of the Chancellery having received the terrible news knew he had to say something to those gathered for the ceremony who were still waiting for the President. "There stood before me a dilemma: what to say to these people. Do you go out and just say that they are all dead, the president is dead, that everyone who flew in the plane is dead?"[105]

Finally Sasin, came to the podium. He spoke briefly, his remarks punctuated with heavy sighs: "Ladies and gentlemen, we have come here to honor the victims of Soviet War Crimes on the 70th anniversary of the Katyn massacre. The President of the Republic of Poland was to be here today. Ladies and gentlemen, unfortunately Mr. President is not here with us. There has been an airplane accident. At the moment, a rescue operation is in progress but everything indicates that… this catastrophe had a tragic course and tragic results. I would like you all, ladies and gentlemen, to pray right now and take part in this mass for all those who died and had been heading here to pray for those murdered in the massacre. The end." [106] He muttered the last two words very silently as he turned from the podium as if he was speaking them to himself.

Krzysztof Sikora, president of the regional council Kujawsko-Pomorskie who was present for the ceremony recalled, "Something tightened in my throat. I looked at the people next to me. They went pale. They distrusted the news. Is this a joke?" [107]

Immediately after hearing the news from Minister Sasin, flags at the cemetery were lowered to half-mast. Someone took the large wreath that the Polish Red Cross contingent had brought to lay at the memorial and placed it against the row of empty chairs that they all now knew would

---

[104] "Wszyscy zaczęliśmy się modlić…" 16 Apr 2010
www.e-sochaczew.pl/sochaczew,wszyscy-zaczelismy-sie-modlic8230,20086.html
[105] "BRUTALNA SMOLENSKA PRAWDA"
4.04.2011 09:45Kategoria: Polityka Odsłon: 3803 37 Komentuj
http://mmariola.salon24.pl/294003,brutalna-smolenska-prawda
[106] Cmentarz Katyński, 10 kwietnia 2010 filmyfrondowe you tube video
[107] "Dla tych, którzy zginęli. Katyń 2" Piotr Zychowicz publikacja: 10.04.2010
http://www.rp.pl/artykul/459625--Dla-tych--ktorzy-zgineli--Katyn-2-.html#ap-1

remain empty. Someone else placed a large Polish flag next to the wreath. One priest was asked to try to calm people down but he was crying and was unable even to recite the rosary. Father Zawislak who was there as one of the representatives of the Polish Scouting Association, was suffering from a sore throat. "I could barely speak. I stood at the pulpit and intoned only the Chaplet of Divine Mercy." [108]

Finally, several priests began saying a mass for the souls of the dead. In the background, the strains of the Polish National Anthem could be heard coming from the ceremonial band.

There was no consolation, only shock and disbelief for those who stood bewildered in the Katyn forest. "Such a disaster. And it is here - in the place of martyrdom of our fathers? Smolensk becomes a terrible, traumatic place for the Polish nation," said Jan Felicki, son of Lieutenant Stanislaw Felicki who was murdered at Katyn. Some of the Katyn families present drew up candles into the form of a cross with the inscription: "To those who died. Katyn2 ".

"Many women wept," said Felicki. "For our nation it is a tragedy far greater than the disaster in Gibraltar and the death of General Sikorski. {In Gibraltar in 1943 a B-24 crash resulted in the death of an estimated sixteen people, including general Władysław Sikorski, the commander-in-chief of the Polish Army and the Prime Minister of the Polish government-in-exile.} .There were killed only a few people-- here reportedly more {than 100}."

"What a miserable thing," said Felicki. "Here were people who came to Katyn, to come together with the president to pray for the souls of the murdered officers. But it turned out that we had to pray for the soul of the President and the others killed." [109]

"We were all shocked. Our friends were killed, longtime colleagues, worthy people. We are with the families. I really do not know what to say" - said Deputy Marek Suski, member of the Polish Parliament. "This

---

[108] "Ksiądz Konrad Zawiślak ze Skierniewic celebrował mszę w Katyniu" by Jolanta Sobczyńska 15 kwietnia 2010 http://www.dzienniklodzki.pl/wiadomosci/244555,ksiadz-konrad-zawislak-ze-skierniewic-celebrowal-msze-w,id,t.html?cookie=1

[109] "Dla tych, którzy zginęli. Katyń 2" Piotr Zychowicz publikacja: 10.04.2010 http://www.rp.pl/artykul/459625--Dla-tych--ktorzy-zgineli--Katyn-2-.html#ap-1)

land has always taken the best of Poles...You know, this whole time I still hoped to wake up on the train to Smolensk {and discover} that it is all just a bad dream" [110]

After celebrating Mass for the souls of those killed in the crash, Katyn ceremonies were immediately terminated. Shocked participants silently got into their buses and went to the train station. The train set off immediately, a few hours before the scheduled departure. They all wanted to get home to Poland, to their families, as soon as they could.

When the tragedy happened, Radoslaw Sikorski, the Polish Foreign Minister was having breakfast with his family. The first information he received came from the head of the Eastern Department in the Ministry of Foreign Affairs at 8:48 am Warsaw time. Sikorski was the first politician in Poland to learn of the crash in Smolensk. He was faced with a dilemma: whether based on a single source of information they should put the entire country into a state of crisis. He sent the first text message to the prime minister and called the Polish ambassador in Russia. Within a few dozen minutes the ambassador was at the wreckage, observing the extent of the catastrophe—all doubts then disappeared. [111]

Sikorski made a call to Prime Minister Tusk. Then he called the Speaker of the Parliament, Bronislaw Komorowski to inform him that according to the constitution, Komorowski was now acting head of state. [112]

It would also be his terrible duty to inform President Lech Kaczynski's brother Jaroslaw of the disaster. Kaczynski was shaving when the phone rang. He was sure that this must be his brother calling to say he had arrived in Smolensk. But instead he heard a stranger's voice. It was one of Minster Sikorski's staff. The minister then took the receiver himself. Kaczynski knew Sikorski. He had no doubt that something was wrong. "I have a

---

[110] Ibid.
[111] Sikorski dzwonił do Jarosława Kaczyńskiego: Mam straszną informację...12.04.2010 0
http://wiadomosci.gazeta.pl/wiadomosci/1,114873,7761052,Sikorski_dzwonil_do_Jaroslawa_Kaczynskiego__Mam_straszna.html
[112] Ibid.

terrible message. There was a tragic accident. It can be concluded that there were no survivors" Sikorski told Kaczynski. [113] Kaczynski remained calm but said to the Foreign Minister, "This is the result of your criminal policy - not buying new aircraft." Sikorski did not respond but merely hung up. [114]

General Marian Janicki, Head of the Government Protection Bureau (BOR) was at home in Krakow on the morning of April 10. At half past eight he went to a shopping bazaar. Suddenly, his phone rang. It was the operations officer saying "Chief, there is a problem with the landing of the Tu-154 near Smolensk. Something is wrong." Janicki thanked him and instructed him to call with any new or more detailed information. Then he immediately called Colonel Jaroslav Florczak, security commander for the Katyn visit. There was no answer. So he called Lieutenant Pawel Janeczk, then commander of the protection of the president. No answer. Both Florczak and Janeczk had been on board the Tupolev and were already dead. The operations officer called Janicki again and informed him that the plane had crashed and there were most likely no survivors.

At the airport in Smolensk were two BOR officers. At the Katyn cemetery there were five. Immediately after the disaster, the five BOR officers at the cemetery went to the Smolensk airfield. Janicki asked them to identify President Lech Kaczynski, his wife Maria Kaczynska, and president Ryszard Kaczorowski (those were the people they were assigned to protect), and their BOR colleagues, and to remain in Smolensk until the last of their caskets was on its way back to Poland.

Janicki was informed that Prime Minister Donald Tusk wanted to go to Smolensk. Jaroslaw Kaczynski also wanted to go. Janicki was told that Kaczynski could not fly with the Prime Minister because there were not enough seats on the plane for everyone the Prime Minister wanted to take with him. He did not want to say anything, but he knew there were actually fifteen vacancies on the Prime Minister's plane. Kaczynski simply

---

[113] Ibid.
[114] Ibid.

did not want to fly on the same plane as his political foe. [115] So, they flew separately.

Upon arriving in Smolensk, Janicki met with his officers. "What I saw, was beyond my worst expectations. I'm talking about their faces, I will never forget. They were in red rubber boots, big, long uniforms and gloves, which they got from the Russians." [116] He learned from the BOR officers that the President's body had been found in the wreckage and secured. Janicki there saw three bodies lying side by side: President Lech Kaczynski, President Kaczorowski and Marshal Putra. The BOR officers assured him that they were with the body of the president the entire time.

Others who were able to be identified were in caskets including some of the BOR officers who had died in the crash. Janicki was asked if he wanted to view the body of the President and he said that he did. The President's body was laying on a stretcher, covered, like the other two, with a white cloth.

Janicki then went to the crash site. "What I saw is indescribable. I started to cry. It was a huge shock. The last time I had cried was at the funeral of my father in 1997." [117]

Polish Prime Minister Donald Tusk and Russian Prime Minister Vladimir Putin now would meet again in Smolensk as they had just three days before. This time they visited the site where President Kaczynski's plane crashed, killing all on board.

It was dark, so the men walked with a group of others, including journalists and cameramen, through the marshy field at the outskirts of the Smolensk air field using the beam of a flashlight to guide them. It was the evening of the crash and the debris from the wreckage still freshly littered the ground. At the Katyn ceremony three days before, Tusk's countenance had been solemn and it still was now on the 10th, but at this time his face

---

[115] Chciałbym się dowiedzieć, czy musieli zginąć by Rozmawiali Agnieszka Kublik and Wojciech Czuchnowski 08.04.2011 http://wyborcza.pl/1,76842,9396354, Chcialbym_sie_dowiedziec__czy_musieli_zginac.html#ixzz1Os3mhgJP
[116] Ibid.
[117] Ibid.

was pale and bore a look of shock and bewilderment combined with that solemnity.

Tusk was handed a wreath and Putin, a bouquet of long stemmed red flowers. Both men took a few steps forward, to a large piece of the aircraft to lay their tributes just as they had at the Katyn memorial three days before. Tusk knelt before the wreckage, and clasping both his hands together in what appeared to be a combination of fervent prayer and anxious wringing, he bowed his head. Putin stayed standing but quickly crossed himself in the Orthodox manner (right to left). As Tusk rose, Putin gently placed his hand on his counterpart's back and, when he had fully stood up, extended his arms to embrace him. This gesture was heart-breakingly touching. The Polish Ambassador to Russia Jerzy Bahr was also present during the visit of Donald Tusk to the crash site. He witnessed Putin embrace Tusk. "It was an awful thing that some people later reported that Putin's embrace could be traced to something other than an expression of sympathy. Putin's gesture was totally spontaneous…it was a human reflex." [118]

On that day, time both stood still and changed forever.

---

[118] "Smiling Tusk and Putin in Smolensk?Ambassador: Tusk was shocked 27/10/2013 http://wiadomosci.dziennik.pl/media/artykuly/441614,usmiechnieci-tusk-i-putin-w-smolensku-na-okladce-tygodnika-w-sieci.html

CHAPTER ELEVEN

PREPARING FOR RETURN TO THE HOMELAND

According to both the Russian and Polish crash investigation reports, the configuration of the aircraft upon impacting the ground created no chance for crew or passenger survival. The cause of death of the seven members of the crew and the 89 passengers was massive multi-organ trauma due to deceleration force on the impact of the aircraft against the ground which was in excess of 100g (100 times the force of gravity). On the basis of the medical expertise, death of all persons on board occurred instantaneously at the time of the crash. [119]

At the moment of the airplane's impact against the ground, the pilot in command was located in the left pilot seat and the co-pilot was located in the right pilot seat. The cockpit, and therefore the crew, was in the upside down position. Both their seatbelts were fastened and they were performing flight procedures. Characteristic injuries on their hands indicated that they were clenched, presumably on the flight controls. Both the pilot and co-pilot were found with the right leg fully stretched forward probably attempting to counteract the rapidly increasing left bank of the

---

[119] Final Report from the examination of the aviation accident no. 192/2010/11 involving the Tu-154M airplane, tail number 101, which occurred on April 10, 2010 in the area of the Smolensk North airfield (the Polish report) and Interstate Aviation Committee Air Accident Investigation Committee Final Report (Russian MAK report)

plane. Both aircraft navigator and flight engineer were found in their seats with their seatbelts fastened. [120]

At the crash scene, Russian investigators divided the site into thirteen sectors and by 1:00 pm had begun the first identification of remains. Firefighters removed the bodies and laid them in a specially prepared place. Photographs and fingerprints were taken, then the bodies were wrapped. By about 3:00pm, 100 places in the city morgue, and 5 places in the 1st Clinic of Smolensk were arranged for receipt of bodies, the evacuation of which began at 3:12pm. By 7:00pm, bodies were loaded on to Mi-26 helicopters and transported to Moscow.

On Sunday, April 11, Polish Health Minister Ewa Kopacz, Head of the Prime Minister's Chancellery Tomasz Arabski, and Deputy Foreign Minister Jacek Najder arrived in Moscow to help identify bodies of the victims of the presidential plane crash. Three groups of Polish experts were in Moscow and Smolensk to work with the Russians. These included forensic experts to assist in identifying the bodies, prosecutors, and aviation accident experts. Psychologists and clergy were also available on site.

Two planes were made available for the victims' families, and the Russians prepared accommodations (150 hotel rooms) in anticipation of their arrival. The Russian government lifted all visa requirements for the family members to facilitate their travel. [121]

As the identification process and autopsies began in Moscow, it was noted that the state of the remains could be divided into three groups: those without any external injuries, those who were severely burned or charred, and mutilated remains. Obviously, the poorer the condition of the remains, the more difficult would be the identification process.

The Polish Health Minister announced that only 14 bodies were so well preserved that identification could take place without any problem. In

---

[120] Final Report from the examination of the aviation accident no. 192/2010/11 involving the Tu-154M airplane, tail number 101, which occurred on April 10, 2010 in the area of the Smolensk North airfield (the Polish report)

[121] Polish ministers in Moscow to help identify crash victims 08:46, April 12, 2010 Source: Xinhua http://en.people.cn/90001/90777/90853/6946782.html

fact, family members identifying these remains remarked that they looked like they were just sleeping and had no outward sign of any injury. [122]

Others were not so easy. Kopacz said that some families refused to view the bodies of loved ones. "I'm not surprised, the view is traumatic", she said. "In many cases we will have to collect research material, which is to do genetic testing to determine identity. We have a list of people with whom we found documents, whose bodies were preserved in good enough condition that there will be no problems for their loved ones to be able to identify them. Unfortunately, I regret to say that this group is a very small number "Kopacz said. [123]

The body of President Lech Kaczynski was first identified by members of his staff on April 10. And later that day by his brother Jaroslaw.

On April 11, shortly after the arrival in Poland of the body of the late Polish President Lech Kaczynski, there was information that the body of Maria Kaczynski was found. Marta, the Presidential couple's daughter was not able to fly, so Maria's brother (the now late) Colonel Konrad Mackiewicz, decided that he would go to Moscow. He did not have a valid passport, so the Polish government took steps to get him an expedited passport. The next day at 6 am he checked in at Warsaw-Okecie airport. There at the Novotel hotel was a collection of families flying to Moscow. At the hotel a DNA sample was taken by ABW officers (Poland's Internal Security and Intelligence Agency).

Mackiewicz ate breakfast and chatted with other families, waiting for the departure. ABW officers circulated among the families and seemed to Mackiewicz to try to discourage them from going to Moscow. They said that the bodies may be difficult to view. They said that if the family declined to go, there were specialists in Poland, who would identify

---

[122] "Lista Pasazerow—obrazenia, rozpoznawanie," 12 Jul 2011 http://pomocnezestawienia.blogspot.com/2011/07/4-lista-pasazerow-obrazenia.html
[123] Kopacz: Tylko w 14 przypadkach możliwa identyfikacja ofiar dżek, PAP / Z Moskwy Darek Zalewski, TOK FM 11.04.2010 18:24http://wiadomosci.gazeta.pl/wiadomosci/1,114873,7759638,Kopacz__Tylko_w_14_przypadkach_mozliwa_identyfikacja.html

their loved ones. Some families gave into this suggestion and did not go. Mackiewicz knew that no matter what he was going to go to Moscow to identify his sister. He had participated for years in the Air Force Institute of Technology in a study of aviation accidents and was used to such sights. Many a colleague he had had to view and identify. [124]

Around 9:00 am, Mackiewicz flew together with a few others to Moscow on a Yak-40. Upon arrival in Moscow, he went under the escort of militia to Tsaritsyn, to the central laboratory. Minister Ewa Kopacz was present as Mackiewicz was shown the body of his sister. Her body was intact; she had all her limbs but had damage to the right side of her face. Her brother positively identified her body. He recognized the scar she had from heart surgery she had undergone in 1955. Mackiewicz was given rings that she had on her fingers and a brooch; he gave the jewelry to Martin Wierzchowski, deputy chief of the chancellery. The minister identified them as belonging to the First Lady. [125]

The Russians once again collected blood (DNA), because they did not trust the samples ABW took. Then Mackiewicz went to questioning by Russian prosecutors which went on for two hours and in which he explained the manner in which he recognized his sister. He was handed the death certificate in Russian, which was later translated by the embassy and the document was brought back to Poland. [126]

Mackiewicz now only had to await the arrival of the caskets in which the victims, including his sister, would be transported back to Poland. He had brought with him the clothes that Marta had prepared for her mother. Russian officials gave him a bag with the remains of his sister's clothes, asking if he wanted to take it, and burn it. He later regretted that he had declined, but at the time he thought it did not seem dignified to bring them on the plane. [127]

That night, he did not sleep, just bathed and dressed, waiting for the casket. As he got a signal that the plane had landed with the caskets, Mackiewicz was directed to take his sister from the laboratory room.

---

[124] "Zmarł brat śp. Marii Kaczyńskiej" 31 Oct 2012 http://niezalezna.pl/34367zmarl-brat-sp-marii-kaczynskiej

[125] Ibid.

[126] Ibid.

[127] Ibid.

A plane arrived from Poland with Ministers Andrzej Duda and Bozena Borys-Szopa, presidential advisors. A woman who had come from Poland to help with the remains promised to prepare the body of the First Lady before closing the casket. Mackiewicz passed on to her the care of his sister. The woman dressed the First Lady and based on photos reconstructed the damaged part of her face. [128]

The Polish embassy told Mackiewicz not to leave his sister's remains for even a moment. "You should guard the body to the end," they told him.

Even though they had reconstructed her face, Mackiewicz asked Minister Borys-Szopa for a black veil because he wanted to take a picture for Marta. "I do not know how she did it," recounted Mackiewicz, "because we were all the time being followed by the Russian security service (even on the way to the toilet), but she managed to obtain the veil. She added roses and took pictures of Maria in the casket. Then I was left alone. I put in her hands a rosary from Pope John Paul II and a holy picture. I let the others go so I could pray." [129]

In his presence the Polish team soldered the casket shut. "The Ambassador told me that it would be an honor for him if he could go with us, so together we went behind the coffin in the funeral procession of honor to the airport. Before entering the aircraft the ambassador said goodbye to me. His wife and the mayor of Moscow were also with us." [130]

After landing they drove to customs and checked that the casket was properly secured. Flowers and a formal farewell were delivered before the First Lady's casket was taken to the Presidential Palace. Her brother followed closely behind, and never let his sister's casket out of his site for even a moment. In this way, he was assured that it was most certainly the remains of the First Lady that were laid to rest next to those of the President at Wawel Castle. [131]

------

[128] Ibid.
[129] Ibid.
[130] Ibid.
[131] Ibid.

By April 12 the bodies of 14 of the victims had been identified on the basis of examination alone. Another 10 people could be identified on the basis of pieces of clothing and special characteristics. Identification of the rest of the victims was difficult due to the extensive damage that passengers of the aircraft suffered during the disaster. Their identification would have to be made with genetic studies. By the evening of April 13 the Russian Prosecutor General's Office released information on the identification of 62 victims.

On April 14, Minister Kopacz reported that, at present, loved ones recognized a group of 20 people, whose bodies could not be identified the day before. "We implored them to try again. It's hard, but thanks to another attempt today we failed to identify only two victims." [132]

That day, 30 caskets were at the airport in Moscow waiting for their return to Poland.

On April 21, Health Minister Ewa Kopacz who had returned to Poland on April 15, again flew to Moscow to obtain information about the progress being made on the remaining 21 victims that had yet to be identified. The remains that had still gone unidentified were those belonging to the following passengers: General Andrzej Blasik, Edward Duchnowski, Grazyna Gęsicka, General Kazimierz Gilarski, Major Robert Grzywna, Mariusz Handzlik, Natalia Januszko, Admiral Andrzej Karweta, Janusz Krupski, General Bronislaw Kwiatkowski, Tadeusz Lutoborski, Warrant Officer Andrzej Michalak, Aleksandra Natalli-Swiat, General Vladimir Potasiński, Lieutenant Arkadiusz Protasiuk, Andrew Przewoznik, Arkadiusz Rybicki, Wieslaw Woda, Edward Wojtas, Stanislaw Zajac, and Lieutenant Arthur Ziętek.

---

[132] Kopacz: identyfikacja genetyczna aż do środy 14 kwietnia 2010, 14:30 (http://www.tvn24.pl)

http://www.tvn24.pl/wiadomosci-ze-swiata,2/kopacz-identyfikacja-genetyczna-az-do-srody,211670.html

Russian Health Minister Tatyana Golikova told Kopacz that DNA testing had been completed and the bodies of the remaining victims of the disaster had been positively identified. [133]

On April 23, at 17:30 at the military airport in Warsaw a NATO transport aircraft Boeing C-17 landed bearing the caskets containing bodies of last 21 victims of the disaster.

In the last days of April, Poland transported the disassociated remains of more than 20 additional people discovered at the Smolensk crash site and identified by genetic testing. Some of them, the remains of 11 identified persons and unidentified persons, were cremated and their cremains buried May 10 at the Powazki Military Cemetery in Warsaw where 28 other victims of the disaster were buried.

Much dispute ensued over the years as to whether or not the Commander in Chief of the Air Force, General Andrzej Blasik was in the cockpit of the plane at any time. Family and some colleagues were adamant that the General would not have imposed himself in this way, and failed to recognize the voice others had identified on the Cockpit Voice Recorder as that of General Blasik. The Russian investigation report however, leaves no doubt that the General was in fact in the cockpit right up until the very moment of the crash.

According to the Russian report:

> *As for the unauthorized person who could have been present in the cockpit during the impact, that person being not fastened and finding himself on the ceiling in the limited area of the cockpit must have sustained severe crushing injuries. Besides, considering the evolutions of the aircraft before the impact (intensively*

---

[133] Smoleńsk. Katastrofa. 21 osób wciąż nie da się zidentyfikować. Zobacz kogo {18 KWIETNIA 2010 http://www.wspolczesna.pl/katastrofa-w-smolensku/art/5712454,smolensk-katastrofa-21-osob-wciaz-nie-da-sie-zidentyfikowac-zobacz-kogo,id,t.html|

> *developing left bank), the initial impact force must have affected mainly the left part of the person's body who instinctively tried to lift himself from the ceiling, leaning on the left hand. The Coroner identified the body of this person as General Blasik based on genetic testing. This person had the main traumatic impact affecting the left side of the chest, abdomen, and pelvis, with the dismemberment of the left arm. Additionally, the body identified as that of General Blasik was found in sector No1, which corresponds with the nose part of the aircraft. The navigator's body was found in the same sector"*[134]

On April 11 the body of the president, was brought back to Warsaw by a Polish military CASA-295. At the airport there was an official ceremony of welcome. After the ceremony, the funeral procession passed through the streets of Warsaw to the Presidential Palace. Along the entire route, approximately 700-800 thousand people lined the streets to bid farewell to their President. Upon arrival at the palace the President's body was placed in a chapel.

On 14 April, 30 more caskets arrived at Okecie-Warsaw airport. On April 15, 34 more caskets arrived back in Poland. On April 16, when the airspace over Poland was closed due to the ash from the eruption of the Iceland volcano, the remains of General Franciszek Gagor, along with seven other caskets was delayed. Before 10:00 pm, two planes carrying the caskets finally arrived at the Okecie airport.

At 5:30 pm on April 23, the 21 caskets containing bodies of victims of the disaster, whose identification on April 18 was not yet possible arrived back in their homeland. The caskets were transported by caravan in a

---

[134] Interstate Aviation Committee Air Accident Investigation Committee Final Report (Russian MAK report)

funeral procession through the streets of Warsaw; some were transported directly to the hometowns of the victims.

As each plane landed returning the remains of the victims of the Smolensk crash to Warsaw, a special ceremony honored their arrival. Soldiers - in the company of the family - brought the casket covered with the white and red flag of the Polish republic out of the plane. Among those gathered at the airport were Marshal of the Sejm Bronislaw Komorowski (now the acting head of state), Prime Minister Donald Tusk, government ministers, and Members of Parliament. The national anthem was played.

"You're back to the homeland, you came back to your loved ones, but today your loved ones are crying. Today, the whole homeland is crying," said Prime Minister Donald Tusk in his remarks. "You're back enveloped in sorrow; enveloped in national mourning; you come back enveloped in glory." The Prime Minister announced the name in turn of each of the people whose bodies were brought out from the plane. "The Polish State and all of us have a duty to the dead and their loved ones...to Honor their memory." [135]

The caskets were transported from Okecie by caravan through the streets of Warsaw where all along the route, Polish citizens lined the streets. The cavalcade of hearses arrived at Torwar Hall (an indoor arena in Warsaw) where a prayer vigil was held. Some families decided to immediately take the bodies of their loved ones. Caskets with the bodies of presidential ministers Wladyslaw Stasiak and Pawel Wypych and employees of the Office of the President--Catherine Doraczyńskiej and Dariusz Jankowski--were taken to the Presidential Palace. They were set on the ground floor of the Palace, in the Hall of Hetmańskiej. [136]

On the sixth day in which caskets of the remains of the victims of the Smolensk crash were returned to Poland, Prime Minister Donald Tusk

---

[135] Generał wrócił do Polski 16 kwietnia 2010, http://www.tvn24.pl/wiadomosci-z-kraju,3/general-wrocil-do-polski,211731.html

[136] "Funeral procession with caskets of 30 passes through the streets of Warsaw" http://www.tvn24.pl/wideo/kondukt-zalobny-z-30-trumnami-przejezdza-ulicami-warszawy,256133.html

greeted them. "This is the sixth day that Poland welcomes its heroes. Here, at the airport we meet them with a kind of honor guard made up of families of the victims, and government soldiers. We keep this vigil to honor the people who gave their lives while in the service... We will remember those who have returned to us from this tragic mission, we will remember their work. But we also remember those who had not yet returned. Every day Poland will be waiting for these 21 caskets to find their way to us. We honor your memory." [137]

---

[137] Generał wrócił do Polski 16 kwietnia 2010, http://www.tvn24.pl/wiadomosci-z-kraju,3/general-wrocil-do-polski,211731.html

CHAPTER TWELVE

WHY?

There is rarely any one single cause of a plane crash, or any other accident. The crash of the Tupolev-154M is no exception. Many factors came together to bring this aircraft to the critical point of the impact. Investigators did rule out any technical or mechanical failure aboard the aircraft. They also ruled out sabotage or explosive device as the cause. This did not stop the conspiracy theorists who continue to contend that the plane was brought down by such a device as a plot by the Russians, backed by Polish political opponents of Lech Kaczynski. There are several other ridiculous theories that can be found circulating on the internet. One is that the Russians brought in giant fog-making machines to create the weather that obscured the pilots' view of the runway. Another contends that there never even was a flight therefore the crash never happened (one piece of "evidence" presented to support this claim was the fact that deputy chancellor Jacek Sasin, when informing the crowd at the Katyn cemetery of the accident, used the words "The President is not with us" instead of saying he was "dead")

The reports of both the Russian Interstate Aviation Commission (MAK) and the Polish Committee for Investigation of National Aviation Accidents point solidly to pilot error as the cause of the crash. The Polish report went farther—to lay a portion of the blame on the poor performance of the Air Traffic Controllers at the Smolensk airfield and the substandard conditions of the airfield itself. [138]

So what were the pilot errors that led to the crash?

The Russian MAK report concluded that the immediate causes of the accident were (1) the failure of the crew to make a timely decision to proceed to an alternate airport once it was apparent that the weather conditions at Smolensk airfield were unsuitable for landing. (2) descent without visual contact with ground references to an altitude much lower than minimum descent altitude for go around (100 meters) (3) no reaction by the crew to the numerous TAWS warnings which led to controlled flight into terrain, aircraft destruction and death of the crew and passengers.

The Polish investigation report was basically in agreement: "The immediate cause of the accident was the descent below the minimum descent altitude at an excessive rate of descent in weather conditions which prevented visual contact with the ground, as well as a delayed execution of the go-around procedure."

The causes and contributing factors of the crash, most of which point to pilot error, can be categorized as follows:

- Failure of the crew to monitor the aircraft's altitude by means of a pressure (i.e, barometric) altimeter during the non-precision approach (i.e, using their radio altimeter instead)
- Late start of final descent which resulted in increased vertical speed of descent the crew failed to correct and therefore maintained until the impact.
- Failure of the pilot in command and crew to terminate descent and go around when they reached their minimum decision height of 100 meters.
- Failure of the crew to respond to TAWS warnings
- Presence of third parties in the cockpit
- Poor Crew Resource Management

---

[138] Final Report from the examination of the aviation accident no. 192/2010/11 involving the Tu-154M airplane, tail number 101, which occurred on April 10, 2010 in the area of the Smolensk North airfield (the Polish report) and Interstate Aviation Committee Air Accident Investigation Committee Final Report (Russian MAK report)

- Psychological pressure on and other psychological factors affecting the pilot in command
- Systemic Failures
- Airport Failures

Failure of the crew to monitor altitude by means of a pressure (i.e, barometric) altimeter during the non-precision approach.

It is clear from the flight data recorder that, during the Tupolev's descent into Smolensk airfield, someone in the cockpit reset the plane's **barometric altimeter** (presumably to silence the TAWS alarm) and from that point on, the navigator, whose job it was to track and read out the plane's altitude, was reading from the plane's **radio altimeter**. A plane's minimum descent altitude (MDA) is the lowest altitude to which a pilot should take the aircraft on final approach when the pilot is landing manually without the benefit of instrument guidance from the airfield. An aircraft must not descend below the MDA until the pilot obtains some visual reference of the airfield. MDA is specified with regard to airfield level. Height above airfield level can only be determined using the **barometric altimeter**, which refers to atmospheric pressure on the airfield. The **radio altimeter** only displays altitude above the ground over which the aircraft is presently flying, and is useless in determining the airfield level. This was particularly true for the Tupolev since the plane had to fly over a valley on the approach to the elevated Smolensk airfield. **Radio altimeter** readings are acceptable for use only when the crew has visual contact with the airfield, which this crew did not. The navigator's reliance on the **radio altimeter** to read out the aircraft altitude resulted in inaccurate altitude readings in relation to the actual level of the airfield. This error resulted in the crew receiving information that the aircraft was about 160 meters higher than it actually was. They were, therefore, not aware of their actual altitude on approach to Smolensk airfield.

Late start of final descent which resulted in increased vertical speed of descent the crew failed to correct and therefore maintained until impact

After passing the runway outer marker, obviously realizing the plane was above the glide path, the pilot increased the aircraft's vertical speed of descent to 8m/sec. To correct this error the vertical speed should not have exceeded 5-6m/sec. The pilot never corrected or changed this excessive speed of descent and, in fact, maintained it until he collided with the first tree. No attempts were made to decrease the vertical speed even when reaching the altitude of the airfield minima of 100 meters. Thus the investigators concluded that the pilot in command was not monitoring the vertical speed at the final stage of descent (below 100 meters). Air accident investigation experience shows that such situations occur when the pilot distracts his attention from the instruments turning his eyes and attention to the space outside the cockpit in order to search for the runway or ground reference (mainly threshold or approach lights), while the other crew members are not monitoring the instruments.

Failure of the crew to respond to TAWS warnings

Descending through 180 meters above the airfield level the Terrain Awareness Warning System (TAWS) issued a "TERRAIN AHEAD" warning. One second after descending through 100 meters the Ground Proximity Warning System (GPWS) issued its audible alert :"PULL UP" requiring the aircraft crew to initiate an immediate go-around, however the crew did not react to either warning and the plane continued its steep descent. Neither of the pilots took immediate measures to terminate descent and initiate climb when the "PULL UP, PULL UP" alert was fired at 105 meters by the radio altimeter. The alert was fired for 12 seconds with no reaction from the crew until they initiated actions to avoid obstacles.

The TAWS systems are designed so that they will not go off on approach to airports that are programmed into the TAWS database. Since many military airports, including the one at Smolensk, are not in the database, investigators found in the course of their work that it was common for military pilots to ignore the TAWS and GPWS warning signals when on approach to military airports. They were even known to silence the "nuisance alarms" by resetting their barometric altimeter (which the Tupolev crew did in this case.)

Failure of the pilot in command and crew to terminate descent and go around.

The pilot in command failed to perform the most critical action—he did not terminate descent and did not go around when reaching the minimum descent altitude of 100 meters while not seeing either the runway or the ground references. The first officer called "go around" just when the navigator called 60 meters (radio altimeter) and the aircraft was about 10-15 meters above airfield level. The yoke was pulled back, however this action was not sufficient to disconnect the autopilot and arrest the sink rate; the airplane continued its steep descent. The crew did not react to the commander's suggestion to "Go around on automatic". The co-pilot confirmed the aircraft commander's "go around" command, but did not take any clear action despite the commander taking none. Nor did the navigator react to the fact of passing the minimum decision altitude without commencing the go-around procedure and he only read altitude until impact with the first tree. When the navigator called 50 meters (radio altimeter) the tower commanded "level, 101" (an order to the crew of the flight --PLF 101-- to level off and decrease descent) with no reply or reaction from the crew.

At 30 meters above airfield level the tower called "Check altitude, level". The crew reacted with an abrupt pull on the control column, the autopilot disconnected the pitch channel, the thrust levers were advanced to takeoff power, and the pull force was increased. The Russian investigators opined that this maneuver of attempting to climb was so abrupt and the resulting aircraft angle of attack was so steep, that even if the aircraft had not collided with the trees, it would have stalled within two seconds which would also have resulted in a crash.

According to analysis made by the Russian investigators, the aircraft could have safely climbed out if the crew had reacted at the point where the first officer called go-around.

The Polish report stated:

> *"Reasons for lack of efficiency in execution of the decision to go around are of a complex character. First of all, the command given by the aircraft commander was not firm enough, and too late. It is likely that the aircraft commander was surprised by a lack of an immediate response of the aircraft to his actions (i.e., trying to initiate go-around on autopilot). The workload on the pilot in command was too heavy. He had to simultaneously analyze the situation, make decisions, carry out operating procedures, supervise correctness of work of less experienced colleagues..., and carry on correspondence in Russian and additionally monitor the situation in the cockpit. Such load, multiplied by the stress influencing mental processes must have caused cognitive overload—omitting important data and difficulties in making decisions.*[139]

Presence of third parties in the cockpit

The Tupolev crew was interrupted several times by third parties appearing in the cockpit in the final stage of the flight. Director of Protocol Mariusz Kazana entered the cockpit about fifteen minutes prior to the crash to determine the status of the landing. This is when Captain Protasiuk informed him that they would probably not be able to land because of the fog. Kazana returned to the cockpit after speaking with President Kaczynski. There is one report that the voice of the head flight attendant,

---

[139] Final Report from the examination of the aviation accident no. 192/2010/11 involving the Tu-154M airplane, tail number 101, which occurred on April 10, 2010 in the area of the Smolensk North airfield (the Polish report)

Barbara Maciejczyk can be heard on the cockpit voice recorder urging Kazana, to no avail, to please leave the cockpit and return to his seat. [140]

During the final moments of the flight, General Andrzej Blasik, Commander in Chief of the Air Force, was also in the cockpit. He participated in reading out the plane's descending altitude, although the navigator was already doing this, and seemed to encourage the crew that the landing could be made (saying "You'll make it easily...be bolder")

Ambient noises could be heard on the cockpit voice recorder which seemed to indicate that during the flight, the cockpit door was left open. This allowed sounds and voices from the passenger cabin to enter the cockpit, and several times someone could be heard telling people to be quiet.

Presence of third parties in the cockpit at the final stage of the flight and conversation with them could have distracted the crew and drawn their attention away from core duties. This is particularly true when, as in this case, the visitors in the cockpit are high ranking officials who, just by their mere presence, add undue stress to the crew. In general aviation, there is an unwritten but practiced rule of "sterile cockpit". In essence, below 10,000 feet, the crew only exchanges flight-related information. Presence of third parties in the cockpit and any communication with them is unacceptable. The crew enters the operation area, requiring concentration on the landing approach maneuver. It is the duty of the aircraft commander to enforce this principle.

Poor Crew Resource Management

Crew resource management (CRM) refers to a set of training procedures for improving air safety. CRM focuses on interpersonal communication, leadership, and decision making in the cockpit--an environment in which human error can have devastating effects. It allows the cockpit crew to work as a team and come up with a common solution rather than individuals

---

[140] "Barbara Maciejczyk. Ta stewardessa probowala ratowac prezydenckiego tupolewa!" 9 Apr 2015
http://www.se.pl/wiadomosci/polska/ ta-stewardessa-probowala-ratowac-prezydenckiego-tupolewa_577884.html

coming up with individual solutions, or relying on the pilot in command to be the sole decision maker without question.

The Polish investigation report noted that crew work on the Tu-154 was chaotic and frequently interrupted by third parties appearing in the cockpit. The pilot in command was burdened with radio communication duty and this limited his ability to receive information from other crew members.

Crew cooperation involved only the performance of the commander's instructions regarding aircraft configuration. There was no reaction from crew members to the aircraft passing below the minimum descent altitude. The crew did not react to passing the altitudes indicated by the barometric altimeter. No crew member noticed or commented on the improper use of the radio altimeter by the navigator on landing approach.

During the entire period of the aircraft's approach to the Smolensk airfield, the crew failed to respond or react to the aircraft commander's deviations from required parameters. The Tupolev's engines ran at low thrust for an extended period (40 seconds), approach speed was higher than planned by almost 30km/h, descent rate was in excess of 5m/s and no crew member reacted. The navigator did not call the steep descent although required, nor did he announce the actual height passing the outer marker, did not announce capturing the glide path, did not announce the required vertical speed for the glide path and did not call approaching the minimum 30 meters above the minimum as required. The Polish investigators noted: ***"What is puzzling is the lack of reaction of anyone present in the cockpit to exceeding critical flight parameters during the approach."*** [141]

When the crew received information in the air about the unacceptable landing conditions at Smolensk, the aircraft commander should have discussed the situation with the other crew members; they should have discussed possible options for making a landing approach or alternative possibilities. Unfortunately such a discussion did not take place. This prevented the pilot in command from having the benefit of a joint

---

[141] Final Report from the examination of the aviation accident no. 192/2010/11 involving the Tu-154M airplane, tail number 101, which occurred on April 10, 2010 in the area of the Smolensk North airfield (the Polish report)

analysis of the problem which might have facilitated reaching a decision on continuing the flight or diverting to another airfield.

The lack of uniform information on the weather at Smolensk and the reaction of surprise of the crew when they learned that the actual weather conditions were in such a variance from the report they had received from their own meteorologist in Warsaw further acted to hinder the decision making process. Upon confirming weather conditions at the airfield in Smolensk, the aircraft commander made a decision to perform a controlled approach ("If possible, we will try to approach, and if the weather is not good enough, we will go around") At the same time this was happening, the co-pilot was having a conversation with the pilot of the Yak-40 aircraft that had just landed in Smolensk. From this pilot, he learned that the visibility was about 400 meters and the bottom of clouds were "way under 50 meters". Despite that, the Yak-40 pilot suggested possibly undertaking the attempt to land ("However, to be honest, you can still try, by all means.") The co-pilot passed this information to the aircraft commander which must have further contributed to confusion and indecision by the pilot ("Well, they managed to do it...what is he saying?")

Analysis of the pilots' conversations in the cockpit indicates the beginning of a phenomenon known as "cognitive tunneling" on the part of the aircraft commander. Cognitive tunneling occurs when it simply becomes impossible for one to attend to all the stimuli in a given situation and a temporary blindness effect can take place as a result; that is, individuals fail to see objects or stimuli that are unexpected and quite often in plain sight or patently obvious. The higher the level of stress influencing a pilot, the more pronounced the cognitive tunneling. The main psychological factors that influenced an increase in stress level at that stage of flight were a high level of situation unpredictability and internal conflict of the aircraft commander. This internal conflict was not a dilemma of whether to attempt an approach or divert to another airfield but how best to make the approach-- how low to descend and what approach procedure to apply. This cognitive tunneling resulted in the pilot only focusing of the approach procedure instead of making a broader decision as to whether or not to divert to another airfield, and at what point to make the divert decision.

During the attempt to make a landing approach the TAWS system warning activated and immediately the barometric altimeter was reset. This action caused the alarm to stop (for some time) but, at the same time, left the pilot without direct information from one of the altimeters, indispensable for establishing real altitude of the aircraft over the surface of the airfield. This led to the situation in which the pilot's plan for his landing approach was based on where he *imagined* the aircraft was in relation to the airfield (which, in this case, was not where the plane actually was). Additionally, misinformation was being relayed to the crew by the Landing Zone Manager and Air Traffic Controller that the plane was "on glide path and on course". It was a factor negatively influencing both the aircraft commander and the whole crew as it was strengthening their conviction that, despite a lack of reference, the location of the aircraft was a lot higher than the glide path and in the final phase of flight a lot under it.

Psychological pressure on the pilot in command

The errors made by the crew, and in particular, the pilot in command were the result, primarily, of psychological pressures present at the time of the approach of the aircraft to the Smolensk airfield.

Clearly during the final stages of the flight of the Tu-154 on April 10th, the pilot in command was experiencing a great deal of stress, primarily brought on by a psychological clash of motives: on the one hand he realized that landing in such foggy conditions was unsafe, on the other hand he faced strong motivation to land exactly at the destination airfield. If he were to decide to proceed to an alternate airfield, the pilot in command expected negative reaction from President Kaczynski, the main passenger. One of the translations of the cockpit voice recorder has Protasiuk saying, "I'm not sure, but if we don't land here, he'll give me trouble."

Discussions of the Tu-154M crew with the Protocol Director and crew of the Polish Yak-40 concerning the information on the actual weather that was lower than the established minima and impossibility (according to the Tu-154M crew opinion) to land at the destination airfield served to significantly increase the psychological stress of the crew.

In the opinion of the Polish investigators, the decision of the aircraft commander to descend past the minimum descent altitude even though he was aware of the unsuitable landing conditions resulted from the need to convince his superiors that there really were no conditions for landing. Information communicated by the Director ("No decision as yet from the President as to what we are doing next"), caused the aircraft commander to continue his plan of performing a landing approach down to the minimum altitude and past it.

The presence of the Air Force Commander in Chief in the cockpit did not directly interfere in the process of piloting the aircraft; he was just an observer of events. However there was pressure which influenced the crew in an indirect way. It was the opinion of the Russian investigators that the indifference shown by the Commander in Chief of the Polish Air Forces to solving the emerging extremely hazardous situation, and in fact giving encouragment to make a landing attempt ("you'll make it easily... be bolder") influenced the pilot's decision to descend below the decision height without establishing contact with ground references.

In an article in the digital magazine Maclean's by George Jones entitled "Were the Pilots of the Doomed Polish Jet Obedient to a Fault?" the author writes:

> *In Western aviation culture, the pilot-in-command (PIC) is used to being de facto in command. A controller—or fellow crew member or passenger or employer—may request or advise a PIC but can't order him...No one outranks the skipper, whether on the ground, flight deck or cabin... What their command authority enables them to do is to refuse requests they consider unsafe.*
>
> *In non-Western aviation culture pilots know their places. A controller isn't called a "controller" for nothing. The authorities aren't unreasonable. As Smolensk regional government spokesman Andrei Yevseyenkov explained, while traffic controllers generally have the final word, they can and do leave things to pilots' discretion.*
>
> *{Complying with the Smolensk Air Traffic Controller's advisement not to land in the poor weather*

> conditions was} a luxury Capt. Protasiuk and Maj. Grzywna may not have had. The word was during the Russo-Georgian conflict of 2008 the president got very huffy with a pilot who thought landing in Tbilisi was too risky.
>
> Former Polish president Lech Walesa was quoted as saying that he had flown a lot "and whenever there was a doubt [pilots] always came to the leaders and asked for a decision." Yes. If the leaders wanted to try one more descent into the murk, a pilot's response in that aviation culture would be to say "Sir!" and pull back the throttles. [142]

A joint group of Russian and Polish expert doctors and psychologists made an assessment of the psychoemotional status of the pilot in command, Captain Arkadiusz Protasiuk . The analysis of Protasiuk's individual personality traits was conducted on the basis of testing results provided by the Polish side. The expert assessment noted that the results of the psychological tests revealed that Protasiuk's dominating character trait was that of conformity (complaisance, subordinacy). The domination of conformity over other character traits makes a person gentle, flexible, and dependent on the opinions of a group or authority due to their strong desire to avoid conflicts. One of the components of conformity is anxiety as a personal quality. An enhanced level of conformity implies an enhanced level of anxiety as a component part. Also, enhanced conformity leads to proportional decrease of independence as a personal quality.

The long period Protasiuk worked as a co-pilot could have also influenced the formation and consolidation of his conformity. From 1997 to 2006 he flew Yak-40s as a co-pilot. From 2000-2008 he was trained and simultaneously flew as a Tu-154 co-pilot. Only in 2006 did he become Captain of the Yak-40 and 2008 Captain of Tu-154, but being a Captain he still continued to frequently fly as a co-pilot.

---

[142] "Were the Pilots of the Doomed Polish Jet Obedient to a Fault?" by George Jonas 17 Apr 2010 http://www.macleans.ca/news/world/wrong-direction/

Much to my surprise, there was no mention in the entire Polish report of the "Georgian Incident" where the pilot refused President Kaczynski's order to fly a plane carrying five heads of state into a war zone to land in Tbilisi. The Russian report itself only dedicated one paragraph to it. This incident would appear to be a critical psychological motivator for Protasiuk during the April 10th flight. Protasiuk was co-pilot on that flight 18 months previously and witnessed firsthand pressure being placed on the pilot, Gregorz Pietruczuk by President Kaczynski and the negative repercussions that resulted for the pilot when he refused to fly the President into what he deemed to be an unsafe area. The President's men brought legal charges against Pietruczuk and Kaczynski called him a coward in the press. While every good pilot either has the natural ability to or learns to compartmentalize—ensuring that personal problems and issues are not in the mind when flying and thereby potentially affecting the pilot's proficiency—this can rarely be one hundred percent. It is inconceivable that Protasiuk was not reminded of the "Georgian Incident" when he was faced, as Pietruczuk was in that case, with the repercussions of failing to carry out the desires and orders of President Kaczynski and on April 10th land his plane in Smolensk, regardless of the danger. One must wonder if Pietruczuk had been piloting the Tu-154M on April 10 instead of Protasiuk the outcome would have been completely different. Given Pietruczuk's refusal to give in to pressure in the interest of safety, it seems probable that he would have, from the time of receiving the ominous weather forecast at Smolensk, acted immediately to divert to an alternate airfield. But Kaczynski, by his own design, had made this impossible, since he refused to allow Pietruczuk to fly him anywhere after the Georgian incident, instead turning the job over to Protasiuk, the more compliant pilot.

Systemic Failures

Both Polish and Russian investigation reports discussed systemic failures that impacted the performance of the Tupolev pilots.

There was an insufficient level of crew training within the 36th Special Regiment and it was obvious that the crew acted on a level which was relevant to their training. They reacted to extremely difficult situations in a way reaching far beyond safety standards, but these standards in the functioning practice of the 36th Regiment were subject to serious lowering. The depreciation of safety standards and incapability of acting in difficult {situations} were caused by a lowering of the level of training (or by a lack of training), primarily in the scope of Crew Resource Management, Operational Risk Management, and Multi-Crew Cooperation. Not less important was discontinuing simulator trainings and training in the TAWS and GPWS systems. The Polish investigators found that, in recent years, in many aviation incidents the Air Force's various mistakes in use of altimeters have been a major cause of incidents. Absence of effective action in this field demonstrated systemic failures of the training process.

Airport failures

The airfield in Smolensk was equipped with a fairly low-tech kind of navigational system called a non-precision approach. Unlike more sophisticated precision approaches in use at major U.S. airports, non-precision approaches do not provide pilots with information about their vertical distance from the glidepath. [143]

The airfield itself was unsafe due to the many terrain obstacles. Many trees that were growing at the end of runway 26 were higher than allowable. There were many such trees along the axis of runway 26, in the area of the approach lights. The trees and shrubs stood in the line of vision of descending aircraft and greatly limited observation of aircraft approaching runway 26.

On the basis of an inspection of the airfield weather station the Polish report stated that the system of measurements and atmospheric observations did not comply with regulations. The location of the airfield weather station was restricting observation of visibility, cloud covering and weather phenomena at the airfield. In order to assess visibility, the meteorologist had to go onto the roof of the building, however, because of mounds, buildings, and aircraft parked around his station he could only see car sheds on the other side of the runway. In such conditions of observation, he

---

[143] "Pilot Error to Blame in Smolensk Crash" by Jeff Weis 12 Apr 2010 http://www.popularmechanics.com/flight/a5579/smolensk-plane-crash-error/

was not able to notice development of fog at the airfield. The closest objects also falsified his measurements of wind, air temperature, and humidity.

The Air Traffic Controllers continued to tell the Tu-154M that they were on the correct glide path, even though they were not. Approach control confirmed to the crew the correct position of the airplane in relation to the runway threshold, glide slope, and course which might have affirmed the crew's belief that the approach was proceeding correctly although the aircraft was actually outside the permissible deviation margin. The ATC had difficulty tracking the aircraft's altitude, relying on verbal confirmation by the crew as to their altitude. This could have been the result of faulty equipment or the ATC's difficulty in understanding Protasiuk's Russian.

The ATC was clearly stressed, agitated, and distracted during the course of the three landings/attempts (i.e. the Yak-40, the Il-76, and the Tu-154). The presence of the MUDC and what might be perceived as micromanaging could have added stress on the controller and interfered with his decision making.

Despite the fact that the Smolensk ATC and MUDC were appropriately concerned about the weather conditions at the airport which should have precluded the Tupolev's landing, their superiors failed to provide them the support, guidance, and decision-making that they needed to be stronger in preventing the landing of the plane. The Operations Center in Moscow failed to issue anything even vaguely resembling an order or even an advisement to the Tu-154M that they needed to divert to an alternate airfield.

Just as there is rarely one single cause of a plane crash, likewise, if any one factor, any one link in the chain of events, is removed from a crash scenario, the crash probably does not occur.

In the case of Polish Air Force 101:

... if the preparation team had not cancelled their request for a Russian guide navigator to lead the flight
... if the preparation team had not chosen Smolensk airfield to take the President's plane into
... if the crew had not reset the barometric altimeter

... if the pilot had immediately made a decision to divert to another airport once learning of the Smolensk airfield conditions instead of trying to approach
... if the pilot of the Yak-40 had told the Tu-154M crew not to even try to land
... if the pilot had not had to assume communication duties with the Smolensk ATC
... if the co-pilot was monitoring the airplane instruments as the pilot looked out the window trying to spot the airfield
... if Mariusz Kazana does not come into the cockpit
... if General Blasik does not come into the cockpit

If any one of these things does not occur, in all probability this crash does not occur. But it did. We can only hope lessons were learned from this terrible, most human tragedy to prevent anything like this from happening again.

Epilogue

In the wake of the accident that killed President Lech Kaczynski, the first lady, and so many other of Poland's best people, the 36th Special Air Transportation Regiment was disbanded. From that point on, the President or other dignitaries would charter commercial flights to get them where they needed to go.

Bronisław Komorowski ran in the Polish presidential election on June 20 2010, to determine who would replace Lech Kaczynski. Jaroslaw Kaczynski also ran saying he would take the place of his recently deceased brother. Kaczynski received 36.46% of votes in the first round, while acting president Bronisław Komorowski received 41.54%. In the second round Kaczynski was defeated—receiving 46.99% of the votes, while Komorowski received 53.01% .

Komorowski ran for re-election in May 2015. He was opposed by Law and Justice (PiS) candidate Andrzej Duda. Duda was elected in the closest presidential election in Polish history, winning 51.5% of the vote to Komorowski's 48.5%. The victory of Duda's Law and Justice party was the latest in a series of electoral victories for eurosceptic centre-right and right-wing parties in Europe. Jaroslaw Kaczynski was re-elected as chairman of Poland's right wing Law and Justice party (PiS) in 2015.

Over the past six years, Kaczynski has spent an inordinate amount of time in a fight for "the truth" about Smolensk and the glorification of his brother's legacy. Kaczynski often personally attended the marches that took place in Warsaw on the 10th of each month to commemorate the crash victims, using them as a tool to help mobilize support for the party.[144]

In the two years following the crash, the bodies of nine of the victims were exhumed at the request of their families when they discovered discrepancies between the Russian autopsy reports and actual physical characteristics of their loved ones.

In March 2012 the bodies of Polish lawmaker Przemyslaw Gosiewski, and Janusz Kurtyk, President of the Institute of National Remembrance were exhumed on the request of their families when they noted discrepancies in the Russian autopsy reports. Military prosecutors determined that in these cases there was no mistaking the bodies. They had been properly identified and released to the correct families.

In August 2012, the body of late conservative lawmaker Zbigniew Wassermann was exhumed. Wasserman's autopsy report contained glaring inaccuracies and described organs as being present that had been surgically removed years before. After his exhumation a new autopsy was performed in August 2012, which corrected the record but did not change the larger conclusions about the cause of his death or the proper identification of Wasserman's remains.

In September of 2012 two more remains were exhumed: those of Solidarity leader Anna Walentynowicz and Teresa Walewska-Przyjalkowski, Vice President of the "Golgotha of the East" Foundation. In this case, the Chief Military Prosecutor's Office reported on September 25, 2012 that based on the results of genetic testing, it was clear that the bodies of the two women had been switched and therefore buried in the wrong graves.

In October of 2012, two more bodies were exhumed: those of former Polish President in Exile Ryszard Kaczorowski and Tadeusz Lutoborski, the chairman of the Katyń Families organization who military prosecutors confirmed were in fact improperly misidentified and switched. As a result, both men were buried under the other's name.

---

[144] "The Plane Crash Conspiracy Theory that Explains Poland" by Ivan Krastev Dec 21, 2015 http://foreignpolicy.com/2015/12/21/when-law-and-justice-wears-a-tinfoil-hat-poland-russia-smolensk-kaczynski/

In November of 2012, the bodies of two priests Father Zdzislaw Krol, Chaplain of the Katyn Families, and Professor Ryszard Rumianek, former rector of the Cardinal Stefan Wyszynski University were exhumed by Polish military prosecutors due to concerns that the bodies may have been exchanged. Testing revealed that the remains of the two priests had in fact been misidentified and confused with each other.

Andrei Kovalyov, the head of the Russian Center for Forensic Expertise, which conducted the autopsies, defended his group's work, and said if there were errors it was because the bodies were very badly disfigured in the plane crash. "We have performed the genetic research and inspections of the bodies to international standard," Kovalyov said. "Any discrepancies, if they exist, are likely rooted not in badly performed autopsies but the fact that the bodies were fragmented. When remains of the numerous victims get mixed up inside the cabin there can be problems regarding the attribution of body parts." Polish Prime Minister Donald Tusk said it's hard to expect perfect reports given "what state the bodies were in after the crash." [145]

The errors made by the Russian forensic teams only added more fuel to the fire for the conspiracy theorists who used the mismanagement of some of the crash victims' remains as proof of either a sinister plot or evidence that the entire crash investigation could not be trusted.

This is the speech President Lech Kaczynski was set to make at the Katyn 70th Anniversary memorial:

> *The alliance between the Third Reich and the Soviet Union, the Ribbentrop-Molotov pact and the Soviet attack on Poland on 17 September 1939 reached a terrifying climax in the Katyn massacre. Not only in the Katyn forest, but also in Tver, Kcharkiv and other known, and unknown, execution sites citizens of the Second Republic of Poland, people who formed the*

---

[145] "Smolensk disaster victim identification" 29 Pct 2012 http://dvi-forensic.blogspot.com/2012/10/spotlight-smolensk-disaster-victim.html

foundation of our statehood, who adamantly served the motherland, were killed.

At the same time families of the murdered and thousands of citizens of the eastern territory of the pre-war Poland were sent into exile deep into the Soviet Union, where their indescribable suffering marked the path of the Polish Golgotha of the East.

The most tragic station on that path was Katyn. Polish officers, priests, officials, police officers, border and prison guards were killed without a trial or sentence. They fell victims to an unspeakable war. Their murder was a violation of the rights and conventions of the civilised world. Their dignity as soldiers, Poles and people, was insulted. Pits of death were supposed to hide the bodies of the murdered and the truth about the crime for ever.

Katyn became a painful wound of Polish history, which poisoned relations between Poles and Russians for decades. Let's make the Katyn wound finally heal and cicatrize. We are already on the way to do it. We, Poles, appreciate what Russians have done in the past years. We should follow the path which brings our nations closer, we should not stop or go back.

All circumstances of the Katyn crime need to be investigated and revealed. It is important that innocence of the victims is officially confirmed and that all files concerning the crime are open so that the Katyn lie could disappear for ever. We demand it, first of all, for the sake of the memory of the victims and respect for their families' suffering. We also demand it in the name of common values, which are necessary to form a foundation of trust and partnership between the neighbouring nations in the whole Europe.

> ***Let's pay homage to the murdered and pray upon their bodies. Glory to the Heroes! Hail their memory!*[146]**

Given the history of animosities between the Polish and the Russian governments, and the terrible tragedy which came to bear on the families of the 96 people who perished in the Smolensk crash, it is understandable that doubts and suspicions would arise. It was not my intent to address these suspicions in any way in this book. If the reader is interested in exploring them, I suggest beginning with the website www.smolenskcrashnews.com (which is in English) and following the trail from there. I myself do not believe the conspiracy theorists. What happened to cause the crash of the Tupolev is clear and explainable by naturally occurring events and the failings of human beings under significant pressure. That is just my own opinion after studying the investigation reports and numerous others sources of information. The reader is invited to make up his or her own mind.

---

[146] "Lech Kaczynski: Seventy years on, it is time the wounds of Katyn were healed" 12 April 2010
http://www.independent.co.uk/voices/commentators/lech-kaczynski-seventy-years-on-it-is-time-the-wounds-of-katyn-were-healed-1942938.html

Appendix

The People

I stated at the outset of this book that I wanted to tell this story from the standpoint of the people involved. Although I believe I have done that throughout this book, there is so much more left untold. There were 96 individual and precious lives lost, each individual with many friends and family members deeply affected by their loss and who miss them every day.

In this section, I present brief vignettes on each of these human lives. These vignettes are not so much to tell you who they were based on their occupation, or position, or contributions they made to their country, although these are very important--but by the very touching and human way in which they expressed themselves as individuals and in which they engendered the affection and respect of their coworkers, friends, and family members.

The four members of the cockpit crew of this flight, I have covered in Chapter Six—the Cockpit Crew. What follows are similar stories of the others.

Joanna Agacka-Indecka
President of the Polish Bar Association

Joanna Agacka-Indecka was born in Lodz on 18 December 1964. A Polish attorney, she was President of the Polish Bar Council from 2007 until her death in 2010. At 43 years old, she was the youngest person ever to be elected to this position.

She loved skiing, and often could be found in competitions with other lawyers. She had recently moved to a new home and changed her headquarters office. For six years she lived between Lodz and Warsaw. In the morning she was in court in Lodz, then a break to read and distribute corporate e-mails, then going to Warsaw to meet the Polish National Regulatory Agency and in the evening - again in her office. "In professional matters she was always honest and perfect. But regardless of the work she always found time for her daughter Kate," says attorney Hanna-Krupowczyk Thicket, a friend from college. "When we left from a long meeting, the first people she called, were her daughter and husband," says attorney Dariusz Wojnar.[147]

Her mother recalled that from the beginning, Joanna was determined that she would be a lawyer. She always did very well in school. She had good grades - in high school and later in college, so that before she passed the MA examination, she had offers from the university but she wanted to be a lawyer and could not do both things. In the meantime, she gave birth to a daughter. She had to give up something. The university was for her perhaps attractive, but earnings there were ridiculously low. In addition, her family had a tradition of lawyers.

As a trainee attorney Joanna spent six months in Chicago. She went at the invitation of U.S. attorneys. She learned everything she could - the work of bailiffs, banks, courts. She got so much from the experience

Her mother recalled that at age thirteen Joanna came with her to Paris. "We were on the island of St. Louis, the Hôtel Lambert - the seat of our emigration, the Polish church. Many years later Joanna went to Paris with

---

[147] "Joanna Agacka-Indecka" Portrety Kobiet, 17 Apr 2010 http://www.wysokieobcasy.pl/wysokie-obcasy /1,53662,7775853, Joanna_Agacka_Indecka.html}

her own daughter. She called me, 'Mommy, do you know where I am?' – 'I know you are in Paris, Juanita.' – 'Yes, but Kasia and I are sitting in the same cafe, where we once sat in front of Notre Dame, which is why I'm calling to tell you.'" [148]

---

[148] "Rozmowa z Elzbieta Agacka-Gajdowska" http://smolensk.muzhp.pl/page-2036/ Interview by Agnieszka Nowakowska March 7, 2014

Ewa Bąkowska
Katyn Families Association activist

The last picture taken of Ewa Bąkowska she was standing at a microphone, probably talking about her grandfather, who was killed in Katyn. It was the day before the crash, Friday, April 9th. She had gone to Kalisz where she was invited to the ceremony of a school which was changing its name to honor her grandfather General Mieczyslaw Smorawiński who was murdered by the NKVD 9 April 1940. He was one of two identified generals during the exhumation in Katyn Forest in 1943 - the second was Bronislaw Bohatyrewicz.

"I won't be going to Katyn, because I want to go to Kalisz," she had told her colleague Danuta Bromowicz. So when Danuta heard about the disaster of the plane crash on April 10, she was relieved. "God, how good that Ewa was not there." But she still hesitated thinking "she wasn't there, was she?" Danuta said, "I could foresee that Ewa would do everything to be here, and here, and here ... She was always conscientious and did not want to disappoint anyone. I had such a tiny hope that she may not have flown."

Ewa was born in Krakow. She studied librarianship and information science at the Jagiellonian University. A year after graduation she took a job at the Jagiellonian Library and worked there until Saturday, April 10, 2010. She was head of the department of scientific information.

She loved books especially memoires, diaries, and literature. She was very focused in her work. She was demanding, but understanding.

A few days before this year's celebrations Ewa Bąkowska called Andrezej Przewoznik, the Secretary General of Council for the Protection of Monuments to Struggle and Martydom. He said that there was still one spot left on the plane so she could fly to Katyn, if she wanted. She was glad even though she had to go to Kalisz the day before ... But she managed to rush all the time. She got on the plane. [149]

---

[149] "Ewa Bakowska", by Renata Radłowska 11.04.2010 http://wyborcza.pl/1,75402,7759637,Ewa_Bakowska.html

Lieutenant General Andrzej Blasik

Commander in Chief, Polish Air Force

Andrzej Eugeniusz Błasik was born October 11, 1962 in Poddębice. He was a military pilot, Lieutenant General of the Polish Army (2007), the commander of the Higher Military School of the Air Force (2007), and Commander of the Polish Air Force from 2007-2010.

"He changed the Polish air force," said commander of the 2nd Tactical Air Wing in Poznan General Vladimir Usarek. "He introduced the F-16 aircraft in Poznan Krzesiny-- it was his child. He built the infrastructure, prepared the whole event, and organized training. Then, as the commander of the Air Force, was responsible for the implementation of these aircraft," said Usarek. [150]

After the crash of the CASA-295 in Mirosławiec in January 2008 in which General Blasik's friend General Andrzej Andrzejewski was killed, he made it a matter of honor to dedicate himself to do everything he could to see that a similar drama never happened again. When a special committee of experts presented the Air Force 25 points to improvements in procedures, Błasik added yet another 30 to it.

"He changed the Polish Air Force: introduced not only F-16s, but CASA and Hercules aircraft. Now he wanted to introduce a new system of flight training. Andrew was a great leader, a friend, a good husband and father, as well as an excellent pilot. Seldom is a superior able to listen to subordinates, give a free hand; it was great to work with him," Usarek added. [151]

He left a wife, Eve Błasik and two children, a daughter Joanna and son Michael.

---

[150] Gen. Andrzej Błasik, "pilot klasy mistrzowskiej"PolskieRadio.pl Wiadomości Informacje 23.04.2011 http://www.polskieradio.pl/5/3/Artykul/202260,Gen-Andrzej-Blasik-pilot-klasy-mistrzowskiej

[151] Ibid.

Krystyna Bochenek
Vice Marshal of the Senate

Krystyna Maria Bochenek (née Neuman) was born 30 June 1953 in Katowice. She was a Polish journalist, politician, senator from 2004 to 2010, and the Deputy Speaker of the Senate seventh term.

In 1976, Bochenek became a journalist for Polish Radio Katowice and worked for many years, with the press and television. She was responsible for the popularization of the culture of the Polish language and the popularization of health. She also prepared nearly a thousand hours of programming on health, including "Medical Magazine" on the radio. She co-wrote the TV program "A to Health."

In cooperation with Silesian newsrooms, she led a campaign raising awareness for the prevention of breast cancer in women under the name "Pink Ribbon". She has helped many social causes including the Great Orchestra of Christmas Charity, the reconstruction of the burnt Silesian Opera building, the Silesian Theatre, and the Mining Families Foundation.

She was married to cardiac surgeon Andrzej Bochenek, with whom she had two children (Thomas—who is also a doctor, and Magdalena).

Donald Tusk wept over the casket of Senator Bochenek. "You were exactly in life and at work as you looked—full of beauty and warmth. I, thanks to you, kept faith in the fact that in Poland in public life kindness and love really have meaning and are not just words. How can I see us today without you? I can see so clearly that you were a real jewel in the crown, and that without you here nothing will be the same." [152]

---

[152] Tusk płakał w swoje urodziny 23 Apr 2010, Fakt24 pl
http://www.fakt.pl/wydarzenia/polityka/tusk-plakal-w-swoje-urodziny/47bhy1p

Anna Maria Borowska and Bartosz Borowski
Representatives of Katyn Families

Anna Maria Borowska was born July 20, 1928. She was one of four children of the officer corps border guard Lieutenant Francis Poplawski who was arrested on 17 September 1939, detained in Kozelsk, and in April 1940 murdered in the Katyn Forest. His family was deported to Kazakstan when Anna was 12 years old. There, they worked hard and were starving. Anna's son Francis recounted, "Mom told me about working in a brick factory, about how they resorted to stealing, not to die of hunger…They had nowhere to sleep; they got potatoes, worked a little milk from the cow, and worked 12 hours in the state-owned farms." [153] They returned to their homeland in May 1946.

"Throughout my life I heard from my mother and my grandmother about Katyn. And now whenever anyone refers to Katyn, we will always remember their deaths" said Francis Borowski. In the crash near Smolensk, he lost his mother and son. [154]

Anna Borowska wanted to go to her father's grave. She had to go by train ten years ago, when she first prayed at the tomb of her father. However, due to her age, it was decided that if there was an opportunity to fly there, she would take it. So she did, on April 10th. Bartosz, her grandson, accompanied her.

"She was pleased with this trip, and my son really wanted to go too, to take care of his grandmother, but also to see, because we all listened to the story since childhood about his grandfather, about Katyn, about his exile to Kazakhstan. Whenever the family is gathered, it is still mentioned, so he was interested. Maybe if she was younger, she would go by herself. But my mother was 82 years old…" said Francis Borowski.[155]

---

[153] "Gorzow zegna dzis dwie ofiary katastrofy pod Smolenskiem"20 Apr 2010 http://wiadomosci.gazeta.pl/wiadomosci/1,114873,7791580,Gorzow_zegna_dzis_dwie_ofiary_katastrofy_pod_Smolenskiem.html
[154] Ibid.
[155] Ibid.

Anna worked and sacrificed for years in the organizations in support of the Katyn families. She became Vice-President of the Katyn Families Association in Gorzow. She was also active in a branch of the Association of Siberian Deportees and Marian Apostolate. Her friends from the organization remember her as being "modest and benevolent, devoted to family and the history of her country." [156]

"I never expected that she would depart from us. And above all, that with her is gone, my son. I cannot deal with that" said Francis Borowski. Bartosz was 31 years old, a graduate in engineering at the Agricultural University in Szczecin. Recently, he married and worked as a truck driver. "They planned to have a child. And now ..." Francis could not continue, his voice breaking.

Bartosz's brother Kamil, added through tears: "His wife was just in Germany. He wrote her a card: 'I love you, see you, to Sunday'. On it, he drew two hearts." [157]

---

[156] Ibid.
[157] "Anna Maria Borowski and Bartosz Borowski" by Dariusz Baranski, 11 Apr 2010, http://wyborcza.pl/1,75402,7759704,Anna_Maria_Borowska_i_Bartosz_Borowski.html#ixzz43XgRfFNr

Major General Taduesz Buk
Commander in Chief, Polish Land Forces

Taduesz Buk was born August 9, 1960 in Mójczy. He was a Major General in the Polish Army and the Commander in Chief of the Polish Land Forces, appointed by President Lech Kaczynski on 15 September 2009.

Hopes were high for Buk when he was appointed as commander of the Army just seven months before his death in the crash in Smolensk. It was a serious time for the army. Buk replaced General Waldemar Skrzypczak, who left the army after a controversy surrounding his statements about the bureaucracy in the Ministry of Defense, which made it difficult to purchase equipment for soldiers on a mission. Decision makers in the Ministry of National Defense and Office of the President knew that after such a big scandal, to save the situation they needed someone different. It fell on Major General Tadeusz Buk, a veteran of the war in Iraq. "Soldiers love him, but it came with blood and sweat," said journalist Peter Bernabiuk. [158]

Stanislaw Szyszka was a friend of the General when they were young. He remembered how, together with the others, they ran through the surrounding forests and the barracks of a military unit. They played at war. "He was a good friend. We went to Mójecką Hill. We made guns out of wood. Together we went to school together; went off together in a field of rye and walked. We helped one another. Tadek was always first. We listened to him," he recalled. [159]

Colonel Janusz Falecki, commander of the Training Centre For Peace in Kielce, met General Buk a year ago. "I took command of the barracks, where he learned about the military, ran as a little boy, climbed the barrels of T-34 tanks." He said that even on the Friday evening before his death, he spoke with the General on the idea of creating a new Training Center Command. "It was his baby, his idea. I was a co-author of the concept. I

---

[158] "Tadeusz Buk: Młody Weteran" Wydawca newsweek.pl 11-Apr-2010 http://polska.newsweek.pl/tadeusz-buk--mlody-weteran,56551,1,1.html

[159] The Catastrophe in Smolensk. General Tadeusz Buk—remember him from his colleagues Kielco" by Paul Wiecek, 11 Apr 2010. http://www.echodnia.eu/swietokrzyskie/wiadomosci/kielce/art/8689181,katastrofa-w-smolensku-general-tadeusz-buk-wspominaja-go-jego-koledzy-z-kielc-zdjecia,id,t.html

listened to him on Friday before his death. He accepted the main theses. It's his baby—it will be realized. He will do everything to make it happen." [160] Commandant Falecki noted that General Tadeusz Buk was a true leader. He faced the difficult task of restructuring the army reducing the ground troops by 11,000.

Dr. Cezary Jastrzębski, a researcher at the Jan Kochanowski University in Kielce, went to high school together with the future General. They were friends, although recently they had rarely seen each other. He remembered Buk as an energetic, active person. "Even in the daily bustle, he was reflective and very emotional, despite appearances, that with a big career in the army he would have to have toughness. This was a man sensitive to all the issues and to daily life..." His voice cracking he recalled their last joint meeting. "It was in December. We talked a couple of hours, even planned a variety of other meetings....Now it does not matter and will not take place." [161]

---

[160] Ibid.
[161] Ibid.

Archbishop (Brigadier General) Miron Chodakowski

Orthodox Bishop of the Armed Forces

Born Mirosław Chodakowski on 21 Oct 1957 in Bialystok, Chodakowski entered the Orthodox Seminary of the Holy Spirit in Warsaw in 1972. He gained holy orders on 17 December 1978. Later, he studied at the Christian Theological Academy in Warsaw. He became the Polish Army's chief Orthodox priest on 1 October 1998. He was conferred the rank of Brigadier Genearl of the Polish Army by president Aleksander Kwaśniewski.

"We still cannot believe it, we lost a man so great that hardly anyone will be able to replace him," said those who knew him. "It is unimaginable loss," said Archbishop Gregory Tomaszuk, director of SP Health Care Centre in Hajnówka. "Archbishop Miron repeatedly visited our hospital, took part in various ceremonies, openings of branches. He demonstrated a very sympathetic attitude to the employees, but especially to the sick. He visited them in the halls, talking. We all now feel tremendous sadness and regret. Orthodox members of the uniformed services also are experiencing the loss. Brigadier General Miron was their spiritual leader and also the shepherd to so many priests.

"It is Archbishop Miron who shaped my way to the priesthood. I was enchanted by his spirituality," said Father Piotr Augustyńczyk. "He was involved in a lot of important moments in my life. It was he who presided at my wedding. Later, he took me to the Holy Land. This trip allowed me to get to know him as a very warm and good-natured priest." [162]

"At the same time he had a phenomenal sense of organization," said the priest Andrzej Misiejuk. "He was the confessor of the clergy. During the retreat of the clergy he presided over devotions. He gave very wise and instructive sermons. Despite his many responsibilities he always had time to meet with the faithful of his diocese," said Fr. Andrzej. [163]

---

[162] "Arcybiskup Miron Chodakowski. Wspomnienie: Byl dobrodusznym i cieplym pasterzem" Urszula Ludwiczak, Andrzej Zdanowicz, 11 APR 2010 http://www.wspolczesna.pl/wiadomosci/hajnowka/art/5711762,arcybiskup-miron-chodakowski-wspomnienie-byl-dobrodusznym-i-cieplym-pasterzem,id,t.html
[163] Ibid.

Fr. Andrzej recalled, "In the management of the Orthodox Military Ordinate he not only cared about holding religious services among the soldiers and the expansion of religious knowledge among the soldiers, but also education, love for the homeland and respect for life, instilling moral principles, promoting Christian values, teaching tolerance for other religions and nations, open to ecumenism and cooperation with representatives of other religions. Every year due to the initiative of Archbishop Miron, Hajnówce organized celebrations of the Polish Army. "[164]

The Archbishop went to Russia with Lech Kaczynski in September 2007 for the first time. There he participated in the ecumenical prayers at the Katyn memorial. On April 10, 2010, in the church of St Nicholas, Archbishop Nicholas James celebrated the "prayer of the dead" for those who perished in the Smolensk crash. Chodakowski's mother and sister took part. Also present were representatives from the clergy, government, and uniformed services. "Life is but a pilgrimage," Archbishop James said in his sermon. "Death is not the end, but only a passage to eternal life. We still pray for the souls of those departed." [165]

---

[164] Ibid.
[165] Ibid.

Czeslaw Cywinski
President of the Home Army Veterans Association

Czeslaw Cywinski was born on March 10, 1926 in Vilnius. During World War II while he was still in high school he participated in underground activities by joining the Vilnius organization-- the Union of Free Poles using the pseudonyms "Skowronek" and "Ryszard"("Skylark" and "Richard"). In the autumn of 1942, he joined the Home Army in Vilnius taking part in the acquisition and accumulation of weapons and ammunition. He took part in combat missions against the Germans occupying Vilnius. [166]

In 1944, he was arrested by the Soviets and deported to a concentration camp when he refused to join the service in the Red Army. He was in exile until 1946. After returning home, he graduated from the Polytechnic and became a civil engineer.

From 1996 he was a member of the Presidium of the Board of the World Association of Home Army Soldiers, and since July 2005 - the president of the World Association of the Home Army.

For over 25 years he chaired the Wilno Brigade "Jurand", which in 1989 was incorporated into the World Association of the Home Army. In July 2005, by an overwhelming majority he was elected President of the World Association of Home Army Soldiers for a three year term. In 2005 the Prime Minister appointed Czesław Cywiński to the Council for the Protection of Struggle and Martyrdom.

Since 2006 he worked with the Museum of the Warsaw Uprising in the collection of exhibits and themes and in conferences and promotional activities. During this period, Cywiński undertook discussions to organize an Army Museum in the capital. He also got support for the development of a Home Army Museum in Krakow.

In September 2009, he was awarded by President Lech Kaczynski the Commander's Cross with Star of the Order of the Rebirth of Poland. [167]

---

[166] http://www.fundacja-ppp.pl/index.php?option=com_content&view=article&id=103%3Appk-czesaw-justyn-cywiski&catid=36%3Abiece&Itemid=64

[167] "Czeslaw Cywinski President of the Armia Krajowa (Home Army) Veterans' Association"
http://smolensk.muzhp.pl/portret/czeslaw-cywinski/

Colonel Zbigniew Debski
Member, Chapter of the Virtuti Military Order

Col. Zbigniew Debski was born November 29, 1922 in the village of Łasin k. Grudziadz in the Pomeranian district of Poland. He was a member of the Chapter of the Order of Military Virtue from September 2008. His nom de guerre was "Zbych-Prawdzic". During the war as an Army soldier, he took part in the Warsaw Uprising in the "Kiliński" battalion. He was awarded the Order of Military Virtue V Class. "Since the beginning of the independent Republic he was in the chapter of the Order of Military Virtue; he was a Home Army soldier," recalled Prime Minister Donald Tusk during the welcoming ceremony on the return of his remains to Poland.

During the Warsaw Uprising Debski took part in several attacks on the Polish telephone company (PAST) building and was the first one to reach the top and post the flag. "I had the honor of displaying the flag on top of the building on this victory. At the time of this action at the PAST building, gradually we moved up, we hoisted a flag to the first, then to the second floor window, then from the third floor. But we still needed to get the flag to the top, so I went there, assisted by my two soldiers nicknamed Ora and Elm", Debski recalled in an interview published in the Oral History Archive on the website of the Warsaw Uprising Museum. "Nurses hastily made the flag which we planted. The way was terribly difficult, because after fires in the ruins of the building, as we came to where all the telephone equipment was; the heat was such that the tin from the equipment was dripping on us. The whole building was on fire and we are in these conditions, but we got to the top. From the beginning we were able to move fast, then as we approached above the embers, with tin dripping on me I got a little burned. We got to the top of the building and there fastened to the ventilation unit the flag in an upright position. A nice breeze just then developed, which unfurled the flag, and it looked very uplifting, giving us great satisfaction. Shouts of triumph and joy were heard in the area, of course, that this place, where so many died, much had been now gained," he said. It was no secret that before the outbreak of the Uprising he had doubts, but at the same time he explained, "We were required in this hour of need. But we were so eager to fight, so much preparing to in some way avenge all those murders, public executions, people sent to the camps. We broke up after this fight". [168] After the end of the Uprising, Debski was a prisoner of several POW camps. He returned to Poland in 1948.

He enrolled at the University of Torun in the department of chemistry, from which he graduated in 1952. After retirement he worked in the chemical plants. He was a co-founder of the Association of Warsaw Insurgents and member of the Presidium ZG IG, as well as co-founder and a board member of the Club of the Knights of the Order of Military Virtue War. [169]

"It is all a matter of chance...that I'm alive. It's all a matter of chance - he said." [170]

---

[168] | Zbigniew Dębski 10 kwietnia 2010, http://www.tvn24.pl/zbigniew-debski,131156,s.html
[169] Ibid.
[170] Ibid.

Leszek Deptula
Member of Parliament

Leszek Deptula was born 25 February 1953 in Zagan. He was a member of the Polish Parliament but also a veterinarian, with a Master's degree in biology. He was married to Joanna Krasowska-Deptula and had two sons, Thomas and Michael. [171]

His wife Joanna remembered:

"We met while studying in Lublin. My husband studied at the Agricultural University at the School of Veterinary Medicine, and I at the UMCS School of Biology. We were a couple for almost the entire time of our studies, and after the fourth year, we were married.

"He was always full of energy; he felt the compulsion to do more than just as much as he should. He was always a well-organized man, able to determine what is the most important thing to do now right away and what can be put off for a future time. I do not know how he did it but he succeeded.

"Getting married I knew that my husband has a career, and therefore it may be that we will often to some extent be dependent on each other. Although I did not know I was getting married to a politician, but I knew that my husband would definitely not make me rich at home in the proverbial slippers in front of the TV – he's not that type of man.... After he finished his internship, he took the first real, serious work as a veterinarian in Wadowice Dolne.

"He was always attracted to nature. He loved all animals. When we were living in Mielec, once I heard the doorbell. I opened the door and found myself facing children with a small mouse caught in a trap ... Another time, in the evening we heard meowing at the door, at that time we did not have a cat. I opened the door, and on the doormat in front of the door sat a cat with a wounded paw, holding it outstretched - probably caught in a trap, and the wound was to the bone. Of course this cat lived for some time in the attic of the clinic. My husband changed the dressings daily, and he fed him, because he was an invalid. After the cat healed, twice

---

[171] http://wiadomosci.gazeta.pl/wiadomosci/56,114871,13698632,leszek-deptula,,20.html

on the mat we found a big, fat mouse - perhaps brought to us in thanks... It sounds like a joke, but animals can show gratitude and appreciate what you did for them.

"In the morning he was at work at the clinic, in the afternoon at the slaughterhouse doing inspections, returning home at night, and often have a phone call, for example, that something is born, and he had to go to work again. The work was actually twenty four hours a day with short breaks." [172]

When her husband was elected, surprisingly, he was more often at home and had more time for his family than ever before. For a week he was working in the Parliament, and then a week was at home and worked in the Mielec office or in the field.

Politics fascinated him, apart from human contact and unpredictability, it is that there is always something new. One person likes to bungee-jump, and another prefers politics ... I think it is comparable, because the emotions associated with such activities are really huge and bring a dose of adrenaline into the bloodstream and makes everything look different. [173]

---

[172] Interview with Joanna Krasowska-Deptula (http://Smolensk.muzhp.pl/page-2100/) Interview by Agnieszka Nowakowska November 5, 2014
[173] Ibid.

Gregorz Dolniak
Member of Parliament

Grzegorz Maciej Dolniak was born 17 February 1960 in Bedzin. He was a Polish politician and entrepreneur, a trained economist, Member of Parliament. He lived in Bedzin - Gzichowie, was married to Barbara (lawyer and politician), and had a daughter Patricia.

At his funeral, Prime Minister Donald Tusk, recalled that Dolniak was one of the founders of the Civic Platform, but there was never a reason for him to exalt himself over others. Tusk said that as the deputy head of the Civic Platform (PO) party he always worked hard, but not for fame; he did not expect awards.

For the head of the Civic Party, Grzegorz Schetyna, Gregory Dolniak was an institution in the parliament. "Without him, this parliament will be different" he said, recalling the hard work and commitment he had in everything he did. "He was a demanding man – requiring the most mainly from himself- the hard work, commitment. He was able to talk to people and have contact with them; he spoke to their hearts and minds…That we will miss" Schetyna stressed. [174]

The President of European Parliament Jerzy Buzek recalled Dolniak's activity and integrity, indicating these traits were his testament. "You know, the loudest member of the team is not necessarily the most important one. And so he was in politics: hard-working, brave and humble," said Buzek. [175]

His wife Barbara recalled the words of Prime Minister Donald Tusk who, when the body of her husband was returned to Poland, said at the airport that he was a man who was "painfully honest." "These were for me and my family tremendously important words. This means that, in his work he was honest, that he valued honor. Each of us, no matter how many years he would survive, would like to hear at the end that one was painfully honest," said Barbara Dolniak. [176]

---

[174] Grzegorz Dolniak "indispensable man" rested in Bedzin 22-04-2010 http://polska.newsweek.pl/grzegorz-dolniak--czlowiek-niezastapiony-spoczal-w-bedzinie,57158,1,1.html
[175] Ibid.
[176] Ibid.

Grzegorz Dolniak, on February 17, 2010 was celebrating his 50th birthday with a large group of friends. He received six liters of champagne as a gift from his fellow members of parliament. A few days before, he had returned from a short ski vacation, tanned and happy.

"He looked forward to the trip to Katyn. We talked about it. It was like a reward to him—he wanted to make a tribute to the Polish soldiers, and he died in this cursed Katyn forest," said Krzysztof Stachowicz, provincial counselor of his friend's tragic death. "The worst part is that he avoided flying. When he went on holiday with his family, he always went by car." [177]

Despite being in the brutal field of politics, he never exceeded the limits of good manners. Elegant, witty, eloquent, he perfected the art of diplomacy. If you said that there are no friends in politics, Dolniak proved this wrong. He had many friends, many people who were kind to him who he won by his predictability, accountability, and by keeping his word.

"I can barely hold back my tears. I knew Gregory from the beginning of his political career. Yesterday we sat next to each other in the Parliament. On Thursday, we were together for dinner," said his colleague in Parliament Jaroslaw Pieta. "Gregory was a warm family man. His wife Barbara and daughter Patricia were the most important people in his life." [178]

---

[177] "Deputy Gregory Dolniak from Bedsin was killed in the crash" by Agata Kestrel 10 Apr 2010, Source: Dziennik Zachodni http://myszkow.naszemiasto.pl/artykul/posel-grzegorz-dolniak-z-bedzina-zgimal-w-katastrofie,375256,art,t,id,tm.html
[178] Ibid.

Katarzyna Doraczynska

Official in the Chancellory of the President

Katarzyna Doraczynski was born October 3, 1978 in Warsaw. She worked in the office of the President since 2007. In 2004 she established and was president of the Factory of the Future Foundation, which promotes the idea of European voluntary service. The Foundation was aimed at providing assistance and equal opportunities for young people who are disadvantaged and socially maladjusted. [179]

Her mother Krystyna and sister Adrianne spoke of her in an interview with Agnieszka Nowakowska

Katarzyna was very active in scouting, going to scouting camps even as a small child. According to her mother, after going on camping trips, she was never again content to just play in the backyard. [180]

Even as adults, Katarzyna and her sister were very close. They frequently met for lunch on the weekends. "When I was driving somewhere, sometimes she used to take my children, especially the older ones. She took care of friends and acquaintances... She kept in touch with friends back to the elementary school, high school, from college. I do not know how she reconciled with her intensive work," said Adrianne. [181] "Kate was always at the gym or at bowling, or a movie theater, or a visit to someone. She and her husband could not sit still at home for five minutes...they traveled by car on wonderful trips." [182]

"She had extraordinary charm. It was enough that she smiled - and then a stranger became her friend. She was well liked, had no conflicts at all. I never heard from Kate that she quarreled with someone, or got angry. She did not like to be angry. She liked to react positively to everything." [183]

---

[179] "Katarzyna Doraczynska," PAP/MHP, http://smolensk.muzhp.pl/portret/katarzyna-doraczynska/
[180] "Rozmowa z Krystyna Dorczynska i Adrianna Pruszkowska," http://smolensk.muzhp.pl/page-2072/
[181] Ibid.
[182] Ibid.
[183] Ibid.

Deputy Chief of the Chancellory, Jacek Sasin, at her funeral, recalled that when he met Doraczyńska two years ago he did not think that they would be so close. He stressed that it soon became apparent that the Presidential Palace "hit a real diamond." He called Doraczyńska as an excellent, conscientious officer, and a person who radiated a smile, goodness and joy. [184] Former Prime Minister Kazimierz Marcinkiewicz said that during the period when they worked together she was for him "a symbol and model of the young generation, young Poland...she treated the work for the state as a service, always worked wholeheartedly," he stressed. [185]

She had wanted to go to Katyn for a long time. For the April 10th ceremony, she was scheduled to go by train but begged one of the ministers to change her to the plane because she had a small child.[186]

She was 32 years old and left her husband Christopher and 4-year-old daughter Hania.

---

[184] "Pozegnanie Katarzyny Doraczynskiej z Kancelarii Prezydenta" 20 Apr 2010 http://wiadomosci.gazeta.pl/wiadomosci/1,114873,7794128,Pozegnanie_Katarzyny_Doraczynskiej_z_Kancelarii_Prezydenta.html
[185] Ibid.
[186] Ibid.

Edward Duchnowski
Secretary General of the Union of Sybiraks (Siberian Exiles)

Edward Duchnowski was born 16 January 1930 in Podbiel. After the outbreak of WWII and the Soviet invasion of Poland, at the age of ten, he was deported with his family by the Russians to Siberia where he stayed during the years 1940-1946 in the Altai Krai. In exile, he lost his father. In May 1946 he returned to Warsaw with his mother and older sister where he graduated in chemistry from the University of Warsaw. In 1980 he began work on the Soviet persecutions and since the mid-90s was its secretary general. Among others his initiative was the establishment of the medal Cross Zesłańców Siberia and the organization of annual marches of still living Siberian exiles.

From December 17, 1988 he was active in the Association of Siberian Deportees. On November 3, 1993, he was appointed Secretary General. He successfully fought for the rights for veterans and for those born in exile. Since 1998, he fought for compensation for the surviving 38,000 Poles who had been deported to the East. Every day he "tramped the halls" of Parliament, the Office of the President or the Office for War Veterans and Victims of Oppression to improve the lives of members of the Union by the relevant resolutions, laws and regulations. [187] He also colaborated with the government on the repatriation of Poles from Kazakhstan. Widely known was his unyielding stance in the fight for truth and the rights of members of the Union. In this attitude he remained faithful to the end. [188]

He enjoyed great authority among the Siberians. Non-confrontational, he always helped resolve any disputes. Open to discussions and arguments of others, he tried to be fair and objective in his opinions and views. He was always ready to help the needy. He liked the presence of other people feeling the need for human contact. He greeted all with a distinctive winning smile, and with women was particularly gallant. Everyone felt good with him, freely, perhaps because he retained a youthful zest for life.[189]

---

[187] "Edward Duchnowski" 10 kwietnia 2010 http://www.tvn24.pl/edward-duchnowski,131158,s.html

[188] "Znani Sybiracy" Zwiazek Sybirakow, http://www.emazury.com/sybiracy/pliki/znani/40duchnowski.htm

[189] "Edward Duchnowski" 10 kwietnia 2010 http://www.tvn24.pl/edward-duchnowski,131158,s.html

Aleksander Fedorowicz
Russian Translator for the President

Aleksander Fedorowicz, personal translator of Russian and Hebrew for President Lech Kaczynski, was born on 27 July 1971. His dream was to serve the Motherland in the uniform of a Polish officer, but this proved impossible due to a heart defect. Therefore, after graduating from high school in 1990 in Bydgoszcz he decided to become a diplomat. He passed rigorous qualifying exams and began studying at the Institute of Political Science of the Moscow University.

After graduation he was sent to work at the Polish Embassy in Tashkent in Uzbekistan as a vice consul. His passion was the search for Polish roots in Uzbekistan. He sought them in cemeteries, in old documents. He wanted to issue a publication on the local Polish exiles. "He discovered this country again. It turned out that descendants of Legionnaires and tsarist exiles live there--people whose roots date back to the Napoleonic era. He was fascinated by their fate. As soon as he came to Bydgoszcz he talked about the Polish roots in Uzbekistan. He lamented the fact that they live in great poverty. He said that you cannot forget them. He began to collect material to document their history. He wanted to publish. He never got to," said his uncle and godfather Roman Kotzbach. [190]

After a few years he returned to Poland and worked in the Ministry of Foreign Affairs as an analyst. But he decided to choose the path of an independent career, so together with a friend he founded the Warsaw office of translators. They performed many important and highly responsible tasks, including translations during the exhumation by the NKVD of murdered Polish officers, policemen and officials, among others, in Katyn. Shortly thereafter he began working with the Office of the President, with President Lech Kaczynski.

---

[190] "W katastrofie prezydenckiego samolotu pod Smoleńskiem zginął bydgoszczanin, Aleksander Fedorowicz" 11 APR 2010
http://www.pomorska.pl/katastrofa-pod-smolenskiem/art/7132065,w-katastrofie-prezydenckiego-samolotu-pod-smolenskiem-zginal-bydgoszczanin-aleksander-fedorowicz,id,t.html

He tried as often as possible to visit family in Bydgoszcz, where lived his gravely ill father and elder brother Darius. [191] In the last days of his life he spent Easter in Bydgoszcz. "We had, the week before a wonderful family celebration - the wedding of my son" said his uncle Roman. "Alexander was so joyful. He laughed, danced. He told us that on April 10 he was flying with President Kaczynski to Katyn. He flew. It was his last trip…Yesterday I opened my computer. So many times we talked on Skype. I saw the entry from Alka: "I'll be back." [192]

He is survived by two children.

---

[191] "Aleksander Fedorowicz," http://smolensk.muzhp.pl/portret/aleksander-fedorowicz/
[192] "W katastrofie prezydenckiego samolotu pod Smoleńskiem zginął bydgoszczanin, Aleksander Fedorowicz" 11 APR 2010
http://www.pomorska.pl/katastrofa-pod-smolenskiem/art/7132065,w-katastrofie-prezydenckiego-samolotu-pod-smolenskiem-zginal-bydgoszczanin-aleksander-fedorowicz,id,t.html

Janina Fetlinska

Senator

Janina Fetlińska was born June 14, 1952 in Tuliglowach. She was a Polish politician, nurse, doctor of medical sciences, and senator.

In 1977 she graduated from the School of Nursing, Medical University of Lublin. She obtained her first degree in social medicine and a second degree in health organizations, and in 1986, she obtained a doctorate degree in nursing.

From 1977 to 2004 she served in various senior healthcare positions in Polish hospitals and clinics.

In the parliamentary elections in 2005, she was elected senator from the Law and Justice Party in the district of Plock. In the parliamentary elections in 2007, she was elected senator for the second time.

"She was one of the busiest senators," said Speaker of the Senate Bogdan Borusewicz. "She was full of ideas that she wanted to pursue. She came with them to me. We talked often. She went beyond the classic type of policy; she was more a social worker. She always remembered that she is a nurse...and she often spoke about the problems of health care." [193]

Her sister Aneta said, "When Nina [this is what relatives and friends called her] organized something, when she undertook any initiative, she took it to the end... She tried to help specifically: families with children, people with disabilities, the promotion of health, the fight against addictions, and especially cigarette smoking." [194]

The bishop of Plock spoke of how she particularly valued the saints Jude Thaddaeus, Sister Faustina and Padre Pio. The latter she had had a dream about when her son Bartosz was one year old. "He came to her in a dream and asked her: 'Where is your Bartek?' Janina woke up and saw that the little boy was standing {precariously} at the balcony railing."[195]

---

[193] "Pogrzeb senator Fetlińskiej. Wychodziła poza klasyczny typ polityka" by Piotr Dązbasz 21.04.2010 http://wyborcza.pl/1,105766,7798721,Pogrzeb_senator_Fetlinskiej__Wychodzila_poza_klasyczny.html
[194] Ibid.
[195] Ibid.

Member of Parliament Marek Suski said goodbye on behalf of Jaroslaw Kaczynski, the President of the Law and Justice Party [Janina Fetlińska was a member of the party] "I remember Janina as a person of great social sensitivity. She chaired the parliamentary prayer group. She was a person of deep faith, always welcoming and eager to help" [196]

She left a husband, Vladimir, and a son Bartosz.

---

[196] Ibid.

LtColonel Jaroslaw Florczak

Deputy Head, Polish Government Protection Bureau (BOR)

Jaroslaw Florczak was born in 1969 in Warsaw. He served 21 years in the Polish Government Protection Bureau (BOR). In 2007, he retired but returned at the request of the head of BOR. He coordinated and supervised the BOR mission for the 70th Katyn ceremony. He had a passion for volleyball and was a member of the national team. He also loved football. In 2007 he worked on the film "Entourage" as a consultant for scenes with actors playing BOR officers.

Beata Florczak, his wife, recounted, "Working in the BOR was his second life. But he never brought work home. Even when I was curious and sometimes I asked him details, he always told me: 'I cannot talk about it, it's a secret ...'" she recalls. [197]

It was LtColonel Florczak's responsibility for the preparation of visit of President Lech Kaczynski to Katyn. "From the first moments when I learned about the tragedy, I had contact with colleagues from Jarek's Office," said Beata Florczak. "They helped me arrange to bring back the body of my husband, organized the care of a psychologist, and supported me at the funeral. Then I could see how my husband was connected with the guys working in the Office. And what a relationship it was." Despite all this help it is difficult to reconcile with the loss. "We have always been an inseparable trio: I, Jarek and our daughter. We miss him so very much." [198]

He was, among others, responsible for protecting the Prime Minister Hanna Suchocka and Prime Minister Waldemar Pawlak. He took part in actions related to the visits of Pope John Paul II and protected President Aleksander Kwasniewski. Major Leszek Kozicki recalled of Florczak, "Always in emergency situations he would rise to the task. I remember during the visit to France with then President Kwasniewski and his wife

---

[197] "Beata Florczak: Bez pomocy BOR moje zycie legloby w gruzach" 21 Jul 2010 http://www.se.pl/wiadomosci/polska/bez-pomocy-bor-moje-zycie-legoby-w-gruzach_146989.html
[198] Ibid.

people in the crowd threw eggs. Jarek sheltered them so that the president did not get hit." [199]

"He was faithful to his service to the end," said Prime Minister Donald Tusk during the welcoming ceremony for the caskets with the bodies of victims of the disaster. "He was my friend. Smooth, firm, experienced officer. A great man, cheerful, with a great sense of humor," said Major Kozicki not hiding his emotions. [200]

LtCol Florczak is survived by his wife and daughter.

---

[199] Pochowano płk. Jarosława Florczaka. Żegnał go m.in. prezydent Kwaśniewski 21.04.2010
http://wiadomosci.gazeta.pl/wiadomosci/1,114873,7799083,Pochowano_plk__Jaroslawa_Florczaka__Zegnal_go_m_in_.html
[200] Ibid.

Lieutenant Artur Francuz
Member, Polish Government Protection Bureau (BOR)

Artur Francuz was born on 10 November 1971 in Warsaw. He served in the Polish Government Protection Bureau for 18 years. Francuz was teasingly called by his colleagues, "the Spaniard". He was fascinated by automobiles.

"He was passionate in many areas of life, a brave officer," said Prime Minister Donald Tusk during the ceremony welcoming back the remains of the Smolensk crash victims. He was assigned to protect Ryszard Kaczorowski (former Polish President in Exile) during his visits to Poland. He was responsible not only for the safety of the president, he also organized his stays in Poland, took care of him, and was his driver," said BOR spokesman Dariusz Aleksandrowicz. "He wanted to go to Katyn. He got a visa, prepared initially, but there was no room. In the end, it turned out that he could fly." [201]

Interested in history, especially World War II, his true passion was automobiles. Shortly before the tragic mission to Smolensk he bought a scooter. He never got a chance to ride it.

Although the official biographical information on Artur Francuk is that he is from Warsaw, Minsk Mazowiecki residents remember that he was "a citizen of their city." Francuk was a student of the Primary School No. 1 in Minsk Mazowiecki (1979-1987) and the Minsk Vocational School Complex No. 2 (1987-1992). "He was always at the side of President Kaczorowski ... to the end of his days ... and you will find us in Bialystok (President Ryszard Kaczorowski was born in Bialystok) missing :(:(:(- wrote someone in a profile on Artur Francuk in a school portal. [202]

---

[201] "W Komorowie odbyl sie pograb ppor Artura Francuza", 21 Apr 2010 http://wiadomosci.gazeta.pl/wiadomosci/1,114873,7797323,W_Komorowie_odbyl_sie_pogrzeb_ppor__Artura_Francuza.html

[202] "Minsk i minszczanie pamietaja..." http://tygodniksiedlecki.com/t9108-minsk.i.minszczanie.pamietaja....html

"My dad would be very happy that everyone remembers him. As I look at all these candles, it's easier on my soul," wrote his 11-year old daughter, Ola regarding condolences and expressions of sympathy from Internet users. [203]

He left his wife Catherine, daughter of Ola and his son Martin.

---

[203] Ibid.

General Franciszek Gagor
Chief of the Armed Forces

Franciszek Gągor was born 8 September 1951 in Koniuszowa near Nowy Sącz. He attended the Mechanized Infantry Officer College at Wrocław, the Adam Mickiewicz University in Poznań, the National Defense University in Warsaw, the NATO Defense College in Rome, and the National Defense University in Washington DC.

In 1991 he was an executive officer/second-in-command at the Polish Military Contingent for Operation Desert Storm. He later became the Deputy Sector Commander of UN Iraq-Kuwait Observation mission UNIKOM between 1991 and 1992. In 1993, as a Colonel, he became the Chief of Polish Armed Forces Peacekeeping Division of the Polish Armed Forces.

He was a key member of the Polish Armed Forces preparations team for Polish accession to NATO, taking care of initial and first rounds of NATO Defense Planning for Poland.

On 27 February 2006, Gagor was made Chief of General Staff of the Polish Armed Forces upon appointment by the President of Poland. He was promoted to General on May 3rd 2006.

He was fluent in English, and communicated in French and Russian. He had an interest in history, English literature, skiing, tennis, volleyball and jogging. He was married to Lucyna and has two children, Katarzyna and Michał. [204]

From an early age he read a lot, he liked to learn. Teachers from Koniuszowa say he was a very ambitious student. Recalls retired teacher - Mrs. Joseph Ogorzałek, "sitting with a book on his lap hidden under the bench. It was difficult to reprimand him, because this incredible urge to read does not reflect negatively on learning." [205]

That he came from a small town, and a large family did not prevent him from developing his passions or from realizing his dreams. Says Lucyna Gagor, his wife, "He was an example of honor and inalienable dignity. The

---

[204] https://en.wikipedia.org/wiki/Franciszek_G%C4%85gor
[205] "General Franciszek Gagor (1951 - 2010)" 2013-04-12 http://www.miastons.pl/59,Ludzie.htm?id=7163}

most prominent military diplomat among officers. He defended the good name of the Polish Army. His life passed in the way of honor. Through hard work and stubbornness he came to the highest position in the Polish Army." [206]

"In our society there is a stereotype that if you're from a small town, there is no chance of a career, to develop your greatest passion. General Franciszek Gagor broke all the stereotypes. His colleagues say that he was in his office at the earliest light and fading at the last." [207]

Despite his demanding schedule General Gągor always made time to visit his family back in Koniuszowa.

The General also had one big dream that he would never realize—to build a ski lift in his family's home town of Koniuszowa. "Since childhood he loved to ski," said his brother Stanislaw. "When he started working at Headquarters, there was already no time. He joked, 'I will build it---it will be my motivation,'" [208]

He died so suddenly and unexpectedly. Quoting a poem of his daughter Catherine: *You went away so suddenly without saying goodbye, not with us for Saturday dinner. We stood in the window, peering, waiting, begging ..."* [209]

---

[206] "General Franciszek Gagor (1951 - 2010)" 2013-04-12 http://www.miastons.pl/59,Ludzie.htm?id=7163

[207] Ibid.

[208] "Mieli tyle do zrobienia, ale nastapil Smolensk" by Paulina Korbut, Maria Mazurek, and Magdalena Stokloas, 10 Apr 2013 http://www.gazetakrakowska.pl/artykul/802327,mieli-tyle-do-zrobienia-ale-nastapil-smolensk,id,t.html

[209] "General Franciszek Gagor (1951 - 2010)" 2013-04-12 http://www.miastons.pl/59,Ludzie.htm?id=7163

Grazyna Gesicka
Member of Parliament

Grazyna Gęsicka (nee Dusyn) was born 13 December 1951 in Warsaw. She was a Polish sociologist and politician, minister of regional development in the government of Kazimierz Marcinkiewicz and Jaroslaw Kaczynski, deputy to the Sejm sixth term. She graduated in sociology from the University of Warsaw, where in 1985 she earned a doctorate in humanities. From 1985-1993 she worked there as a lecturer in the Institute of Sociology.

Since 2007 she was a member of the PiS party in the district of Rzeszow. But she did not focus only on politics. She was the author and co-author of a dozen books and over 30 articles in Polish and foreign books and journals.

"When we met privately, she always talked about her grandson. She loved him and was proud of him," said a colleague Voivod Podkarpacki. As women, they both chatted about cosmetics or clothes. However, almost every conversation finally turned to professional issues. Grazyna Gęsicka was 59 years old and had a great career still ahead of her. She was cited as a potential candidate for leader of the PiS party if Lech Kaczynski had not won it. [210]

She left a husband, Janusz Gęsicki (sociologist) and a daughter Clara.

---

[210] "Grazya Gesicka, the most important woman in the PiS" 11-04-2010 Newsweek (Polish) http://polska.newsweek.pl/grazyna-gesicka--najwazniejsza-kobieta-w-pis,56547,1

Brigadier General Kazmierz Gilarski
Commander in Chief of the Warsaw Garrison

Brigadier General Kazimierz Gilarski was born May 7, 1955 in Rudołowicach. He was appointed Deputy Commander of the Warsaw Garrison in 1993 and promoted to the rank of colonel. In 2005 he was appointed Commander of the Warsaw Garrison. On 11 November 2006 he was nominated to the rank of Brigadier General.

He was married, and had a daughter and a son. He was interested in military history, sports and tourism.

His daughter, Katarzyna, recalled that her father's decision to go into the army "stemmed from the fact that his older brother, who had done it, impressed him when he came home in uniform. These were the times when the uniform was associated with respect...Tata grew up in the country and...truthfully, his choice of a military academy was a way for dad to escape to the big city." [211]

"The command, which he held for the past three years, was associated with ceremonial duties. Mother accompanied him wherever she could. Tata could call at four o'clock and tell my mother: 'About seven o'clock we have an event, evening dress required.' Mama pretended to be upset-- that she did not have time, that she couldn't go, then at the appointed time she came out ready to meet him...my mother I think liked this whole crazy work-related dad. [212]

"Tata in spite of so many duties always had time for us. He shared tasks with mom. Dad was with us doing homework and teaching us morals. We got the most help from him in science and essays in the Polish language. When I had completely no inspiration, I asked him to help me. We sat together and he got me back on various topics, themes, sometimes he even wrote something for me. I got so used to it that without him I could not write a composition. [213]

---

[211] Rozmowa z Katarzyna Gilarska Re: General Kazimierz Gilarski," http://smolensk.muzhp.pl/rozmowa-z-katarzyna-gilarska/

[212] Ibid.

[213] Ibid.

"I think my dad liked all living creatures. He treated them with respect. He grew up in the countryside, among nature, so it always attracted him. We inherited his sensitivity to the plight of abused animals. Together we fed homeless cats and to our home were drawn all the animals as if there was a magnet - squirrels, cats, neighbor's dog—one was always standing at the gate." [214]

"Dad was a master at organizing interesting social events. He would arrange everything so that no one had to think of anything, he always had everything ready. It was never boring, there was always something going on - it seemed obvious and natural. When we met with people, it was not improvisation. Dad always said that a good show must have its screenplay so he always seamlessly steered it so that it was fun and interesting. It was simply brilliant." [215]

"He had a tremendous gift of storytelling, and burst into uncontrollable laughter, and although some of the stories we already knew by heart when we heard his laughs, how other people laughed, it was new to them and so for us it was as if we heard it the first time." [216]

"The 'script' was a key word for my dad at work—it was the basis for his work. Each state ceremony must be written, signed, accepted. Very often we were laughing about this at home asking him: "You have a script?" Though not in writing, but in his head he always had everything planned. When I was in high school, I wanted to go somewhere alone with my friends for the first time, so I asked my father for permission. He asked: 'What are you going to do there? I will consider it, but please leave me the prepared script.' In school, we laughed at this all day and then wrote quite seriously 'Script for Kasi's dad". On the same day my dad looked in disbelief, read it, and as promised, let me go. He just wanted the script." [217]

---

[214] Ibid.
[215] Ibid.
[216] Ibid.
[217] Ibid.

Przemyslaw Gosiewski
Sejm Deputy

Przemysław Gosiewski was born 12 May 1964 in Slupsik. He was a Member of Parliament in the IV, V and VI terms from the Law and Justice party, Member of the Council of Ministers and Deputy Prime Minister in the government of Jaroslaw Kaczynski, and chairman of the parliamentary partyof Law and Justice.

He grew up in Darłowie. His father, John, was a teacher of history, and a member of the Communist Party. His mother, Jadwiga, was a pediatrician and was involved in political activities within the local PiS party in the Slawnoo district.

Gosiewski was married twice. With Margaret Gosiewska, whom he divorced, he had a son. With his second wife, Beata Gosiewska, he had a son and a daughter.

"Gosiewski was known as a hard man, without sentiment enforcing the duties of party colleagues. But in dealing with journalists he was different. Always open, willing to cooperate, often smiling, patiently enduring even the dumbest questions." [218]

---

[218] "Gosiewski: Great workaholic by Peter Śmiłowicz" 02-04-2015 http://polska.newsweek.pl/sylwetka-przemyslawa-gosiewskiego-katastrofa-smolenska,artykuly,360694,1.html&usg=ALkJrhjI6_1aJ6iiJI-XSWxxQ1yB-JCjVw

Monsignor Bronislaw Gostomski
Chaplain to former President in exile Kaczorowski;
Pastor of Katyn Families in London

Bronislaw Gostomski was born on 9 November 1948 in Sierpc in the diocese of Plock, into a family with strong religious roots. In 1966 he entered the Higher Seminary in Plock where after six years of study he was ordained a priest on 18 June 1972. Following a brief period as an assistant Parish Priest he was directed by his bishop to continue his studies at the Catholic University of Lublin in 1974. In 1979 he gained his Masters Degree in history. Little did he know how strongly history would play a part in his life.

In December 1979 he began his pastoral work in England, serving in the Polish Parish of Our Lady Mother of the Church in Ealing, west London, the Polish Parish in Peterborough and then Bradford. This was a difficult period in Poland's history. On the one hand the joy of the election of a pope from Poland; on the other the political difficulties at home, ending in the imposition of martial law in December 1981. The Polish exiled community lived these events and Father Gostomski lived it with them. Wherever he served he became known as a fervent patriot, ever optimistic and full of joy. Not only was he assiduous in the spiritual development of his parishes but he fostered good ecumenical contacts with followers of other religions.

In 2003 he was made Parish Priest of St Andrew Bobola Church in London's Hammersmith district. Here his keen historical consciousness developed deeper on being appointed Chaplain to the Polish Ex-Combatant Association (veterans of the Polish Army during the Second World War.) He had a great affinity with the old soldier exiles and their families born and raised in exile. With his spontaneous love and openness he also gained the trust and devotion of the new wave of Poles settling in England, this time not as political exiles but in search of a better future for themselves and their families. Put simply he was a true father to his parishioners." [219]

---

[219] "Tributes to former Bradford priest killed in air crash" http://www.thetelegraphandargus.co.uk/news/8092994.Tributes_to_former_Bradford_priest_killed_in_air_crash/

Bronislaw Gostomski was not originally scheduled to fly to Smolensk on April 10th. But when the wife of former Polish President in exile Ryszard Kaczorowski was unable to go, Gostomski went in her place.

Anna Spyrka, 36, was married to her husband by the much-loved priest, who she described as a "brilliant people's man." She said: "He knew how to speak to the smallest child, to the oldest person. He never used his knowledge to make anyone feel inferior and never spoke to anyone in a patronising way. It is such a loss."[220]

---

[220] Ibid.

Mariusz Handzlik
Undersecretary of State

Mariusz Handzlik was born June 11, 1965 in Bielsko Biala. He was a Polish diplomat, the Undersecretary of State in the Office of the President of the Republic of Poland and since October, 2008 in charge of foreign policy. Handzlik earned a Master's degree in sociology of international relations from the Catholic University of Lublin. [221]

Waldemar Piasecki knew Handzlik from the time he studied at Catholic University of Lublin. While Handzlik was in a Polish Embassy post in Washington DC in 1994, he and Piasecki met often--most often in the company of Professor Jan Karski, a Polish war hero and Righteous Gentile whom Handzlik had befriended in Karski's final years. They talked about politics and about Polish relations with their new their strategic ally – America. In the climate of these meetings they began to enjoy the American drink "Manhattan". [222]

In 1998, Handzlik was diagnosed with a brain tumor. The only chance was a neurosurgical procedure. He asked Karski advice what to do. The professor left no doubt: "Only the operation and only in America." He went and all ended happily. [223]

Piasecki recalled "I remember how with professor Karski, we celebrated the successful end of his treatment in a restaurant. Mariusz, with a shaved head after surgery and the way he was dressed reminded of us of Kojak. We raised a toast with "Manhattans"—a toast to his head." [224]

Handzlik and Karski played chess on Tuesdays. On July 13, 2000, in his apartment in Chevy Chase, Maryland Karski fell ill and began shaking with cold. Alarmed, Handzlik started to call an ambulance. Karski sternly responded: "Minister Handzlik, Check! Your move." Karski won the game,

---

[221] https://en.wikipedia.org/wiki/Mariusz_Handzlik
[222] "Mariusz Handzlik. Farewell" Dziennik Kzwiazkowy Polish Daily News April 10, 2010
http://dziennikzwiazkowy.com/wydarzenia/mariusz-handzlik-pozegnanie/
[223] Ibid.
[224] Ibid.

then agreed to be taken to Georgetown University Hospital. He was placed in intensive care and died shortly thereafter.

Karski was both a citizen of Poland and the United States and an honorary citizen of Israel. He was proud of each country. After Karski's death, Handzlik came up with the idea of decorating his coffin with not only the flag of Poland but also the American flag, and the flag of Israel with the Star of David. When he told this to the high official of the Polish Embassy, he was told: "Impossible! It's against protocol." [225] Handzlik took it upon himself, therefore, to do what was necessary to honor his departed friend's desires. He was able to obtain an authentic Star of David from the collections of the Jewish Historical Institute in Warsaw and an American flag which had flown over the White House. When Jan Karski's coffin was brought to the cathedral of Saint Mateusza it was wrapped only in the white and red of the Polish flag. After the service, Handzlik took from his pocket the Star of David and reverently placed it on the Polish flag. The American flag joined the casket on the Mount of Olives cemetery. There were few people at the service, but Mariusz Handzlik, who came with his wife, daughters Iwona and Julka, and son Janek, who had been born in Washington, completed his mission according to the final wishes of his friend Jan Karski. [226]

Unfortunately, Handzlik's marriage broke up. It was probably one of the costs of his own public service and professional dedication to everything he did for the next position.

Katyn was for him one of the most important priorities. As a great friend of America, Handzlik shared the view that Poland should not forget those brave Americans who, when they told the truth about Katyn, risked their careers and often lost them. He worked on giving them high Polish awards, even if only posthumously. [227]

Throughout it all, he was dedicated to passing on the lessons of his late mentor Professor Karski. Once he recalled the professor asked his "student" Handzlik, the last thing he should do as a diplomat traveling to an important function. Handzlik tried to figure out the answer but

---

[225] Ibid.
[226] Ibid.
[227] Ibid.

without success. Finally he surrendered. The professor looked at him with a sense of superiority. "What should he do before leaving? ... Pee. You never know when you will have the opportunity next time, and the imperative of the bladder cannot supercede the imperative of the Republic," Karski said finally. Handzlik jumped up and kissed Karski's hand uttering one word: "Master!" [228]

---

[228] Ibid.

Roman Indrzejczyk
Chaplain to the President

Roman Indrzejczyk was born on 14 November 1931 in Żychlin in the province of Lodz. He was ordained in 1956. After the imposition of martial law 13 December 1981 Indrzejczyk followed the prophet of the Old Testament and refused to shave as a sign of mourning. In the 1980s he welcomed in his parish meetings the National Commission of "Solidarity" and the Citizens' Committee.

For twenty years he served as chaplain in the Psychiatric Hospital in Tworki; the next dozen years he was pastor. He was twice a national minister of health (1961-1976; 1989-1994). As the pastor he participated in the ecumenical movement - he was a member of the Polish Council of Christians and Jews, for some time its Vice-President.

He became the Chaplain to the Polish president December 23, 2005 after Lech Kaczynski won the election. Although previously the post was held by military chaplains Lech Kaczynski asked the Polish Primate for Indrzejczyk to be appointed his chaplain.

He used to say about himself that he is an ordinary priest and that he had a propensity for seeing the goodness in people and telling them so. [229] {1}

---

[229] "Roman Indrzejczyk," http://smolensk.muzhp.pl/portret/ks-roman-indrzejczyk/

Lieutenant Pawel Janeczek
Member, Polish Government Protection Bureau (BOR)

Lt. Paweł Janeczek, was born 16 Apr 1973 in Zvolen. From an early age he was physically fit. In the 1980's and 1990's he coached judo in Radomiaku. "It was with pain that I learned about the crash of the government plane. I knew that Pawel was on the aircraft because I knew that he was the chief of security and bodyguard for the president," said Lech Falkiewicz, judo trainer in Radomiaku. "Paul was a great man, helpful, polite. Such people rarely are found," said the coach. [230]

Besides his passion for judo, Janeczek also loved motorcycles and running marathons. He was fluent in English and Russian. Though Janesczek competed in national judo competitions, he failed to win a medal at any major event. However, thanks to practicing judo, he was very athletic and it helped him in finding a job in the anti-terrorist police brigade in Radom in the mid-1990s. He then moved to Warsaw.

For about 12 years he worked in the State Protection Office. In late 2004, he married the Polish journalist, Joanna Racewicz. He met Joanna while sitting next to each other on a plane. Because she was a well known and publically recognized, their marriage was discrete, away from Warsaw, away from paparazzi. [231]

In an interview for the weekly "Gala" she spoke about her husband. "He is a unique man--good, caring, sensitive, very masculine, smart, and honest. He is mentally strong, resolute and noble. He would help me when I came from work tired or sad...He convinced me that the world does not end at work. He was wise and had the ability to understand that the simple

---

[230] "Shock and disbelief. What were Paul and Artur Janeczek Ziętek who died in the crash? We got to the people who knew them" Roman FURCIŃSKI 12 APR 2010, http://www.echodnia.eu/radomskie/wiadomosci/art/8689781,szok-i-niedowierzanie-jacy-byli-pawel-janeczek-i-artur-zietek-ktorzy-zgineli-w-katastrofie-dotarlismy-do-ludzi-ktorzy-ich-znali,id,t.html

[231] "Paweł Janeczek, oficer BOR, był mężem znanej dziennikarki TVN Joanny Racewicz. Zginął z prezydentem pod Smoleńskiem" (mag) Echo Dnia 14 KWIETNIA 2010 http://www.gazetalubuska.pl/artykuly-archiwalne/art/7849199,pawel-janeczek-oficer-bor-byl-mezem-znanej-dziennikarki-tvn-joanny-racewicz-zginal-z-prezydentem-pod-smolenskiem,id,t.html

things are the most beautiful-- that together you can enjoy every moment. There is nothing better than knowing that there is someone to whom you can go back to—someone waiting for you with dinner, freshly brewed tea, with stories about the whole day. With my husband I always felt safe," she said. [232] On April 23, 2008 they had a son, Igor.

A few years ago a young Pawel Janeczek, consulted a gypsy woman who prophesied that he was going to die a tragic death. That prophecy came true on April 10, 2010.

"Today we cannot believe what happened. Pawel is no longer with us, a gypsy foretold the tragedy, which I learned by telephone while at school in the classroom," says Wojciech Kacprzak, Janeczek's brother-in-law. [233]

Pawel's parents live in Zvolen. They learned about the crash of the media. They had last seen him just before Easter. He would have celebrated his 37th birthday on April 16. [234]

---

[232] Ibid.

[233] "The Crash Killed Officer Przasnysza" 14 Apr 2010 http://kuriermlawski.pl/W-katastrofie-zginal-oficer-z-Przasnysza-,93973

[234] "Paweł Janeczek, oficer BOR, był mężem znanej dziennikarki TVN Joanny Racewicz. Zginął z prezydentem pod Smoleńskiem" (mag) Echo Dnia 14 KWIETNIA 2010 http://www.gazetalubuska.pl/artykuly-archiwalne/art/7849199,pawel-janeczek-oficer-bor-byl-mezem-znanej-dziennikarki-tvn-joanny-racewicz-zginal-z-prezydentem-pod-smolenskiem,id,t.html

Dariusz Jankowski
Official in the Chancellery of the President

Jankowski worked in the office of the President since 1993. He led the Organizational Service Team. During the presidency of Lech Kaczynski he specialized in organizing his visits to East.

He was 55 years old and left a wife and two children.

Natalia Januszko
Flight Attendant

Natalia Maria Januszko was born July 27, 1987 in Warsaw to Isabella and Gregory. After graduating high school, she studied zoology at the Animal Sciences Department of Animal SGGW in Warsaw. From 2007-2008 she worked as a flight attendant for Polish LOT airlines. On February 16, 2009 she began working in the 36 Special Air Transport Regiment as a senior flight attendant. She had flown approximately 247 hours before the crash. She was only 22 years old at the time of her death, the youngest person killed in the Smolensk crash. [235]

"She loved to fool around and make silly faces. She had a great sense of humor, able to amuse everyone, and her laughter was very contagious," Ania Krolikowska, close friend of Natalia from high school, told "Newsweek." "Natala was always smiling, full of energy and enthusiastic life," confirms Nadia Januszko, another friend from that period. In spite of the same name they are not related, but always called themselves sisters.

Natalia loved animals and horseback riding. Her dream was to be a veterinarian. Deciding to take a year off from her studies, she took a job as a flight attendant, as her mother once was. "She always liked to travel," said Joanna Brzozowska, a friend from college. "Flying was for Natalia adventure. On the refrigerator were dozens of magnets: Shanghai, Rabat, Brussels, St. Petersburg. Soon she was to be flying to in Washington and New York. To go to the United States had been her dream. She was to go the following week," says childhood friend Magda Niestryjewska. [236]

"She was so beautiful. Even wearing just a white T-shirt she looked like she was wearing a stylish tailored suit. She loved good movies and good music. She was always watching and listening to something different than everyone else. She had her own taste," said Ana Krolikowski. [237]

---

[235] https://pl.wikipedia.org/wiki/Natalia_Januszko
[236] "Zginęła z prezydentem. Miała zastępstwo" http://www.fakt.pl/Zginela-z-prezydentem-Miala-zastepstwo,artykuly,69132,1.html
[237] "Natalia Januszko – stewardesa z tupolewa" by Filip Gańczak 20-04-2010 http://polska.newsweek.pl/natalia-januszko---stewardesa-z-tupolewa,57010,1,1.html

"Above all, she loved animals. In her home lived dogs and cats. Her mom was getting mad, but together they would give others the gift of a pet," says her friend Magda. "She gave to me a gift—a dog Philo. To this day he is with me. She had a Labrador. She called him Barnej." [238]

---

[238] "Zginęła z prezydentem. Miała zastępstwo" http://www.fakt.pl/Zginela-z-prezydentem-Miala-zastepstwo,artykuly,69132,1.html

Izabela Jaruga-Nowacka
Member of Parliament

Izabela Jaruga-Nowacka was born 23 Aug 1950 in Gdansk. She was Sejm Deputy, President of the Labor and Union Party, and deputy prime minister in the government of Marek Belka. She was the wife of Professor Jerzy Nowacki, rector of the Polish-Japanese Institute of Technology in Warsaw. She had two daughters, Barbara and Catherine.

In an interview published in the Polish news magazine "Newsweek", journalist Zofia Wojtowska remembered Izabela: [239]

"She was a politician, a feminist, sometimes shocking, often a "Mother Teresa" helping the injured, single mothers, nurses, pensioners, and veterans. I could on forever. But first she was a woman--smart, beautiful, well-dressed. This is why I dared to approach her and start a conversation. We were talking about the upcoming referendum on the abortion law. Izabela Jaruga-Nowacka was the first politician with whom I spoke in my professional life. Such discussions one does not forget. Especially since the referendum quickly came down to the situation of women in Poland. Discrimination based on sex, bullying, equal opportunities. Her contagious conviction was that in the new Poland everything is possible.

"She had a contagious laugh. She did not stop laughing when she came in 1993 to the Parliament as a Labor Union deputy. She was a colorful bird among members of Parliament whose frowning was evidence of the sense of helplessness and uselessness in the Houses of Parliament. She became increasingly important in politics without losing anything of being a woman.

"Perfect makeup. Nice shirts. Good shoes. Big necklaces. Scarves and beautifully arranged hair. Similar were her emotions. Because when she laughed, it was real. But she also raged and screamed for real. She often had tears in her eyes, not only during meetings with single mothers or of

---

[239] "Izabela Jaruga-Nowacka And God took the woman" By Zofia Wójtowska 03-04-2015 http://polska.newsweek.pl/kim-byla-izabela-jaruga-nowacka-v-rocznica-katastrofy-smolenskiej,artykuly,360718,1.html&usg=ALkJrhjsrdbKq0yoFGZiIabVreI6Rn3ZNg

abused women but also on the parliamentary tribune, when she spoke about their problems.

"She spearheaded the adoption, in 2005, of the law against domestic violence, when she was a deputy prime minister in the government of Marek Belka." [240]

---

[240] Ibid.

Josef Joniec
Chairman, Parafiada Association

Father Joseph Joniec was born on 12 October 1959 in Laskowa near Limanowa. Along with his parents and siblings he lived there until 1973 when a fire completely destroyed his family home. After the fire, the family moved to Wilkow near Krakow. After finishing elementary school he enrolled in the Piarist School in Krakow and was admitted to the Minor Seminary of the Piarist Order. August 16, 1977 he made his first religious profession, assuming the patron Saint Christopher. He was ordained on May 18, 1985. After his ordination he served as pastoral minister in Lowicz, then in the parish of Hebdów and in the parish of the Holy Name of Mary in Krakow-Rakowice. [241]

Since 1990 he performed his pastoral work in the parish of Our Lady Queen of Believers in Warsaw Siekierki, where he was a catechist, catechetical inspector, university chaplain, parish priest (1995-2001), and first rector of the Piarist college (1990-1999). The Piarists were dedicated to working with children and young people of all levels of education, including the scouts, athletes, and university students in Poland and beyond its borders. [242]

The greatest achievement of his life was his involvement in the creation and promotion of the education of young people through faith, culture and sport. In 1992 he founded the Parafiada Association, a non-governmental and non-profit association which has become an important link in the process of education of young people in Poland, and was also developed in many European countries, especially on the Polish eastern border. The principal aim of the association is to promote the development of children and youth from various social environments, permitting children and youth to preserve their identity and simultaneously to integrate with the community at local, regional, national and international levels. The Parafiada Association cooperates with parishes, schools, sport clubs and

---

[241] "o. Józef Joniec SP," http://www.bieg-jonca.pl/jozef-joniec-sp/
[242] Ibid.

orphanages targeting children and youth who have fewer opportunities due to socio-economic, educational or geographical difficulties. [243]

The invitation for Father Joseph to participate in the official state delegation at the ceremony in the Katyn Forest on April 10 came from the President of the Republic Lech Kaczynski as a tribute to the activities of the Parafiada Association undertaken earlier in the educational program "Katyn ... Save from Oblivion". The aim of this program was to honor the memory of the heroes of the Katyn massacre, and at the same time restore their names in the collective memory of the Nation by planting 21,857 oak trees. Each oak commemorates a particular person who was killed in Katyn, Kharkiv and Tver. The program had already involved nearly 3,000 institutions in Poland and abroad. Lech Kaczynski patronized the project; two days after returning from Katyn on April 12, a Katyn oak tree was to be planted in the presidential gardens in a suburb of Warsaw. [244]

"Father Joseph Joniec was very cheerful man, always smiling, and this joy he passed to others," said Dariusz Karnowski volleyball coach, educator and president of the Parish Sports Club "Unitas Tuchola", since 2002. "He was a friend to everyone. Although there were many people in his Parafiada Association everyone was under the impression that Father Joseph was there for him and only him."

Notes Father Gregory Radzisz, an associate of the Parafiada Association for 24 years, "Father Joniec never refused anyone time and attention; never out of his mouth fell the words, 'I do not have time, please come back later.' He just could not finish the conversation and coldly go away when someone needed this conversation. He was a very cheerful man. Always smiling. Always focused on young people, also on the problems of educators. And always tried to solve their problems or identify the individuals who could help in this." [245]

---

[243] "Parafiada Association from Poland is looking volunteers for an non formal education project" http://www.evs4u.ro/evs-opportunities/parafiada-association-from-poland-is-looking-volunteers-for-an-non-formal-education-project

[244] "o. Józef Joniec SchP," http://www.sanktuarium-pijarzy.pl/?page_id=4000

[245] "Parafiada Association from Poland is looking volunteers for an non formal education project" http://www.evs4u.ro/evs-opportunities/parafiada-association-from-poland-is-looking-volunteers-for-an-non-formal-education-project

"I worked with Father Joseph for fifteen years," said Maria Kujel, who for 20 years worked in the Parafiada Association. "In conversations sometimes we sketched visions of various projects, ideas for Parafiada programs, saying that it will happen in a few years. Then it seemed unreal. But in retrospect, I see that these visions came true and turned out to be real. Father Joseph always saw a lot farther than I did…than all of us… Many times I witnessed ordinary people who came to him experiencing some difficulties in life, just to talk, to thank him for his help and identify the way out of trouble. Shortly before the crash in Smolensk when Father Joseph on the way back to Warsaw to one of the Parafiada camps for children from the orphanage, he had a very serious car accident. A truck was crossing the road when a wheel fell off and it completely destroyed the driver's side of the car Father Joseph was riding in. But to Father Joseph, nothing happened! The police officers who arrived at the scene of the accident heard people saying that 'it is probably some intervention of the saints' … Father Joseph said to them, that God had for him another death planned. The young man who was driving Father Joseph was also shocked by what he saw. While he was driving Father Joseph to Warsaw the young man truly opened up, talking, and finally confessed. He said that he had to confess, 'I met on the road an angel,' he said, "and he helped me make important life decisions."[246]

---

[246] Ibid.

Ryszard Kaczorowski
Former Polish President in Exile

Ryszard Kaczorowski was born 26 November 1919, in Białystok, Poland. He completed his education at a school of commerce. He was also a Scouting instructor of a local branch of the Polish Scouting Association. Following the Invasion of Poland in the beginning of World War II he clandestinely recreated the scouting movement (which had been delegalised by the Soviet authorities). In 1940, when he was only 21, he was arrested by the NKVD for his clandestine activities running messages for the underground movement. He was sentenced to death. He sat on death row for three months before his sentence was changed to ten years in a concentration camp in Kolyma in the northeast Arctic. [247]

Following the Sikorski-Mayski Agreement of 1941 he was set free and enlisted in General Władysław Anders' Army. After its evacuation from the Soviet Union, Kaczorowski joined the 3rd Carpathian Rifle Division, where he completed divisional secondary school. He fought in most major battles of the Polish 2nd Corps, including the Battle of Monte Cassino. After the war he remained in the United Kingdom as a political emigrant. Until 1986, he worked in business as an accountant. [248]

Between 1989 and 1990 he served as the last President of Poland in exile. As such he was the public representative of Free Poland. After the Communist regime fell apart, Kaczorowski resigned his post as Poland regained its independence from the Soviet sphere of influence and Lech Wałęsa was elected as the first democratically-elected president of Poland since World War II. He also passed the presidential insignia to Wałęsa, thus ending the 45-years long episode of the Polish government in exile. [249]

Ryszard Kaczorowski's last home was in London. He had two daughters with wife Karolina, Jadwiga Kaczorowska, who has two children Zenek and Wanda Szulc, and Alicja Jankowska who has three children, Ryszard,

---

[247] https://en.wikipedia.org/wiki/Ryszard_Kaczorowski
[248] Ibid.
[249] Ibid.

Marcin and Krystyna Jankowska. He frequently visited Poland and was treated according to the Polish law on former presidents of the state. [250]

On his 90th birthday he came to his hometown of Bialystok. The city awarded him honorary citizenship and a local university dedicated to him a library.

"I have two souvenirs, very important to me, which are waiting for me to take them with me to the grave. It's a rock from Monte Cassino, and a handful of earth from under the oak trees in the park in Zwierzyniec. These oaks make up the monument of the Constitution of May 3..." said Kaczorowski. [251]

---

[250] Ibid.
[251] "Ryszard Kaczorowski, the last president of Poland in exile – memory" 10.04.2010 http://wyborcza.pl/1,105742,7752837,Ryszard_Kaczorowski__ostatni_prezydent_RP_na_uchodzstwie.html

Lech Kaczynski
President of the Republic of Poland

Lech Aleksander Kaczyński was born 18 June 1949 in Warsaw, the son of Rajmund (an engineer who served as a soldier of the Armia Krajowa— Home Army-- in World War II and a veteran of the Warsaw Uprising), and Jadwiga (a philologist at the Polish Academy of Sciences). As a child, he starred in a 1962 Polish film, *The Two Who Stole the Moon* with his identical twin brother Jarosław. [252]

He graduated from the school of law and administration at Warsaw University. In 1980 he was awarded his PhD by Gdańsk University. He later assumed professorial positions at Gdańsk University and Cardinal Stefan Wyszyński University in Warsaw. [253]

In the 1970s Kaczyński was an activist in the pro-democratic anti-communist movement in Poland (the Workers' Defense Committee) as well as the Independent Trade Union movement. In August 1980, he became an adviser to the Inter-Enterprise Strike Committee in the Gdańsk Shipyard and the Solidarity movement. After the communists imposed martial law in December 1981, he was interned as an anti-socialist element. After his release, he returned to trade union activities, becoming a member of the underground Solidarity movement. [254]

In 2001 he founded the Law and Justice (Prawo i Sprawiedliwość – PiS) political party, usually labeled 'conservative' by the media, with his brother Jarosław. Lech Kaczyński was the president of the party between 2001 and 2003.

Kaczyński married economist Maria Kaczyńska in 1978. They had one daughter, Marta and two granddaughters named Ewa and Martyna. [255]

Former deputy head of the Presidential Chancellery Robert Draba met Kaczynski when he sought the position of director of the Legal Office. Already at the first meeting, Draba said, "I was struck by his unusual openness, directness and naturalness. He was able to make the other

---

[252] https://en.wikipedia.org/wiki/Lech_Kaczy%C5%84ski
[253] Ibid.
[254] Ibid.
[255] Ibid.

person feel very comfortable in his company. I remember how after a year of working together, he suggested that we call each other by our first names. He did not like how people he worked closely with called him 'Mr. President.' [256]

"He had an excellent memory for numbers-- in his cell phone was listed barely six names, the rest of the numbers to his co-workers he knew by heart. He was a sensitive person, open and caring for the well-being of others. [257]

"I think that most of his colleagues {experienced} his concern for them. I remember his commitment when Elzbieta Jakubiak began to have health problems. At the time he was mayor of Warsaw. He spent several hours a day with her."[258]

In a similar vein, also Jan Ołdakowski, Law and Justice deputy and director of the Museum of the Warsaw Uprising recalled, "When my father had a heart attack, I had the impression that he was well treated {thanks to Lech Kaczynski}. I remember that morning as I came to see him, Dad was gone ... It turned out that the president learned of my situation and at night called professor Zbigniew Religa and asked him for help. That evening an ambulance came from the Institute of Cardiology, picked up my dad and took him there." [259]

The President was exceptionally warm to children. "At the farewell for Minister Ewa Junczyk-Ziomecka I was there with the whole family. The president met my son Frances. At some point, the President came up to a crowd of guests. Lech Kaczynski smiled, patted my son on the head," says Marek Opioła, Law and Justice deputy and friend of the presidential family. [260]

For the President, his wife Maria was always first

"After a late return from the presidential office, he always quietly entered the bedroom where she slept, so that he did not wake her up. He did not want his wife to feel in any way tired because of his own work," said Draba. Unfortunately, once it happened by accident. On that occasion he returned quietly to the bedroom, he puts his leg under the blanket, under

---

[256] "Lech Kaczynski Never Wanted to Wake his Marylka" 16 Apr 2010 http://www.se.pl/wiadomosci/polska/nigdy-nie-chcia-budzic-swojej-marylki_136524.html
[257] Ibid.
[258] Ibid.
[259] Ibid.
[260] Ibid.

which sat the dog Titus. He suddenly felt his favorite pet angrily bring his teeth down on his big toe. The President could not stop himself—he shouted ... {and thereby woke Maria}"- smiles Draba. [261]

Two days after the Smolensk crash, the editors of the National Review published as essay by Charles Crawford who served as British ambassador in Warsaw from 2003 to 2007 which succinctly sums up Lech Kaczynski politics and his vision for the Poland he loved:

"I had met the Kaczynski family on numerous occasions. They came across as smart, amusing, private, determined, and far-sighted Polish patriots. Conservative? For sure. But not snooty, paternalistic conservatives. Rather, their conservatism was based on rock-hard core beliefs and unshakable private integrity. Yet it was not free-market conservatism: They liked a strong state, and fretted in almost left-wing ways about the Polish underclass. They were uneasy with tycoons and capitalists; they suspected (presciently?) that too much easy money sloshing around would do more harm than good. The Kaczynskis' overriding ambition was for Poland to be strong. (Since 1795, Poland has been free and independent for only 40 years.) Lech Kaczynski was a fastidious constitutionalist. He did not want Poland slipping back into the ruinous feuding of the 1930s.....Lech Kaczynski wanted Poland to be strong in Europe. But he also wanted Western Europe to grasp that while it had prospered after World War II, Poland had been left at Yalta to rot under Soviet misrule. The values of "modern Europe" had been formed without Poland's rightful participation; Poland was not automatically bound by them....He struck defiant postures against Putin's Russia, but lacked the diplomatic guile to build international alliances and make much of a difference....Yet his unwavering insistence on integrity and constitutionality made a real difference. I was asked on the BBC and CNN whether Poland would now slump into political instability, given that so many top officials died in the plane crash. I replied, "Of course not." Poland today is in deep sorrow, yet it is coping firmly and democratically with this calamity. That is Kaczynski's towering achievement, for Poland and for Europe."[262]

---

[261] Ibid.
[262] "A Very Polish Conservative" by THE EDITORS April 12, 2010 Remember Lech Kaczynski.
http://www.nationalreview.com/article/229525/very-polish-conservative

Maria Kaczynski
First Lady

The First Lady was born as Maria Helena Mackiewicz 21 Aug 1942 in Machowo (near Kobylnik, now Belarus) to Lidia and Czesław Mackiewicz. Her father fought in the Vilnius Armia Krajowa (Home Army), while an uncle fought in the Polish II Corps of Gen. Władysław Anders at the Battle of Monte Cassino; another uncle was murdered by the NKVD (Soviet secret police) at Katyń.

She studied transport economics and foreign trade in Sopot at what is now the University of Gdańsk. After graduating in 1966, she worked at the Maritime Institute in Gdańsk, where she met Lech Kaczyński in 1976. They married in 1978. In addition to her native Polish, Maria Kaczyńska spoke English, French, Japanese and some Spanish and Russian. [263]

Since childhood, she had health problems. She was born with a heart defect. Maria's mother at the instigation of doctors moved with her to Rabka, because the local climate better served the sickly girl.

In Rabka, Maria finished high school, but chose a college on the other side of the Poland - in Sopot at the School of Maritime Transport Higher School of Economics (now the University of Gdansk). After graduation, she started working at the Maritime Institute in the laboratory where she studied prospects for the development of freight markets in the Far East.

Maria met her future husband through a friend of the Marine Institute. "It was in January 1976. I remember that day was very frosty. With Leszek, we really hit if off right away." [264]

The wedding took place in 1978. Two years later, Kaczynski's daughter Marta was born. After a long maternity leave Maria never returned to work. In the 1980s, she took care of her daughter, gave English and French lessons and assisted her husband in opposition and underground activities.

---

[263] https://en.wikipedia.org/wiki/Maria_Kaczy%C5%84ska
[264] "Maria Kaczynski Said I Live The Moment, I am Happy With What is Now" Newsweek PL, 11 Apr 2010
http://polska.newsweek.pl/maria-kaczynska-mowila--zyje-chwila--ciesze-sie-tym--co-jest-teraz,56539,1,1.html

She remained constantly by his side and on October 23, 2005 he won the presidential election.

As the spouse of the president she sponsored charities and participated in many charitable activities. Very important to her was the promotion of her own country in the world-- to eliminate false negative stereotypes in the assessment of Poland and the Polish people. Her active participation in charity events is evidenced by the many awards that she received. [265]

Maria was interested in the arts - theater, music, ballet. She liked traveling, because through traveling, she learned about the life and customs of other nations. She valued family life. She loved to spend time with their grandchildren: Ewa and Martyna. [266]

When asked in an interview if she was afraid of passing, she said: - "I do not think about it. I'm living the moment, I am happy with what it is now. I do not analyze the past; I do not live in the future." [267]

The Kaczynski's daughter Marta, in an interview by Marta Legieć, recalled her mother and her childhood. [268] "I was happy. This was due to {my mother's} approach to life, which was extremely optimistic. She was a bit like Anne of Green Gables or like a character similar to the Little Prince. She was able to enjoy the small things and to see the beautiful details of everyday life, so that she always left people smiling.

"A friend's daughter once gave me a Barbie doll. I still have it at home. In those days, there were no shops where one could buy doll clothes. Mom decided to take matters into her own hands and sewed really beautiful things. She outfitted my doll with a coat with a fur collar, various dresses

---

[265] "Maria Kaczyńska & # 8211; Polish real lady" http://polki.pl/maria-kaczynska-8211-prawdziwa-dama-polski,we-dwoje-lifestyle-jej-portret-artykul,10068092.html

[266] "Maria Kaczynski Said I Live The Moment, I am Happy With What is Now" Newsweek PL, 11 Apr 2010 http://polska.newsweek.pl/maria-kaczynska-mowila--zyje-chwila--ciesze-sie-tym--co-jest-teraz,56539,1,1.html

[267] Ibid.

[268] " Anne of Green Gables – Maria Kaczyńska in the eyes of her daughter", 7 Apr 2016, WP Kobieta http://kobieta.wp.pl/kat,132002,title,Ania-z-Zielonego-Wzgorza-czyli-Maria-Kaczynska-w-oczach-swojej-corki,wid,18256433,wiadomosc.html?ticaid=116eef

and suits--Ken got even pajamas. I was proud, because no one had such clothes for their dolls.

"Mama knew four languages, was a translator and taught English at home. Several times a week students would come to our house. In the eighties it was an opportunity to practice my character (she laughs). I had to be patient, not enter the room and ask for something. I was very pleased with myself when I succeeded. But when I was a teenager, we flew abroad. I could not remember if my mother once taught Spanish so I was surprised when she suddenly began to speak freely in this language."

Then there was Maria's sense of humor. Szymon Majewski, a Polish journalist and actor, had a particularly fond memory of her reaction to his joke, which concerned the famous photo of the First Lady boarding the government plane with a plastic bag. Someone had made {a picture of} a mock-XRay scan of the bag, showing hidden in there, supposedly, sandwiches for the president. When Majewski came one day to the Presidential Palace in a TVN (Polish television network) car, a BOR officer gave Majewski a plastic bag in which there were two sandwiches and a note from the First Lady, "Mr. Simon, you discovered what was inside. P.S. Please don't leave any crumbs. Maria Kaczyńska". [269] {4}

After the incident, Majewski praised the class and a sense of humor she has. Marta recalled, "From time to time, different people write to me who are concerned that Dad had to have his wife make sandwiches for him, even when travelling by plane. The story of the sandwiches lingers all the time. And absurd in itself would be if my parents had to take a meal on board. Yes, Mama had with her a plastic bag, but it was a sweater for Dad, she bought a while ago. It was just after an illness and she wanted him to have it on the airplane so that after removing his jacket, he would have something to keep him warm."

---

[269] Ibid.

Sebastian Karpiniuk
Member of Parliament-Sejm Deputy

Sebastian Marek Karpiniuk was born 4 December 1972 in Kolobrzeg.

"The month of April is cursed for us," said Bozena Strembska, aunt of Sebastian Karpiniuk. She cannot come to terms with the enormity of the tragedy of her family. Her nephew tragically died in the plane crash near Smolensk. Twenty years earlier he buried his mother, Danuta Karpiniuk. She died in April and also tragically - horribly burned in apartment fire. [270]

"They were both so young ... They were not even forty," lamented Bozena. Deputy Karpiniuk - for her simply Bastuś - embarked on his last journey almost directly from the tomb of his mother. Because on April 6, 2010, in Kolobrzeg Cathedral a service was held dedicated to the memory of Danuta Karpiniuk. Sebastian was there. He prayed long and intently. "And on April 10 he was gone ..." - says Bozena. "God, why is fate so cruel?" [271]

When his mother died, Sebastian was only 18 years old. The fire that took his mother's life broke out suddenly in her apartment. She managed to escape from the flames, but suffered terrible burns and died shortly thereafter in the hospital. Her beloved son had to watch as she died.

"Then he went back to school, much more serious and mature than most of us. Just grown up in this one tragic day," says Rafal Kolikow a friend and schoolmate of Karpiniuk.

After this terrible tragedy Sebastian lived with his father Marek. His aunt and grandmother tried to take the place of his lost mother. "If only he had not boarded the Tupolev ... He was very much afraid to fly, and during landings experienced panic attacks. But he was ambitious and the flying was required. It was for him stronger than fear," said Deputy Jerzy Kolakowski. [272]

---

[270] "The tragic story of a family Karpiniuków"
http://www.fakt.pl/Tragiczna-historia-rodziny-Karpiniukow,artykuly,69824,1.html
[271] Ibid.
[272] Ibid.

Robert Wegrzyn, a fellow Member of Parliament, recalled his colleague in this way: [273] "He scrupulously prepared everything; he was a demon for work. In my opinion, his desk says a lot about a man. Sebastian, had everything evenly arranged, thematically sorted, and in perfect order. When summer came and we were to visit his hometown of Kolobrzeg for a week, he carefully planned all our activities: sightseeing, a visit to a friendly eatery, playing tennis, trips to concerts...a joint boat ride...a race.

"He was very well liked by his fellow party members but I think that the politicians of other parties also held him in esteem, because Sebastian was just an awfully nice guy. He captured people with his characteristic smile. It is true that he liked to show off in the media. Newspapers sometimes wrote about him that he was overly concerned about his hairstyle. He laughed at this, although he actually had attached great importance to his appearance. He always wore a well-cut suit, ironed shirt, a well-chosen tie.

"He had one weakness – he was terribly afraid of traveling by plane. He always sat in the rear of the plane because he felt that the front seats are the most dangerous. The people who flew to Katyn {ceremony} did so either by virtue of their position or because the tragedy 70 years ago personally touched their family. Sebastian did not fit in either of these categories. I tell myself that as a man passionate in history he wanted to see Katyn, to be a part of the historical event." [274]

"Combative, enthusiastic...he was a fighter, the leader of the group, but in a positive sense," recalled his father, Marek at the memorial service for his son. "He liked to stand out. Once in high school, when he went to the prom he was the only one who sported a white suit, the rest wore black." [275]

"I also remember how we caught him smoking a cigarette. Then he became an opponent of smoking. He fumed when he saw me with a cigarette. Because of my addiction we could not watch the football matches

---

[273] "Sebastian Karpiniuk: Terribly stunner" by Robert Wegrzyn 06-04-2015 http://polska.newsweek.pl/ludzie-ktorzy-zgineli-w-smolensku-sebastian-karpiniuk-newsweek,artykuly,360712,1.html

[274] Ibid.

[275] "Sebastian Karpiniuk. The boy from the sea" ed. Agnieszka Niesłuchowska Act. 10.04.2011 http://wiadomosci.wp.pl/kat,1329,title,Sebastian-Karpiniuk-Chlopak-znad-morza,wid,13303156,wiadomosc.html?ticaid=116a70

together. I smoked, so Sebek locked himself in his room and watched alone. As a goal scored, both of us were screaming but in our own room. [276]

"When he came for the weekend from Warsaw to Kolobrzeg, still he lived his work. Until late at night we talked about politics; he told me about the Diet, of the difficult work in the committee. Pressures and conflicts, which have occurred. He was very active, always struggling with something, but I noticed that shortly before his death, he was muted, withdrawn—he was quieter," said his father. [277]

Six months before his death Polish newpaper "Fakt" published a photo shoot of Sebastian and his fiance Carolina. They were smiling, happy to pose for photos on the beach. He's in a white shirt and light blue jeans, she in a white dress. He spoke then about his love, which began 17 years earlier. The beautiful brunette he met at a disco. "All the men's eyes were attracted {to her} but I decided to try it. I do not even remember to what songs we danced. I only know that they were very slow pieces," Karpiniuk told "Fakt"

---

[276] Ibid.
[277] Ibid.

Vice Admniral Andrzej Karweta
Commander in Chief, Navy

Andrzej Karweta was born 11 Jun 1958 in Jeleń village, Poland. In 1977 he started studies at the Polish Naval Academy in Gdynia and graduated in 1982, with the rank of Lieutenant Junior Grade. In the following years he took up further studies, including Defense Politics at the Polish National Defense University in Warsaw (2006) and Royal College of Defense Studies in London.

Most of his early career was with minesweeping units of the Polish Navy. From 1992-1996 he was chief of staff and second in command of the 13th Minesweeper Division and later he became its commander. In 2002 he became deputy commander of the Underwater Warfare Division in Supreme Allied Commander Atlantic (SACLANT), and was a Polish representative in SACLANT headquarters. In 2005 he returned to Poland and served as the second in command of the 8th Coast Defense Flotilla in Świnoujście. On 3 May 2007 he was promoted to Rear Admiral and became a deputy chief of Polish Navy Staff in Gdynia. On 11 November 2007 he was promoted to Vice Admiral and appointed the Polish Navy's commander-in-chief. [278]

Karweta's daughter, Mariola, remembered her father for his love of planting and gardening. He could never get enough of it. Even on the day before his fateful flight to Smolensk he had bought some plants and seeds and had planned to take advantage of the lovely weather to do some planting. But he first had to fly to Smolensk for the ceremony. It was to be a short trip, so he anticipated being able to get some gardening in that weekend after he returned. "Perhaps he flew out of obligation because he was a great patriot," said his daughter Kamil. "Dad sang the national anthem to us, instead of lullabies. He did it almost every night before bedtime." [279]

"His backyard was his passion—his pride and joy... He looked after each tree," said Commander Krzysztof Marciniak, subordinate and neighbor Andrew Karwety. Recently, we were together at an exhibition of Navy

---

[278] https://en.wikipedia.org/wiki/Andrzej_Karweta
[279] "Mariola Karweta: Bardzo lubiłam być Twoją żoną by Irena Łaszyn"
8 APRIL 2011 http://www.dziennikbaltycki.pl/artykul/389923,mariola-karweta-bardzo-lubilam-byc-twoja-zona,7,id,t,sa.html

equipment in Qatar. After returning, despite the fatigue of eleven hours of travel, the Admiral only changed shoes and immediately went to take care of his plants." [280]

On Sunday, 11 April 2010, in Gdynia sailors raised the flag of the ship "Lightning" to half-mast. In memory of their commander it was said: "His passion inspired us to the best work for the Navy. He hated incompetence and discontent. At the same time he rewarded initiative and dedication in his subordinates. He was able to respond rapidly to crisis situations, and he mastered the outstanding skills of command. He always acted honorably and in accordance with naval tradition. Commander, help us to go on in our sailor's watch. "[281]

November 11, 2007, he was appointed by the President to the post of commander of the Navy. As such, he had to travel between Gdynia and Warsaw. In Warsaw, he experienced his work as "claustrophobic". In meetings there with politicians, he found they wondered whether it was worth spending money on the Navy. Then as he returned to Gdynia, he gathered friends and told them what was going on in Warsaw. Sometimes he said that he felt there was probably no hope for the navy. But he returned to his headquarters in the morning and continued fighting. He said to his superiors: "Do not give me another promotion, give me ships."[282]

His career moved him through all levels of command, including the national military representative at NATO headquarters in Norfolk, Virginia. He studied at the prestigious Royal College of Defense Studies in London. [283]

Karweta with his wife Maria have two daughters and a son.

---

[280] "Wiceadmirał Andrzej Karweta; morze i ogródek"
notował: Hubert Orzechowski
http://polska.newsweek.pl/wiceadmiral-andrzej-karweta--morze-i-ogrodek, 56703,1,1.html

[281] "Admirał floty Andrzej Karweta (11.06.1958 - 10.04.2010)"
Marcin Górka, sla, pcg 08.04.2011 19:20 http://wiadomosci.gazeta.pl/wiadomosci/1,114892,9402873,Admiral_floty_Andrzej_Karweta__11_06_1958___10_04_2010_.html

[282] Ibid.

[283] Ibid.

Mariusz Kazana

Director, Ministry of Foreign Affairs Diplomatic Protocol

Mariusz Kazana was born 5 August 1960 in Bydgoszcz. He was a graduate of the School of Law and Administration at Warsaw University and Postgraduate Foreign Service in the Polish Institute of International Affairs in Warsaw. He completed internships at the International Institute of Public Administration in Paris and the Institute of Political Studies in Paris. Since 1988 he held various positions in the Polish Ministry of Foreign Affairs. [284]

In Bydgoszcz, as a teenager he coached pole vault and later went on to dedicate himself to scouting activities, becoming an instructor in the Polish Scouting Association.

All his professional life he spent working in the Ministry of Foreign Affairs. He was the first secretary of the Polish Embassy in Paris (1992-1996), advisor to the minister of the Department of Europe-West and Western Europe (1996-1999), and counselor at the Polish Embassy in Paris (1999-2003). He served as head of the Department of the Common Foreign and Security Policy in the Department of the European Union (2003-2005), deputy director of the Department of Strategy and Foreign Policy Planning (2005-2006), Minister-Counsellor and Director of the Office of the Director General (2006), and Director General of the Foreign Service (2006-2007).

February 11, 2008, he was appointed Director of Diplomatic Protocol. He accompanied the President of Poland and the Prime Minister in their travels abroad and handled their guests during their visits to Poland. And although it was a difficult task, requiring tremendous professionalism and prudence, he had the ability to make quick decisions - often in difficult circumstances.[285]

He was a lover of art, the author of many projects promoting Polish culture and art. He believed that art is an important part of diplomacy.

---

[284] https://pl.wikipedia.org/wiki/Mariusz_Kazana
[285] O Patronie, Fundacja Imienia Mariusz Kazana, http://mariuszkazana.org/katalog2/katalog/MariuszKazana.htm

As the Director of Diplomatic Protocol he was highly respected by his colleagues in the Diplomatic Corps and had many friends among the heads of diplomatic missions in Poland. He was a man full of kindness, optimism and humor. He loved people and dedicated his whole life to selflessly helping others. Regardless of others' positions he behaved with great class, demonstrating sensitivity and courage in solving difficult cases. He was known for his elegance and impeccable manners and his unique ability to win people over. He was well liked by his colleagues from the Ministry. In the memories of friends he will remain the model of integrity, wisdom and peace. [286]

---

[286] Ibid.

Janusz Kochanowski
Ombudsman and Civil Rights Commissioner

Janusz Kochanowski was born in Częstochowa on 18 April 1940. He graduated from the School of Law at the University of Warsaw and completed his court training in the capital city of Warsaw between 1964 and 1966. He obtained his doctoral degree in 1980. [287]

He took the floor in almost every case pervading society - ranging from the threat of swine flu to too loud television commercials to tax rates. He was the most colorful advocate for civil rights in the history of the office.[288] He was the author of more than 100 works on criminal law, administrative law and international relations, part of which were published in English and German.

After being elected to the post of Ombudsman in January 2006, Kochanowski quickly gave it unprecedented momentum, addressing virtually every issue present in public life. Outspoken on a wide variety of issues, he did not hide his conservative views, criticizing feminists and homosexuals and even a concert performance by Madonna which fell on a religious holiday. [289]

He was known for his sharp tongue, strong feelings and diligence. His political sympathies and declared views aroused controversy on the left side of the political scene and among some lawyers. "There are no rights and freedoms without well-functioning institutions of a strong rule of law - created by free citizens. There are no free citizens and a strong state without civil society that promotes civic virtues and a sense of responsibility for the common good," he said in the Sejm. [290]

He was a supporter of investigation and inspection saying that "truth and transparency are core values of public life." But he defended the representatives of authority when he believed journalists had abused

---

[287] https://en.wikipedia.org/wiki/Janusz_Kochanowski
[288] "Janusz Kochanowski: rzecznik wszechobecny"11-04-2010 http://polska.newsweek.pl/janusz-kochanowski--rzecznik-wszechobecny,56545,1,1.html
[289] Ibid.
[290] "Janusz Kochanowski" by Bogdan Wróblewski 10.04.2010 http://wyborcza.pl/1,75402,7754651,Janusz_Kochanowski.html

their freedoms by using "provocation." Most recently, he was best known for his amazingly fierce dispute with Health Minister Ewa Kopacz on introducing vaccines against swine flu. Kochanowski, who himself became ill, demanded prosecution of the minister. [291]

Two years ago, Janusz Kochanowski filed complaints by Katyn families against Russia to the Court of Human Rights in Strasbourg.

He was married to a Polish philologist, Ewa and had two children: Marta, a lawyer, and Mateusz, a law student.

---

[291] Ibid.

Brigadier General Stanislaw Komornicki
Chancellor of the Virtuti Militari Military Order

Stanislaw Komornicki was born July 26, 1924 in Warsaw. When Poland was occupied in 1939, Komornicki went underground to continue his education in secret. In February 1940 he was sworn in as a member of the Polish Victory Service, adopting the code name "Nalecz" (corresponding to the name of the Komornicki family coats of arms).

During the Warsaw Uprising he commanded an assault platoon in the Old Town. He participated in numerous battles and was wounded. For his efforts in defense of Warsaw, he was awarded the Order of Military Virtue V Class and the Cross of Valour. As one of 160 Army soldiers drafted into the Kosciuszko Division he was a company commander in the 6th Infantry Division. While with this unit, he participated in the Pomeranian battle, the assault on Kolobrzeg (where he was again wounded) and operations against Berlin. He led a branch of the Polish Army which drove to the Elbe River to meet up with U. S. Army units. He was presented the Cross of Valour.

After returning to Poland he served on the border with Czechoslovakia. He studied history at the University of Warsaw. In 1958 he graduated from the Academy of General Staff as a lieutenant colonel.

Komornicki retired from the service in 1975.

In an on-line blog, Malgorzata Pierski, who, through her father, knew General Komornicki since she was a child wrote of the General: "{He} is an unusual figure. It was the soul of the man--always ready to express himself and always having something to say which spoke to your heart." [292] He was an ardent patriot devoted to the Warsaw Uprising, and other national uprisings. Asked once about the January uprising (of 1863), he said that "it seemed that this kind of action did not make sense, but they did it, and thanks to them were able to raise the next generation of Poles."

He enjoyed great respect among colleagues from the Association of Warsaw Insurgents. Everyone knew his unusual biography. As a soldier he forged a combat route through the Old Town and Czerniakowski,

---

[292] DZIENNIKARSTWO Żegnaj generale…14 APR 2010
http://piekarska.blog.pl/?tag=stanislaw-nalecz-komornicki

and "was the one who crossed the Vistula with a report and returned to the burning Warsaw to once again cross the Vistula River." [293] He was threatened with exile to Siberia. As he recalled in an interview: "I did not go to Siberia as a result of my participation in the Warsaw Uprising but I was lucky enough to come to the Elbe and Berlin. I owe it to the soldiers and officers in the sixth division who preserved me, and I did not go east-- I just went to fight. "[294]

"Vitam impendere vero" (Life for the truth) was the life motto of General Komornicki. In an interview published on the website of the Museum of the Warsaw Uprising, he recalled that on 1 August 1944 when he got word that his unit was to prepare for the Uprising, "I began packing... I took socks, handkerchiefs, a small pair of theater binoculars; my mother even put a jar of jam. In a word, it was pointless. On the other hand I did not take the things that I had in the house already prepared for emergencies. I had a pre-war steel Polish helmet; I had shovels, boots that I got before the Uprising in the fire service. But those shoes were normal for a fireman in uniform. Out on the street, it would make me stand out to German patrols, so I chose not to take them. " [295]

In 1993 he was appointed by the president to serve as the Chancellor of the Order of Military Virtue War. In 2008 he began a fourth term in this position.

---

[293] Ibid.
[294] Ibid.
[295] "Stanisław Nałęcz-Komornicki" 11 kwietnia 2010
http://www.tvn24.pl/stanislaw-nalecz-komornicki,131164,s.html

Stanislaw Jerzy Komorowski
Undersecretary of State for Defense

Stanisław Jerzy Komorowski was born 18 December 1953. He started his diplomatic career almost by chance, without any prior diplomatic experience, by applying for a position in the Foreign Ministry opened at the time by Minister Krzysztof Skubiszewski, who was seeking to renew diplomatic services in Poland after the regime change in 1989. In 1991, he was appointed as Skubiszewski's chief of staff. Between 1994 and 1998, he was the Polish ambassador to the Netherlands and, between 1999 and 2004, he was the Polish ambassador to Great Britain. He played a role behind the scenes in the diplomatic events leading to Poland's acceptance to NATO as well as the European Union.

He was Deputy Foreign Affairs Minister and between 2007 and 2010 Deputy Minister of the National Defense. In the Department of Defense he was responsible for foreign affairs and, among other tasks, he negotiated the US missile defense system to be deployed in Poland.

The U. S. Ambassador Feinstein said "Minister Komorowski was our invaluable partner on bilateral defense issues of vital importance to both countries, including Missile Defense and the upcoming rotation of Patriot Missiles in Poland. With Minister Komorowski seated across the table from our negotiators during U.S.-Polish talks on a Status of Forces Agreement, we knew we would come up with an agreement that met both sides' needs, and we did. His energy, his leadership and his mastery of security issues will be sorely missed by his American colleagues at the United States Departments of State and Defense. America mourns a true friend." [296]

Komorowski was an avid skier and ski instructor as well as tennis player. During his university years, he was an active member of the Academic Ski Association (his father was a member of the International Ski Federation.) One of his passions was parks and gardens and, for a short time in 1990, he had a small gardening company; with his wife Maria Komorowska they created three gardens before they closed the company. His other passion

---

[296] https://en.wikipedia.org/wiki/Stanis%C5%82aw_Komorowski

was French culture. As a student he spent his vacations in France. Later, at the end of his life, he rebuilt the garden at the Komorowski's *Dziewanna* villa on the outskirts of Warsaw. [297]

He was married three times and had three sons – Karol and Maciej with his first wife Irena and Jerzy with his second wife Maria. His third wife was Ewa.

Komorowski was not originally scheduled to travel to Smolensk on April 10th but when Polish Defense Minister Bogdan Klich's mother was admitted to the hospital, he asked Komorowski if he would go in his place, so he did.[298]

---

[297] Ibid.
[298] Ibid.

WO2 Pawel Krajewski
Member, Polish Government Protective Services (BOR)

Warrant Officer Pawel Krajewski was born in 1975 in Szczytno, but grew up in Mazovia, Przasnysz.

Krajewski, due to his work, had to travel a lot however, he was always in telephone contact with his wife, and despite the distance they always made decisions together. "I love him, and he loved his children with all his heart," said his grieving wife Ursula. [299]

Pawel and Ursula Krajewski were married in the parish of Christ the Saviour in Przasnysz. On July 29, 2010, they would have celebrated their 10th wedding anniversary.

"Family for Pawel was the greatest value. It must be emphasized, he was an exceptional father. Every evening after a bath, when Ula prepared the children for sleep, Pawel read them stories. .. He loved his children; he was caring, sensitive, always organizing family time. He was a good swimmer, took his children to the pool, was interested in martial arts, parachuting, diving, and mountain climbing," said his wife's sister Małgorzata. [300]

"Pawel Krajewski made his last flight, while defending the security of Polish President Lech Kaczynski" Adam Rapacki, Undersecretary of State in the Ministry of Internal Affairs and Administration said before the start of the funeral mass for Krajewski. "In the eyes of his superiors he will always be smiling, cheerful and friendly. He loved what he was doing. For 14 years he served in the BOR, and for five years he worked in the personal protection of the president. He was a professional. He lived with courage-- diving, mountain climbing, active in scouting. It's hard to find words of consolation in the face of such a tragedy." [301]

---

[299] "The Crash Killed Officer Przasnysza" 14 Apr 2010 http://kuriermlawski.pl/W-katastrofie-zginal-oficer-z-Przasnysza-,93973
[300] "The Crash Killed Officer Przasnysza" 14 Apr 2010 http://kuriermlawski.pl/W-katastrofie-zginal-oficer-z-Przasnysza-,93973
[301] "Ostatnia droga Pawła Krajewskiego i Jolanty Szymanek-Deresz" by Adam Małachowski, Rafał Kowalski, PAP 19.04.2010
http://wyborcza.pl/1,105766,7790832,Ostatnia_droga_Pawla_Krajewskiego_i_Jolanty_Szymanek_Deresz.html

Reverand Colonel Marek Wesolowski, chaplain of the BOR spoke at Krajewski's funeral. "Whenever I talked with Pawel, I remember how he spoke of his wife Ursula and children: Daria and Gabriel. I remember concocting plans for the future...Comforting are the words of Scripture: 'The angel says no one lives for himself, we die for the other.' You, Pawel, died as a sacrifice for your country, you died for others." [302]

---

[302] Ibid.

Andrzej Kremer

Undersecretary of State in the Ministry of Foreign Affairs

Stanislaw Andrzej Kremer was born 8 August 1961 in Krakow. He graduated in 1984 from the School of Law and Administration of the Jagiellonian University. Seven years later, he defended his doctoral thesis at the same university and received the degree of Doctor of Law.

He was secretary of state in the Ministry of Foreign Affairs since 2008, responsible for legal affairs and consular treaties. He was part of the negotiations and later signatory to the Polish-American agreement on the stationing of anti-missile bases in Poland. He began his diplomatic service in 1995 as the Polish Consulate General in Hamburg. For two years, he also worked at the Polish embassy in Bonn. In 2001-2005, he was Consul General of Poland in Hamburg. From 2007 he was director of the department of legal treaties in the Ministry of Foreign Affairs. [303]

Polish journalist Marcin Wojciechowski recalled Kremer in this way: "He said that being a consul is the only profession where one day you handle someone from the elite, and the next day you take care of the homeless. And to each of them you must behave with the same class. He knew how to do this. He has never refused to talk with reporters. Patiently he explained, presented arguments, and could listen - even take criticism - and learn from it. His good-natured smile, warmth, and natural kindness made me want to talk to him and be around him. His work has led to a significant improvement in relations with Russia. The difficult, gradual dialogue with Moscow was in fact his initiative.

"It was unfortunate that Kremer's life ended on Russian soil. The last time I saw him was in Katyn on Wednesday at a ceremony attended by Prime Minister Donald Tusk. I was glad that we were going to meet again on Saturday. I hoped we might have been able to exchange a few words. It is a shame that I was unable to do this." [304]

---

[303] "Andrzej Kremer," 10 Apr 2100, http://www.tvn24.pl/andrzej-kremer,211477,s.html

[304] "Andrzej Kremer" by Marcin Wojciechowski 11.04.2010 From Wyborcza Poland http://wyborcza.pl/1,75402,7758788,Andrzej_Kremer.html#ixzz42VazX0HB

"He certainly could have made a career in science, but he chose the service of diplomacy," said Professor Jerzy Stelmach, Kremer's colleague from the School of Law at the Jagiellonian University. "He took life seriously...Service was very important to him."

His younger brother, John Kremer, a spokesman for the Court of Appeal in Krakow, recalled his brother's smiling face. "He was positive about people. A good negotiator, balanced and fair," he said. [305]

Andrzej Kremer was married and had three sons.

---

[305] "Andrzej Kremer: seriously he took professional life" 11 Apr 2010 http://www.gazetakrakowska.pl/artykul/243341,andrzej-kremer-na-serio-bral-zycie-zawodowe,id,t.html

Rev. Chancelor Zdzislaw Krol

Chaplain (1987-2007) Warsaw Katyn Families Association

Father Zdzislaw Krol was born 8 May 1935 in Zdzieborzu. He was ordained on August 3, 1958 in Warsaw Cathedral by Cardinal Stefan Wyszynski. At the Catholic University of Lublin he received a doctorate in canon law. Since 1967 he was notary of the Department of Pastoral Care of the Warsaw Metropolitan Curia of the Archdiocese of Warsaw, and from 1979-1992 he was the chancelor. He participated in planning the visits of Pope John Paul II to Poland. [306]

Father Krol was chaplain of the Warsaw Katyn Families in the period 1987-2007 and a member of the Council for the Protection of Struggle and Martyrdom. He was also a vicar bishop and secretary of the Archdiocesan Council of Leviticus, as well as a member of the Episcopal Council. Since 1992, he held the position of rector of the Warsaw parish of All Saints, where after retirement he was a resident. [307]

Father Krol devoted himself to the work of the Catholic media. He was chairman of the Programme Council of the monthly "Messages of the Archdiocese of Warsaw," the weekly "The Catholic Review" of Catholic Radio and a member of the College of Consultors of the Archdiocese of Warsaw. [308]

As pastor of All Saints parish in Warsaw, his homilies always gathered crowds, coming to the church on Grzybowski Square, often from distant districts of the capital. He contributed to the restoration and construction of many elements of the church including an elevator for the disabled, renovated staircase, and the creation of a plaque commemorating Poles who rescued Jews during the occupation. In the homilies that he delivered, he spoke for insurgents in Warsaw and Polish soldiers and the intention of

---

[306] https://pl.wikipedia.org/wiki/Zdzis%C5%82aw_Kr%C3%B3l
[307] Ibid.
[308] "Ks. Zdzisław Król - warszawski kapelan rodzin katyńskich" http://ekai.pl/wydarzenia/wydarzenia/x28054/ks-zdzislaw-krol-warszawski-kapelan-rodzin-katynskich/

veterans, reminding others of the need to remember the patriots, but also expressing the joy of a free homeland. [309]

From March 31, 2000, Fr. Krol was chaplain of the Warsaw Katyn Families. In 2001 he was awarded a commemorative medal and diploma of honorary member of the Polish Society of the Righteous Among the Nations, an honorific used by the State of Israel to describe non-Jews who risked their lives during the Holocaust to save Jews from extermination by the Nazis.

---

[309] Ibid.

Janusz Krupski
Director of the Office for War Veterans and Repressed Persons

Janusz Krupski was born May 9, 1951 in Lublin. He was a Polish historian, member of the democratic opposition to communist rule in Poland during the People's Republic of Poland and a government official.

Krupski acquired his degree in history at the Lublin Catholic University in 1975. While there he became friends with other future opposition leaders, such as Piotr Jegliński. Between 1977 and 1988 he was the chief editor of the independent, non-censored, underground journal *Spotkania* ("Meetings"). [310]

In 1980 he joined the Solidarity movement, and served on the coordinating committee of its Gdańsk branch. During the state of martial law in Poland he was persecuted by the communist authorities. After ten months in hiding he was arrested and interned by the authorities in a special Internment Camp. His mother made numerous appeals for his release on his behalf (Janusz himself refused to make them) but they were turned down. [311]

In 1983, with the end of martial law he was released. However, soon after he was seized by the communist secret police, the *Służba Bezpieczeństwa* (Security Services), taken to the Kampinos Forest and burned with a mixture of phenol and lysol. The perpetrators had actually been ordered by their commander, to have Krupski strip completely naked before the acid was dumped on him so that the mixture would burn through his skin, damage his internal organs and kill him. They were supposed to have had thrown his body into a nearby water reservoir afterward. However, the policemen had been in such a hurry that they only made him take off his jacket and boots and as a result, the thick sweater he was wearing prevented most of the damage, saving his life. [312]

Joanna Puzyna met her future husband Janusz Krupski in the late 1970s at the Catholic University of Lublin. Joanna studied psychology and worked with the mentally handicapped; Janusz was acting in the

---

[310] https://en.wikipedia.org/wiki/Janusz_Krupski
[311] Ibid.
[312] Ibid.

anti-communist movement. His future wife was impressed that he was brave and uncompromising. During martial law Janusz Krupski had to hide, and his bride helped him find another hiding place. However, in autumn 1982, he was caught and briefly interned. A year later they were married. [313]

"We did not have housing, jobs, or prospects. Despite this, we decided to get married. We loved each other and the natural consequence was the children who were our happiness," said Joanna Krupska. [314]

Those were difficult years for the couple. Joanna worked in a classroom with severely autistic children. Her salary was not enough to support the whole family, and Janusz was out of work, and blacklisted, targeted by the police. [315]

Over the next few years the couple relocated from Warsaw to Lublin and back. In the end, they settled in a cottage 50 km from Warsaw. The first son, Peter, was born in 1985. Shortly thereafter came Paul, Tom, Luke, and Hansel. Some of the births Janusz attended himself. Their sixth and seventh children-- Mary and Therese were born when the couple moved into a house in Grodzisk. For the first year the family had to live there without running water, because no one could dig a line to the house. [316]

"Our children were not accustomed to luxuries," said Joanna Krupska. "For children, moderate poverty is a better environment than wealth. The ability of self-restraint is better than the possibility of meeting all the needs and desires." [317]

This was the legacy Janusz Krupski left.

---

[313] "To będą trudne święta" by Witold Dudziński
Tegoroczne święta Bożego Narodzenia miały być takie jak co roku. Nie będą: katastrofa smoleńska wszystko zmieniła
http://www.niedziela.pl/artykul/93651/nd/To-beda-trudne-swieta
[314] Ibid.
[315] Ibid.
[316] Ibid.
[317] Ibid.

Janusz Kurtyka
President of the Institute of National Remembrance

Janusz Marek Kurtyka was born 13 August 1960 in Kraków and obtained his degree in the History and Philosophy Department of the Jagiellonian University. He had been a historian at the Polish Academy of Sciences since 1985 where he specialized in Polish medieval and communist era history, modern history and historical methodology. He finished his PhD in 1995. He authored more than 140 academic publications.

In Poland, Kurtyka was a member of the democratic opposition to communism and an activist with the Independent Students Union and the trade union Solidarity. Between 1989 and 2000 he was the president of the Kraków office of Solidarity in the Historical Institute PAN.

After the Institute of National Remembrance (a Polish government-affiliated research institute which investigates both Nazi and Communist crimes committed in Poland) was created in 1998, Kurtyka was the first president of its Kraków branch. In April 2005 he was recommended by the Board of the Institute for the position of the president and was approved by the Polish Sejm and Senate in December of that year. He took his oath of office on December 29, 2005.

Days before he died he called for "the results of the Russian investigation into Katyn massacre to be declassified and for the Russian archives to be opened". The post which was left open by his death was considered particularly problematic due to the difficulty there would be in replacing him. [318]

"He lived at the headquarters of the Institute of National Remembrance (IPN) in Warsaw. Friends warned that it could end badly. I persuaded him to move, because sleeping where you work is a nightmare. But he did not even think of it," said a friend of Kurtyka, professor Ryszard Terlecki. When Kurtyka would come on Fridays to Krakow, he first went to bookstores, from which he came out laden with books. Then he visited all his friends. Here it was as if he had come back from another planet. He

---

[318] https://en.wikipedia.org/wiki/Janusz_Kurtyka

said to his friends, 'I'm terribly jealous of you, that from your window you have a view of the normal world',"said a friend. [319]

"Last Friday, as usual, he came to the Krakow branch of IPN. I saw him just in passing in the corridor; he was wrapping up the details of the March of Remembrance of the victims of Katyn in Krakow. The next day he boarded the presidential Tupolev, which was flying to Katyn." [320]

Kurtyka left a wife and two children. Friends agree that he devoted a lot of time to his sons (one is a student of archeology, the second a history student at the Jagiellonian University.) For them, he dressed in camouflage and went running through the woods. "We played paintball. He wanted the guys to have fun," said Marek Lasota, director of the Krakow branch of IPN. The first question colleagues had at the news of the crash: if Kurtyka's sons were flying with him.[321]

When Kurtyka, in 2005 became the head of the IPN he was criticized by some for politicizing the institute. "Janusz was sure that what he was doing was right, and he knew what he was doing. He never backed away from troubles," said professor Terlecki. "He was incredibly strong, even courageous. Strong and very involved in what he was doing," he added. Colleagues acknowledge that he was a born leader, instantly making decisions. Friends and acquaintances agreed that he could be called "noble." "He had a mission to restore national memory," said Jaroslaw Szarek, IPN historian. [322] "Always surrounded by books, he could sit all night in the archives," said a friend, Wojciech Frazik. [323]

Janusz Kurtyka had plans and future ambitions. "He thought about taking up politics-- running for parliament," explained Marek Lasota, director of the Krakow branch of IPN.

---

[319] "Janusz Kurtyka: swój świat miał w Krakowie" by Marta Paluch 11 KWIETNIA 2010
http://www.gazetakrakowska.pl/artykul/243176,janusz-kurtyka-swoj-swiat-mial-w-krakowie,id,t.html
[320] Ibid.
[321] Ibid.
[322] Ibid.
[323] Ibid.

Reverend Andrzej Kwasnik

Chaplain Katyn Families Association

Andrzej Krzysztof Kwaśnik was born November 10, 1956 in Warsaw. He was a Catholic priest of the Archdiocese of Warsaw, chaplain of the Federation of Katyn Families (2008-2010), and chaplain of the Warsaw Police (2008-2010). [324]

Father Kwasnik was ordained on June 3, 1984, and then he worked as a vicar in Warka, in Pruszkow, and in the parish of the Annunciation in Warsaw. From October 1995 to June 2007 he was a parish priest in the Descent of the Holy Spirit parish in Stara Iwiczna. From 1 July 2007 he served as the parish priest of St. Thaddeus the Apostle in Warsaw. In 2008 he succeeded Fr.. Zdzislaw Peszkowski as chaplain of the Federation of Katyn Families. [325]

He was a Chaplain representing motorcyclists and the chaplain of the riot police in Warsaw and the District Police Headquarters in Piaseczno. He celebrated Mass for motorcyclists, where they prayed for the victims of road accidents. In Stara Iwiczna every year, several hundred bikers came to the mass. "Father Andrew was a very sympathetic, open man. He took motorcyclists under his wing although initially we were strangers to him. He helped us with his knowledge and contacts," said Tomasz Woźniakowski, rider and organizer of the mass in Stara Iwiczna. "He was very busy; he held various functions in the Church. At the same time he was well organized...it did not happen that he was not prepared for something, that he did not foresee any situation." [326]

"He was a great priest, joyful, smiling. A friend, devoted to the Katyn affair. He cared about every man, every need," recalled vice president of the Federation of Katyn Families, Krystyna Brydowska.

---

[324] https://pl.wikipedia.org/wiki/Andrzej_Kwa%C5%9Bnik
[325] Ibid.
[326] Ks. Andrzej Kwaśnik (10.11.1956 - 10.04.2010) by Katarzyna Wiśniewska, pcg 09.04.2011
http://wiadomosci.gazeta.pl/wiadomosci/1,114892,9404468,Ks__Andrzej_Kwasnik__10_11_1956___10_04_2010_.html

Brydowska said that Father Kwasnik was only accidentally on board the plane that crashed in Smolensk. "He was supposed to go by train, but always on the Divine Mercy Sunday is organized a pilgrimage to Czestochowa for the Katyn families. Because he had to lead this pilgrimage, he flew on April 10th to Smolensk."

"He was an open person with a great sense of humor, which stole the hearts of the people. He tried to help every policeman. He fostered values, which we often forget in everyday life," said Rafał Marczuk, from the press team of the Metropolitan Police.

LtGeneral Bronislaw Kwiatkowski
Operational Commander of the Armed Forces

Bronislaw Kwiatkowski was born May 5, 1950 in Mazurach. He served in the Polish Armed Forces since 1969 commanding the Polish military contingent in Syria, the 6th Airborne Assault Brigade, and the Multinational Division Central South in Iraq. In connection with the reorganization of the Armed Forces, on 15 August 2007, he became the Operational Commander of the Armed Forces. His military service would have been completed May 5, 2010, after which the general was to retire. [327]

He was married to Krystyna, with whom he had two daughters, Kamila and Edyta.

Krystyna Kwiatkowska, as the wife of an officer of the Polish Army often experienced stressful situations. "In the 40 years of our marriage, more than half the time, my husband spent outside the home. They were shorter or longer business trips. He served in the most dangerous regions of the world after receiving an order from the Ministry of Defense. He understood that Polish participation in the many missions as a NATO ally strengthened the credibility of the United Nations and the interests of our country in the international arena.[328]

"My husband, as Operational Commander of the Armed Forces often visited his troops: 16 times he visited Iraq, 14 times to Afghanistan, and 4 times to Chad. He created and closed the contingent in Iraq, created and closed the contingent in Chad. When he participated in missions, he was present at the closing of each coffin with the body of a fallen soldier, thanking him for his supreme sacrifice. While in Poland, he participated in the funeral of every fallen soldier, giving him a last tribute. [329]

"What a blow was the death of my husband 21 days before retirement."

In a final farewell to Kwiatkowski, Col. Zdzisław Śliwa, of the Baltic Defense College remarked: "He was with us in the Polish Military Contingent in Afghanistan less than two weeks ago. He came not only

---

[327] https://pl.wikipedia.org/wiki/Bronis%C5%82aw_Kwiatkowski
[328] "Apel żony śp. gen. Bronisława Kwiatkowskiego i wywiad" Opublikowano 19 listopada 2012, autor: emka http://hej-kto-polak.pl/wp/?p=65349
[329] Ibid.

with Easter wishes. He thanked the troops for their service and wished them luck in their next assignment. None of us thought that he was the soldier whose luck would run out … [330]

"On April 1 on the Base at Ghazni, Afghanistan, General Kwiatkowski accompanied the Minister of National Defense. On his face you could not see the fatigue of his long journey-- for each of us he managed a hearty smile, he held out his hand, said a few words. He gave us faith, strength and hope." [331] As Generał Kwiatkowski, together with the other members of the delegation boarded the helicopter to leave he waved his hand goodbye in friendship. "It never occurred to anyone's mind that this would be our last meeting." [332]

General Kwiatkowski was set to retire in May. "In the end, it would be the time for a normal life. To drink coffee together without haste, to eat breakfast together," said Krystyna Kwiatkowska. She was proud that her husband was invited on the Presidential plane to Smolensk on 10 April, especially since he was never in Katyn and wanted to pay homage to the murdered soldiers. "If it was not for the disaster, everything would be different. My husband put off everything for later," said Krystyna. They had a lot of plans. On Friday, April 9, the general had ordered a new car because the old one was already very worn out. "All the time I was waiting, he promised that when he retired he'll make up for all the arrears." [333]

Less than a year after his death, there was born a granddaughter— Hannah. Bronislaw Kwiatkowski has always dreamed of grandchildren and planned with his wife how it would be when they were grandparents.

---

[330] Text: Anna Pawlak, Press and Information Section PKW Afghanistan http://do.wp.mil.pl/info/pamieci-generala-kwiatkowskiego/

[331] "Mieli tyle do zrobienia, ale nastąpił Smoleńsk"Paulina Korbut,Maria Mazurek,Magdalena Stokłosa 10 Apr 2013
http://www.gazetakrakowska.pl/artykul/802327,mieli-tyle-do-zrobienia-ale-nastapil-smolensk,id,t.html

[332] Text: Anna Pawlak, Press and Information Section PKW Afghanistan http://do.wp.mil.pl/info/pamieci-generala-kwiatkowskiego/

[333] "Mieli tyle do zrobienia, ale nastąpił Smoleńsk"Paulina Korbut,Maria Mazurek,Magdalena Stokłosa 10 Apr 2013
http://www.gazetakrakowska.pl/artykul/802327,mieli-tyle-do-zrobienia-ale-nastapil-smolensk,id,t.html

They laughed then, that they would take care of their grandchildren so well that their daughter would not even notice when her children had grown up. Krystyna Kwiatkowska emphasizesd that her husband would have been very proud of Hani. Recently, at the cemetery Hannah said she knows who is buried here: "My grandfather. He was a general and he flew in the plane." [334]

---

[334] Ibid.

Brigadier General Wojciech Lubinski
Personal Physician to the President

Wojciech Lubiński was born 4 October 1969 in Ryki. In 1994 he graduated from the School of Medicine of the Military Medical Academy in Lodz. He worked as a doctor in the Military Unit in Osterode, and then at the Military Hospital of Tuberculosis and Lung Diseases in Otwock. In 1997 he obtained a first degree specialization in the field of internal medicine; three years later he majored of pulmonology. He was the spokesman of the Military Medical Institute, and since 2008 the deputy commander of the Central Clinical Hospital at the Ministry of Defense.

Since 2006 he was the personal doctor of Polish President Lech Kaczynski.

He was married to Beata and had two children: Marysia, 6 and Johnny one year old.

In the weeks before the crash, Jadwiga Kaczynski, mother of President Lech Kaczynski, was fighting for her life and she was admitted to the hospital as her health deteriorated. Dr. Lubinski managed to save her life.

Brig. General Marek Maruszyński, former director of the Military Medical Institute in Warsaw remembers: "He was a cheerful, wonderful man, dedicated to his work." 41-year-old Dr. Lubiński usually accompanied President Kaczynski on foreign travel, and therefore was on the airplane flying to Smolensk. [335]

Patients valued Dr. Lubinski's professionalism and human approach to the patient. He cared for, among others, 20-year-old Oksana Prots who, in November 2008 was admitted to the hospital in Szaserów-- badly burned after an explosion of gas cylinders. [336] "I remember how with such sensitivity, understanding and professionalism he took care of the girl and other Ukrainians and Belarusians, who, being in a difficult situation, were sent to the hospital through our foundation. The doctor never asked for money," said Cajetan Wroblewski, vice-president of the "fundacji

---

[335] "Gen. brygady dr hab. Wojciech Lubiński (4.10.1969 - 10.04.2010)" by Agnieszka Pochrzęst, 11.04.2010 http://wyborcza.pl/1,75402,7760062, Gen__brygady_dr_hab__Wojciech_Lubinski__4_10_1969.html
[336] Ibid.

Proksenos" "Oksana, whose body was burned over 75 per cent almost completely regained her health. On April 24th she got married." [337]

"He was an involved father. He loved his family and tried to ensure that his wife and children had everything they needed. He was often on the phone with his wife and daughter. He always said that once he had achieved his scientific objectives, he wanted to devote more time to family. The way to meet the family dream was to buy a house. [338]

"He paid great attention to detail; always impeccably dressed: tie, suit, shirt with cuff links, and when at the hospital - a snow-white physician's coat. He liked the uniform, believed that we should wear it with pride - after all, few doctors have been in uniform…He had a rare ease in formulating sentences. When I asked how he does it, he answered: 'Never tell everything you know. But always know what you're talking about' … it was his credo. [339]

"He was able to win people over. As deputy commander he would often hit his fist on the table and make a decision, but he always explained his reasons. [340]

"I remember the surprise when one day Wojtek said that he could not participate in a conference, because he had to fly out with the president. I thought, where and why? Then we found out that he was the doctor for the President of Poland. He never boasted that he held such a function. Once we knew, we understood his absence. He did not talk too much about his service. He said that he made this decision after talking to the president. He was discreet. [341] In February of this year, after defending his doctoral dissertation, there was suddenly confusion. There were people in black suits, and soon afterwards entered the presidential couple with congratulations. It was evident that they were good friends. [342]

"Wojtek wanted to go to Katyn. He said that every Pole, and even more so, every soldier should go there. The day before, at 11:00 at night

---

[337] Ibid.
[338] "Dr. Wojciech Lubinski," http://www.sluzbazdrowia.com.pl/smolensk/sylwetka.php?o=48
[339] Ibid.
[340] Ibid.
[341] Ibid.
[342] Ibid.

we talked about work. Wojtek said that he was tired, and in the early morning he was flying to Katyn. We said goodbye. Information about the crash seemed improbable, impossible. Wojtek had so many plans, dreams, everything in front of him. And the family, small children. What they will do?" [343]

---

[343] Ibid.

Tadeusz Lutoborski
Representative, Katyn Families Organization

Tadeusz Lutoborski was born 6 June 1926 in Warsaw. He graduated in law at Warsaw University and economics at the Central School of Planning and Statistics in Warsaw. Then he was assistant professor at the Warsaw School of Economics. [344]

After the outbreak of World War II, his father, Adam, a reserve lieutenant in the 46th Cavalry Regiment was arrested by the Soviets and interned in the camp in Kozelsk. In April 1940 he was killed at Katyn. He was identified by the documents he had on him. He also had on him, among other things, a picture of his son at his first communion. [345]

In 1943 Tadeusz Lutoborski was a member of the Army. He attended a clandestine school in Warsaw in 1944, graduating a month before the outbreak of the Warsaw Uprising, in which he participated as part of the Fourth Circuit AK "Kaliska Redoubt". His mother in 1944 was sent to the Nazi concentration camp Bergen-Belsen where she died in 1945. In the same camp his aunt, Jadwiga Lutoborska, also died. While in the camp at Dachau in 1941, his grandfather, Edmund Lutoborski died.

He was a member of the Communist Party until 1989. He served as president of the Association of Katyn Family in Warsaw for two terms elected in 1995 and 1998. [346]

---

[344] https://pl.wikipedia.org/wiki/Tadeusz_Lutoborski
[345] "Tadeusz Lutoborski," http://smolensk.muzhp.pl/portret/tadeusz-lutoborski/
[346] https://pl.wikipedia.org/wiki/Tadeusz_Lutoborski

Barbara Maciejczyk

Flight Attendant

Barbara Maria Maciejczyk was born 26 August 1981 in Biala Podlaska. She graduated high school in 2002 and continued her studies at the Department of Slavic Studies, University of Warsaw, at the School of Communication and Social Media in Warsaw. She joined the 36th Special Air Transport Regiment 22 January 2007 and from 16 February 2009 she worked as a flight attendant, having almost 1400 hours flight time.

Her family remembered that she loved to fly, following in the footsteps of her father and brother, who were pilots. Those who flew with her claim that she could be firm and when it came to safety--she did not hesitate to discipline VIPs. She was to keep even the Prime Minister seated in his place. So no one was surprised that 14 minutes before the crash, on the plane's cockpit voice recorder, could be heard the voice of reason—as Barbara Maciejczyk --addressing the Director of Protocol, Ministry of Foreign Affairs: "Sir, let's go back." Unfortunately, no one listened to her. It seems that just before landing approach she also implored General Blasik to leave the cockpit. Also to no avail. [347]

"She was a very stubborn and headstrong girl. Above all ambitious," said her parents. "She loved (the work of flight attendants) right away. She could already imagine seeing the world. Even two or three days without flying caused frustration and impatience. She saw so many states, cities, in such a short time! Some of us may live to be one hundred years old and not have this experience," her mother recalled the enthusiasm of her daughter. [348]

---

[347] "KATASTROFA SMOLEŃSKA To ona ratowała tupolewa" http://www.fakt.pl/polityka/stewardessa-barbara-maciejczyk-nie-chciala-ladowac,artykuly,536965.html

[348] "Dzień, w którym runęło niebo. Wspomnienia rodzin ofiar katastrofy smoleńskiej" http://fakty.interia.pl/raporty/raport-lech-kaczynski-nie-zyje/wspomnienia/news-dzien-w-ktorym-runelo-niebo-wspomnienia-rodzin-ofiar-katastr,nId,1713701

Barbara Maminska
Director in the Chancellery of the President

Barbara Maminska was born 10 November 1957 in Pruszkow. Her father, Tadeusz Osinski (code name "Tek") was a partisan soldier of the Home Army in the Lublin region of Poland. [349]

Maminska was a long time employee of Lech Kaczynski in Warsaw City Hall where she served as director for human resources and training and, since 2005, in the Office of the President, where she served as director of the Office of Personnel and Distinctions. She was responsible for preparing all nominations and dismissal from positions of successive governments, prime ministers, ministers, generals, and promotions, and appointments of judges. It was she during various ceremonies in the Presidential Palace who would read the names of those persons receiving awards.

Working closely with veteran communities throughout the country, Maminska always came up with ideas to honor others. She conducted her own search for people and historical events that eluded formal recognition. She found, for example, the names of the soldiers, railwaymen and customs officers, who on 1 September 1939 defended access to the bridges on the Vistula River in the area of Tczew and Szymankowo. From this little known incident of resistance came the first victims of the war, because the Germans, on September 1 shot the resisting railway workers and their families. Mamińska found descendants of the murdered families and prepared the documentation for the awards, [350]

Another of her personal achievements was her organization of a separate ceremony to honor women persecuted in communist prisons and mothers who gave birth to children in prisons.

As director, during the celebrations Maminska took over the role of master of ceremonies. It was with great grace and poise, and a beautiful, warm voice that she led the ceremonial handling of nominations and awards. [351]

---

[349] "Barbara Maminska," http://smolensk.muzhp.pl/portret/barbara-maminska/
[350] Śp. Barbara Mamińska. Wspomnienie Opublikowano 9 lutego 2013, autor: emka http://hej-kto-polak.pl/wp/?p=43841
[351] Ibid.

During the ceremony in Katyn, with the same calm, clear voice she would have read the names of the citizens of the Russian Federation awarded by the President in recognition of outstanding achievements in research and revealing the truth about the Katyn massacre. She carried those awards with her on the plane on April 10. [352]

"Basia was generous in her work and with full conviction that everything has a deep meaning. Meticulous, demanding, but always very cheerful," wrote her coworker Janina Jankowsa. "She was a pillar of our office, always there, always with the initiative," said Jacek Sasin, the deputy head of the Presidential Chancellery. [353]

Barbara Maminska was married to Christopher Mamiński, railway activist of "Solidarity." They were married in the Warsaw City Hall by Lech Kaczynski. She had a son Radoslaw Sosinski.

---

[352] Ibid.
[353] Ibid.

Bozena Mamontowicz-Lojek

President of Polish Katyn Foundation

Bozena Mamontowicz-Łojek was born 22 December 1937. She was a Polish historian of ballet and theater studies and a social activist. She was president of the Polish Katyn Foundation and founder of the Warsaw Katyn Families. [354]

She was a graduate of the National Ballet School in Warsaw and a dancer with the Central Team of the Polish Army and opera houses in Warsaw and Lodz.

Since 1961 she was the wife of historian George Lojek whose father Leopold was murdered in Katyn. After the death of her husband in 1986, by involving herself in the commemoration of the Katyn massacre, she fulfilled his last will that she "... always and consistently raise publicly the issue of the Katyn massacre and demand her punishment" [355]. She became the co-founder of the Katyn Families in 1988. She was president of the Polish Katyn Foundation and secretary of the Independent Committee of Historical Research of the Katyn Massacre. [356]

"There is something symbolic in the death of Dr. Bozena Łojek near Katyn," said Stanislaw M. Jankowski, Krakow journalist and historian associated with the Institute of Katyn and the Independent Committee of Historical Research of the Katyn Massacre. "In her apartment she met with our committee. She organized trips to Katyn, protests, and celebrations." [357]

June 29, 1993, together with the then Deputy Minister of National Defense Bronislaw Komorowski, Bozena opened the Katyn Museum in Fort Czerniakowskie in Warsaw which showed the fate of Polish prisoners

---

[354] https://pl.wikipedia.org/wiki/Bo%C5%BCena_Mamontowicz-%C5%81ojek
[355] "Bożena Mamontowicz-Łojek" Jarosław Osowski, domi 11.04.2010
http://wyborcza.pl/1,75402,7760106,Bozena_Mamontowicz_Lojek.htm
[356] https://pl.wikipedia.org/wiki/Bo%C5%BCena_Mamontowicz-%C5%81ojek
[357] "Bożena Mamontowicz-Łojek" Jarosław Osowski, domi 11.04.2010
http://wyborcza.pl/1,75402,7760106,Bozena_Mamontowicz_Lojek.htm

from Kozelsk, Ostashkov and Starobelsk. Some of the hundreds of photographs and documents came from the exhumation conducted in the summer of 1991.

"Her entire apartment was filled with the documents of Katyn. We owe much to her diligence and her dedication," said Marek Tarczyński. [358]

Every year at the Royal Castle in Warsaw, she held seminars on Katyn. For each was prepared a newsletter sometimes numbering 400 pages. In these "Katyn Notebooks" edited by Mark Tarczyński, Bozena gathered photos and materials from different authors. There were 24 volumes published. The next was being prepared for the 20th session which was to take place on April 17th.

"I'll meet there anyway, without Bozena," said Marek Tarczyński. [359]

---

[358] Ibid.
[359] Ibid.

Stefan Melak
President of the Katyn Committee

Stefan Melak was born 13 Aug 1946 in Warsaw. He studied law at Warsaw University from 1965-1974. In 1974, together with his brothers, he founded the Circle of National Remembrance and in 1979 Melak, along with Father Wenceslas Karłowicza created the Katyn Conspiracy Committee. Since 1979 he was a member of Poland's pro-independence political party.

In a somewhat conspiratorial action on July 31, 1981 in the so-called Valley of the Katyn Cemetery at Powazki cemetery in Warsaw, Melak had placed Poland's first "Monument of Katyn," which was made of granite in the shape of a cross with the words "Katyn 1940" on the front. The statue was made by Melak's brother, Arkadiusz and weighed several tons. "More than a year we are preparing this monument, because the existing wooden or metal crosses disappeared—taken away by so-called unknown perpetrators. {The} daring action to place the monument involved people from Lublin, Warsaw University, drivers and laborers," Melak recalled in an interview. [360] After only a few hours, the statue was removed after the protest and intervention of the Soviet Embassy. In 1985, the Polish communist authorities set up in the same place a monument with the inscription "Polish soldiers - victims of Nazi fascism resting in the land of the Katyn 1941." In defense of the stolen statue Melak appeared before the Congress of "Solidarity" in Oliwa. He finally succeeded in recovering the statue in July 1989. "For eight years our monument was kept in some wooden crates," recalled Melak.[361] It was replaced to its original location and unveiled on September 8, 1995. [362]

During martial law Melak was interned by the communist authorities for anti-communist activities and participation in Solidarity meetings. In the 1980s he cooperated with an independent Polish publishing house, organizing pilgrimages and lectures and independence rallies for which

---

[360] Stefan Melak 10 kwietnia 2010, http://www.tvn24.pl/stefan-melak,211498,s.html

[361] Ibid.

[362] https://pl.wikipedia.org/wiki/Stefan_Melak

he was subjected to repression by the communist authorities.³⁶³ He was publisher and editor of the Polish underground, in which in the years 1983-1989 he published several books and numerous posters, leaflets, brochures, etc. He also organized the printing and distribution of many daily underground Solidarity newspapers. ³⁶⁴

As the chairman of the Katyn Committee, Stefan Melak, fought for many years to commemorate the Polish officers murdered by the NKVD in Katyn, Kharkov and Miednoje. He was an independent activist in the hardest of times. "Melak was one of the first to proclaim the truth about Katyn boldly and openly," said Prime Minister Donald Tusk during the welcoming ceremony for the coffins with the bodies of victims of the Smolensk crash. ³⁶⁵

---

³⁶³ Stefan Melak 10 kwietnia 2010, http://www.tvn24.pl/stefan-melak,211498,s.html
³⁶⁴ https://pl.wikipedia.org/wiki/Stefan_Melak
³⁶⁵ Stefan Melak 10 kwietnia 2010, http://www.tvn24.pl/stefan-melak,211498,s.html

Tomasz Merta
Undersecretary, Minitry of Culture

Tomasz Merta was born 7 November 1965 in Legnica. He was appointed to the position of undersecretary of state in the Ministry of Culture and National Heritage and the General Conservator on November 4, 2005.

He was married to Magdalena Pietrzak-Merta. They had three daughters.

In a tribute to Merta, United States Senator Sherrod Brown, (D-Ohio) addressed Congress on 14 April 2010: [366]

> *"Mr. President, I rise as a result of the resolution offered earlier today commemorating the tragic deaths of so many Polish leaders, especially the death of Tomasz Merta, who is the Minister of Culture in Poland. I worked with Tomasz Merta a couple times over the last 25 years. In the early 1990s, he was a very young man, was still in his twenties, and he worked with Ohio State's Mershon Center, where I worked, helping his country's government transition from communism to democracy. We worked on everything from curricula writing to training teachers. I worked with him again when I was a Member of Congress. This time I went to Ukraine, and he helped us train Ukrainian teachers, helped write curriculum, and helped those Ukrainian teachers teach government courses on civic education in Kiev.*
>
> *"...His whole career was all about love of country, all about democracy, all about doing the right thing. He, in the 1990s and since, was a prolific writer. He wrote articles about democracy, articles about teaching democracy, articles about building democracy. He was*

---

[366] "Tribute To Tomasz Merta" Capitol Words vol 156, number 52, 14 Apr 2010 http://capitolwords.org/date/2010/04/14/S2275_tribute-to-tomasz-merta/

so important to this country. He was one of the youngest leaders who was killed on this terrible, tragic flight.

"He had a terrific future...We will all miss him. Tomasz was a devoted husband, the father of three daughters.

"I last saw him several years ago in Kiev. I so appreciate what he did. As I will say now in Polish: I offer my deep condolences to the people of Poland for this tragic loss. Tomasz and some of his friends taught me some Polish. I must admit I read it, but the pronunciation he helped me with... I am so sad about his loss. I am so sad for his country. I am so sad for his wife and his three beautiful daughters. I know that country will mourn his loss as it mourns the loss of so many other Polish patriots."

Captain Dariusz Michalowski
Member, Polish Government Protection Bureau (BOR)

Dariusz Michalowski was born 24 July 1975 in Warsaw. Although he was born in Warsaw, he grew up in Moscow, where his mother was a diplomat in the Polish Embassy. Hence his colleagues gave him the nickname "Moskwa." [367]

He began his basic military service in 1994, graduating from the School of Non-Commissioned Officers and Younger Professionals Special Operations. In 1996, as a soldier Michalowski was appointed to professional military service as commander of Group 1 PSK (Polish Special Forces). In April 1997, for outstanding achievement in the Special Forces, Michalowski was assigned to serve in the State Protection Office (BOR). In 2002 he graduated from the Higher Police School in Szczytno and was promoted to the rank of second lieutenant. During his service in BOR, Michalowski protected among other presidents Aleksander Kwasniewski (1995 - 2005) and Lech Kaczynski (2005 - 2010).

Thirty-five year old Dariusz Michalowski was one of the most experienced officers of the Government Protection Bureau. He practiced martial arts and was Fluent in English and Russian. He was passionate about running-- competing in marathons in Warsaw.

In the farewell to Michalowski, were the mournful sounds of police orchestra, standard bearers and honorary salvo. The funeral ceremony was attended by relatives and friends, dozens of BOR officers and above all his mother, fiancée and son, Victor. As Victor stood before the tomb of his father covered with countless wreaths and flowers, he tossed onto it a white teddy bear. [368]

In a touching goodbye letter Michalowski's finacee, Justyna Piotrowska, wrote: "You were my whole life. Every day I miss your hands on my hands.

---

[367] https://pl.wikipedia.org/wiki/Dariusz_Micha%C5%82owski
[368] "Pożegnanie oficerów BOR, którzy zginęli pod Smoleńskiem" by Wojciech Grejciun, Piotr Machajski 23.04.2010
http://warszawa.wyborcza.pl/warszawa/1,34889,7809189,Pozegnanie_oficerow_BOR__ktorzy_zgineli_pod_Smolenskiem.html

Your lips on my lips. I miss the daily rituals. The coffee, which you brought me in bed has now lost its flavor" [369]

---

[369] Ibid.

Stanislaw Mikke

Vice-chairman of the Council for the Protection
of Struggle and Martyrdom Sites

Stanislaw Mikke was born on 11 Sep 1947 in Lodz. He graduated in law at the University of Warsaw. Although he spent most of his adult professional life in Warsaw, he grew up in Czestochowa and began his education and his legal training there. Since the 1980s he worked as a lawyer in Warsaw, active in local government. [370]

For years, he was heavily involved in the disclosure of the Katyn crime (his uncle was killed in a Soviet labor camp). Mikke participated in the exhumation of victims of the Katyn massacre in Katyn, Kharkov, and Miednoje Bykivnya. The result of these works was two books, including "Sleep, Courageous" which left the printing press on April 9, 2010. He brought 120 copies of book with him on the plane on April 10, 2010 to give out at the ceremony in Katyn. In addition, he published the books: "As Long as I Live, Do Not Come", "Sweet Lemons", as well as hundreds of socio-legal columns and numerous short stories.

"My husband set his alarm clock for the fifth time," recalled Mikke's wife Bozena of the morning her husband boarded the plane to Smolensk. "I woke up at twenty minutes to four. My husband was calling to find out the phone number of the military airfield. It's a small apartment, so I heard. Then he called to the airport. I looked at my watch - it was quarter to four. He asked the dispatcher what time the presidential plane was flying to Smolensk for the ceremony - at six or seven o'clock...He doubted whether the program was correct... that the time was a mistake. He wanted to make sure that it was at seven. My husband {went to} Katyn in April every year and the plane always flew to Smolensk at six in the monring... {But this time he was flying with President Kaczynski for the first time} and that is probably the reason for the change in the departure time....My husband left home at 5:30 or 10 minutes later. Much earlier than he should have....He had a wreath of Polish advocacy, and 120 copies of the second edition of his book, to distribute it to all passengers.

---

[370] https://pl.wikipedia.org/wiki/Stanis%C5%82aw_Mikke

"For my husband discovering the truth about Katyn, Kharkov, Miednoje was a mission and passion. His uncle, Stanislaw Mikke, died of exhaustion in Arkhangelsk, where he was exiled with his family - his wife and five children. And there is his grave. Stasio got his name from him.

"My husband had a choice - to fly on April 7 with the Prime Minister or April 10 with the president. Andrew Przewoźnik, which for years has worked, he asked him: "Tell me when." He waited until the last minute, to decide." [371]

---

[371] "Torańskiej wywiad o Smoleńsku" Interview with Teresa Torańska 03-10-2012 http://polska.newsweek.pl/toranskiej-wywiad-o-smolensku,96584,1,1.html

Justyna Moniuszko
Flight Attendant

Justyna Moniuszko was born July 6, 1985 in Bialystok. She graduated from Christopher Baczyński High School in Bialystok in 2004 and continued her studies at the School of Power and Aeronautical Engineering, Warsaw. In 2006 she was elected the first ever Miss Warsaw University of Technology. She was a long-standing member of the parachute section of the Aero Club of Bialystok performing more than 250 parachute jumps. She became a pilot of remote control gliders and was active in scouting with the 93rd patrol Bialystok.

From 1 May 2008 to 30 November 2008, she worked as a flight attendant at LOT Polish Airlines. 1 December 2008 she joined 36 Special Air Transport Regiment as a senior flight attendant. She had flown about 425 hours.

Her memorial mass was attended by more than 300 people. "Justyna was a very polite girl...smiling...I've never seen her sad," said Margaret Polecka, her neighbor. "She was always helpful. Before she started to parachute jump all her free time was devoted to scouting," said Karolina Sarosiek. [372]

Her motto was: "The road to the goal is as important as the goal itself."

"On March 29 she welcomed us - a group of journalists - on board a government plane to Kosovo, where she flew to meet with Polish soldiers. She was one big smile," said the journalist of "Gazeta" Wojciech Szacki. "She teased with journalists. Reminded us of the takeoff rituals - the cells off, stow luggage, fasten seatbelts ... We were not ashamed to admit, we were not very disciplined passengers, so she had to repeat it after a few times, but even though she tried to sound firm, in her eyes and the corners of the mouth still she is smiling." [373]

---

[372] Stewardessa Justyna Moniuszko. Zginęła w katastrofie, od dziecka skakała ze spadochronem (zdjęcia) (adek) / Kurier Poranny 13 Apr 2010
http://www.to.com.pl/polska-i-swiat/art/6341844,stewardessa-justyna-moniuszko-zginela-w-katastrofie-od-dziecka-skakala-ze-spadochronem-zdjecia,id,t.html
[373] Zginęła stewardessa - białostoczanka Justyna Moniuszko Pcg 10.04.2010
http://bialystok.wyborcza.pl/bialystok/1,105840,7755948,Zginela_stewardessa___bialostoczanka_Justyna_Moniuszko.html

Aleksandra Natalia-Swiat

Member of Parliament

Alexsandra Natalia-Swiat was born 20 Feb 1959 in Oborniki Slaskie. In 1982, she graduated from the School of Management and Informatics, University of Economics in Wroclaw; then in 2004, she graduated from the management studies program at the Wroclaw School of Banking. In 2005, as a member of the Law and Justice Party, she was elected deputy in her fifth term of office for the district of Wroclaw. In the Sejm, she chaired the Public Finance Committee

Her husband, Jacek Swiat is also a member of Parliament, elected deputy in 2011. They married in 1985.

Though married for 24 years, Natalia-Swiat admitted she is not a "big fan of such a life where one is married but living apart: one in one city, the second in the other." [374]

She enjoyed sports, especially basktetball, and martial arts. In her quiet times she enjoyed reading mystery or crime stories, "mostly those with a moral background. I do not like stories where on where every page is pointless spilling of blood. I like the classics, like Agatha Christie." [375] She also enjoyed trips to the woods with her family, walking, bike riding, and "a bathtub full of hot water, foam, and bubbles"

When asked by a journalist if, when she was a child she wanted to be a politician, she replied, "I do not know of a child who would like to be a politician. I wanted to dance. I really like to dance, but now that happens very rarely." [376]

Natalia-Swiat never got a driver's license, never even sat behind the wheel of a car. "I do not have time for it," she said. But she did feel it was important to take time "to take care of yourself, your appearance, you always have the time.... Each of us likes to look good. And besides, when

---

[374] "Aleksandra Natalli-Świat: Bycie królową mi nie grozi" by Robert Migdał, 22 May 2009
http://www.gazetawroclawska.pl/artykul/120458,aleksandra-natalliswiat-bycie-krolowa-mi-nie-grozi,8,id,t,sa.html
[375] Ibid.
[376] Ibid.

you have contact with people when you're a public figure, the look is a sign of respect for those who you talk to. Therefore, I believe that one of my responsibilities is to look appropriate for the situation." [377]

When asked by a journalist if she ever looked back on a day or her life and had regrets…thought of something she could have done better or not done, she answered, "There are many things that I do that I could do better or differently. But I try to remind myself not to…not to go back to that. I say to myself: 'It is difficult, a closed chapter.' There is no use crying over spilled milk. I try to look to the future and not 'the pit' of the past." [378]

"But most is my dream to travel. My youth fell during the times in which the world was not open to us. You could not freely travel abroad. I would like to make it up …"[379]

---

[377] Ibid.
[378] Ibid.
[379] Ibid.

Janina Natusiewicz-Mirer
Activist, Art historian, Archaeologist, Polish free trade union activist

Janina Natusiewicz-Mirer, was born in Brest-Litovsk 1 January 1940. She graduated from the University of Wroclaw where she studied art history and archaeology. During World War II, as a child, she was deported to Siberia. In 1947, she returned with her mother to Poland and settled in Jawor in Lower Silesia with her family. In the second half of the 1960s she began working at the State Enterprise Workshops for the Conservation of Monuments in the Scientific and Historical Documentation Laboratory.

When she and her husband, university professor Simon Mirer, were living in Krakow they were jointly involved in opposition activities. Since 1980, she collaborated with the democratic opposition and United Solidarity movement during the time of martial law. Together with Solidarity co-founder Anna Walentynowicz, whom she befriended, she founded the Foundation for the Promotion of Sacred Art.

"Janka was something of a mentor, a good spirit of Mrs. Walentynowicz, who did not make any important decision without consulting Janeczka. Besides Janka prepared all of her events and accompanied her in almost all travel," said Janina's brother. [380] The trip to Katyn was the culmination of their joint activities aimed to commemorate the victims of the Katyn massacre, and all those who died there. [381]

"Janina Natusiewicz-Mirer was principled, consistent, but above all modest," recalled her late husband's brother Viktor Mirer. [382] She came from a family of intellectuals. Her father and brother Marian were lawyers, and the oldest of the siblings, Richard, was a professor and head of the Department of Drawing at the Technical University of Wroclaw. "From

---

[380] "Janina Natusiewicz-Mirer," http://smolensk.muzhp.pl/portret/janina-natusiewicz-mirer/

[381] "Ofiara smoleńskiej katastrofy, Janina Natusiewicz-Mirer, również była związana z Legnicą"
http://www.portal.legnica.eu/aktualnosc-709-ofiara_smolenskiej_katastrofy_janina.html

[382] "Pryncypialna i skromna" 23 April 2010 Wpisany Przez Redakcja
http://nowagj.pl/to-i-owo/wspomnienia-wspomnienia/3482-pryncypialna-i-skromna-.html

the home she had a patriotic upbringing, and she gained a solid education," said Viktor Mirer. [383]

Natusiewicz-Mirer's last joint initiative with Anna Walentynowicz was a conference on the future of Poland organized on December 19 which was held in the Parliament building where the first lecture was delivered Lech Kaczynski. "Janina dynamically acted politically, but due to her innate modesty she is always in the background and quiet," said Viktor Mirer. [384]

Before their flight to Smolensk Janina together with Anna Walentynowicz wrote a letter to Lech Kaczynski thanking him for the opportunity to participate in the celebrations, because the trip to Katyn was to be the culmination of their joint efforts to commemorate the victims of the Katyn massacre.

---

[383] Ibid.
[384] Ibid.

2 Lieutenant Piotr Nosek
Member, Government Protection Bureau (BOR)

2nd Lieutenant Piotr Nosek was born in 1975 in Krasnik. He served as a BOR agent for 15 years.

"He was one of the bravest and best trained," spoke Prime Minister Donald Tusk during a welcoming ceremony for the coffins of the victims of the disaster. "He was one of the best officers specializing in personal protection," recalled a former BOR classmate. [385]

He practiced karate and other martial arts, was fascinated with military weapons and was an excellent shooter. "He collected different types of weapons, including knives and bayonets," said a former BOR officer. "We ran together for shooting competitions in Poland. He was a gunsmith." [386]

Nosek left a daughter.

---

[385] "Podporucznik Piotr Nosek (09.1975 - 10.04.2010)" 13.04.2010 http://wiadomosci.gazeta.pl/wiadomosci/1,114873,7767389,Podporucznik_Piotr_Nosek__09_1975___10_04_2010_.html

[386] Ibid.

Piotr Nurowski

President, Polish Olympic Committee

Piotr Nurowski was born June 20, 1945 in Sandomierz. In 1967 he graduated from the School of Law of the University of Warsaw. In the years 1973-1980 he twice served as President of the Polish Athletics Association. When he was elected for the first term, he was 28 years old and was the youngest president of a national sports association in the world.[387]

After a period of activity in the youth movement, in 1981, Nurowski was an employee of the Ministry of Foreign Affairs. In the years 1986-1991 he was a Counsellor in the Embassy in the Moroccan capital, Rabat.

Nurowski had a lifelong passion for sport. While a student of Sandomierz high school, he was the announcer at the local stadium. After graduating, he won the competition for sports announcers on Polish Radio.[388]

As member of the Polish United Workers' Party in the second half of the 1970s, he served as head of the department of propaganda and culture of the Provincial Committee of the Communist Party overseeing the Metropolitan newspapers and television.[389]

From 1991-1992, Nurowski was director of the trading company Solpol. In 1992 he became involved in the creation of television station Polsat. In February 2005, he was elected President of the Polish Olympic Committee—a position for which did not receive a salary.

"He did not lock himself in the office of the President of the Polish Olympic Committee. He tried to always be with the players. He knew them all by name because Piotr Nurowski simply loved sports and athletes. Nurowski was the eleventh president of the Polish Olympic Committee, but for most people, in Polish sports, he was something more. He was not

---

[387] "Piotr Nurowski" 10 Apr 2010, TVN24, http://www.tvn24.pl/piotr-nurowski,214339,s.html

[388] Ibid.

[389] https://pl.wikipedia.org/wiki/Piotr_Nurowski

just the president, he was a friend of the sport, a friend of athletes," said Troika Otylia Jedrzejczak. [390]

Under his direction as Olympic Committee President, in 2009, Poland acquired a record number of six medals in the Winter Olympics in Vancouver.

"He knew how to listen to people, always found time for us. He will be very much missed," said pole vault champion Monika Pyrek. [391]

---

[390] "Piotr Nurowski, przyjaciel sportu i sportowców"
tow, PAP 12-04-2010 http://polska.newsweek.pl/piotr-nurowski--przyjaciel-sportu-i-sportowcow,56600,1,1.html
[391] Ibid.

Bronislawa Orawiec-Loffler
Representative of the Katyn Families

Bronislawa Orawiec-Löffler was born 16 February 1929 in Poronin near Zakopane, the daughter of Bronislaw and Helena. Her parents were involved in the resistance movement, hiding people sought by the Gestapo, and assisting in smuggling people across the border, for which they were imprisoned.

In the years 1947-1952 she studied at the School of Dentistry at the Medical Academy in Krakow. From 1953-1989 she worked in her profession in Nowy Targ, as director of prosthetics, where she was the only one in the region to perform wax castings intended for local hockey players.[392]

Because of her vital energy her friends gave her the nickname "Halny" which refers to the warm mountain winds in the Tatra Mountains. She actively participated in many patriotic activities. Since the 1980s she belonged to the Federation of Katyn Families organizing meetings and school competitions on the subject and organizing commemorations in the form of plaques and planting oak trees.

Bronisława Orawiec-Löffler's aunt was Aniela Gut-Stapińska, a cultural activist, poet, and novelist, and her uncle was Colonel Francis Orawiec, commander of the 2nd Regiment of Riflemen, who was murdered Katyn in 1940 by the NKVD. Her family preserved a letter written by Colonel Orawka from the camp in Kozelsk, which was submitted to the Institute of National Remembrance in Krakow. Bronislawa for many years wanted to personally pay tribute to her uncle's memory in the Katyn forest. In 2001, she was the initiator of the exhibition "Katyn - the fight for the truth" in Poronin. In 2005 she was questioned as a witness in the Branch Commission for the Prosecution of Crimes Against the Polish Nation in Krakow in the murder at Katyn of her uncle, Francis.[393]

Marrying February 27, 1954, her husband was Wieslaw Löffler, a civil engineer, who died on November 26, 2003. They had a daughter, Anita and grandson Luke.

---

[392] https://pl.wikipedia.org/wiki/Bronis%C5%82awa_Orawiec-L%C3%B6ffler
[393] Ibid.

Lieutenant Colonel Jan Osinski
Field Chaplain of the Armed Forces

Jan Kazimierz Osinski was born 24 March 1975 in Michowie. In 1995 he entered the Seminary of St. John the Baptist in Warsaw with the intention of becoming a priest of the Military Ordinariate of the Polish Army. He was ordained a priest on May 27, 2001. Father Osinski's first parish was the military parish in Deblin. In November of 2004 Osinski became the personal secretary to Bishop Tadeusz Ploski. In the same year he became a correspondent for the Military Ordinariate for Vatican Radio. In November 2005 he was appointed chaplain of Military Justice. In 2007 he was entrusted with the offices of Vice-Chancellor of the Curia Field Polish Army and the first Air Base in Warsaw, and chief chaplain of Railway Security Guard at the General Headquarters of Railway Security Guard in Warsaw. In 2008 he began doctoral studies at the School of Law and Administration at the same university.[394]

In 2009 he was appointed to the office of the Deputy Secretary General of the Synod of the Military Ordinariate in Poland.

"He was well suited to the army!" said Tadeusz Szlendak, a former colleague. "He had a look! He was a good child from a God-fearing family. Oh, when I learned {of his death}, I could not sleep all night, but I cried." [395]

Danuta Remiszewska, Deputy Director of school, taught Jan Osinski history. "He stood out against the background of the class. He was a great teacher. He had his own mind and was able to defend himself. Curious about the world, sympathetic. I remember at the prom he was not ashamed to dance with a young child of one of the teachers. He had leadership qualities. I remember him at the altar."

Colleague Kazimiera Kowalska recalled, "My son Jacek entered military service in Deblin. Father {Osinski} met him there and said to him 'Come to me, if you have problems.' He is proud of his countrymen.

---

[394] https://pl.wikipedia.org/wiki/Jan_Osi%C5%84ski
[395] "Ks. ppłk. Jan Osiński cieszył się każdym dniem życia by Ewa Czerwińska"13 April 2010 http://www.kurierlubelski.pl/artykul/243760,ks-pplk-jan-osinski-cieszyl-sie-kazdym-dniem-zycia,2,id,t,sa.html

Always he is thinking about his hometown....We're getting ready to do the unveiling of a monument dedicated to the victims of World War II. Father John joined in the preparations. When I came to Michowa on holiday, he always asked me 'what's new?' [396]

"Father Jan was a deacon in my parish for 10 years... I only remember that he was extremely smiling and cheerful, and so positively proud that he was a military chaplain. Life is very strange ... Although, as my colleague said, 'it would seem that they are already dead, and we live. But they woke up to life, and we still die ...' I'll see you someday in the clouds ... " [397]

---

[396] Ibid.
[397] "ks. Jan Osiński 14.04.2010"
http://www.tokfm.pl/Tokfm/1,105765,7770398,ks__Jan_Osinski.html

Colonel Adam Pilch

Field Chaplain, Evangelical Church of the Armed Forces

Adam Pilch was born June 26, 1965 in Wisla. He completed his theological studies at the School of Theology of the Evangelical Christian Theological Academy in Warsaw in 1989. He was ordained July 15, 1990 in Sorkwity. For three years, he was the vicar of the parish of the Holy Trinity in Warsaw, then two years as administrator. The rest of his life he spent as pastor of the parish of the Ascension in Warsaw. Since 1995 he was the dean of the Warsaw Military District in the rank of major and since 1999 deputy of the Bishop of the Evangelical Military in the rank of colonel. Since November 2009 he held the position Supreme Evangelical Chaplain.

Colonel Pilch participated with soldiers in peacekeeping missions in Kosovo, Lebanon, and Chad. He has participated in numerous international conferences and seminars.

"The late Father Adam Pilch was a man who was ecumenically open. His pastoral ministry was not limited only to the faithful of the Church, of which he was a priest. As a priest he was sincerely devoted to anyone seeking a relationship with God. Firmly holding the biblical words, he could give support in many different situations—whether a man is lost or is experiencing joy. He wanted always to help a man gain faith in the Savior," said Paul Anweiler Bishop of the Lutheran diocese of Cieszyn. [398]

"For 15 years I was friends with him, working closely in organizing monthly ecumenical worship celebrated in the temple every first Monday of the month. I cannot imagine a better priest in this place, taking care of these prayers despite a growing number of other activities. These are the devotions, the most important point is to read the Bible and homily. I helped him in the search for volunteers, which sometimes was not easy. He

---

[398] "Ks. Adam Pilch Zostal Pochowany w Warszawie"
Publikacja: 24 Apr 2010
http://katowice.tvp.pl/1701729/ks-adam-pilch-zostal-pochowany-w-warszawie

always enjoyed when he could persuade a priest or a lay Catholic to help him, and he always thanked him warmly... He was a very modest man, best evidenced by the fact that he refused to accept the appointment as bishop of the field--he did not care to be a general." [399]

Colonel Pilch left a wife Cornelia and a daughter, Eme.

---

[399] "Ks. Adam Pilch (26.06.1965 - 10.04.2010)"Jan Turnau 09.04.2011 http://wiadomosci.gazeta.pl/wiadomosci/1,114873,9404802,Ks__Adam_Pilch__26_06_1965___10_04_2010_.html

Katarzyna Piskorska

Katyn Famlies Representative

Katarzyna Piskorska was born in 1937, the daughter of Thomas and Maria Piskorski who had two daughters: Anna and Katarzyna. She lost her father at the age of two years, when he was interned in Starobelsk, and later shot in Kharkov. [400]

During the Warsaw Uprising she lived with her mother in Warsaw at ul. Nowy Zjazd. Raised from birth in the spirit of love for the homeland and the values of scouting she held secret scout meetings in the apartment of her parents and helped her mother in helping Jews by hiding them in her house on Nowy Zjazd. [401] During the uprising, she learned how to dress battle wounds and she helped sew belts for guns [402]. When their house was destroyed during the uprising they moved to the home of her grandparents - Przemyslaw and Anna Podgorski.

In 1956, she passed the exams at the School of Sculpture at the Academy of Fine Arts in Warsaw and at the School of Biology, University of Warsaw, but was removed from the list of students in both departments for political reasons. She finally graduated from the School of Sculpture at the Academy of Fine Arts in Warsaw in 1962.

After graduation, in the years 1962-1964, she worked as an art teacher. After a long illness she returned to work in 1968. She moved to the National School of Fine Arts, where she taught sculpture until 1980 when she was dismissed for political reasons. [403]

During the time of martial law in the 1980's Piskorska, supported resistance activities, collecting money, providing her house for meetings and its basement for an offset printing machine on which were printed independent publications. She also hosted and hid underground Solidarity activists. [404]

---

[400] https://pl.wikipedia.org/wiki/Katarzyna_Piskorska
[401] "Katarzyna Piskorska"osa, domi 11.04.2010 http://wyborcza.pl/1,75402,7760216,Katarzyna_Piskorska.html
[402] Ibid.
[403] https://pl.wikipedia.org/wiki/Katarzyna_Piskorska
[404] Ibid.

"She was very benevolent, kind, and cheerful. An artistic soul," remembered Col. Marek Tarczyński, Secretary of the Polish Katyn Foundation. "It was Kasia who prepared the decorations for all our annual Katyn sessions at the Royal Castle and banners for processions, which were organized on behalf of the redemption of Russia's Katyn investigation in 2004." [405]

Her pre-war house at 104 Powsinska was built by her grandparents in the 1920s. This house had an unusual history: it was destroyed during the May 1926 coup, September 1939 campaign and the Warsaw Uprising in 1944. Each time it was rebuilt by the family. The house on Powsinska Street attracted passers-by. {3} Before the door could be found, two slender clay boxes, part of an exhibition, which Piskorska had arranged in her magical garden. When one strolled through the garden after her, one had to be careful not to trample a clay mouse or coiled animals of unknown species. [406]

Michael Horbulewicz stayed with Katarzyna Piskorska during a period of his studies. "She fried my pancakes with apples. I remember the first days. My room was not ready yet, so I sat in the studio - full of paintings and sculptures. For a new, slightly frightened student it was a place with the best stories. Friends who also lived with the artist still repeat them. I remember her cheerful disposition, but also a formidable inner strength. All alone, she took care of the family home - a former insurgent headquarters, art garden, a place full of history, the last memento of her father." [407]

---

[405] "Katarzyna Piskorska"osa, domi 11.04.2010 http://wyborcza.pl/1,75402,7760216,Katarzyna_Piskorska.html
[406] Ibid.
[407] Ibid.

Maciej Plazynski
Head of the Polish Community Association

Maciej Płażyński was born 10 February 1958 in Młynary. He began his political career in 1980 as one of the leaders of the Students of Solidarity, coordinating the sit-down strike at the Gdansk University in autumn of 1981. [408]

He was governor of the Gdańsk Voivodship from August 1990 to July 1996, and was elected to the Sejm (the lower house of the Polish parliament) in September 1997. He was the longest serving Marshal of the Sejm of the Third Republic of Poland.[409]

In January 2001, he founded the Civic Platform political party with Donald Tusk and Andrzej Olechowski. He left the Civic Platform for personal reasons and at the time of his death was an independent Member of Parliament. He was later chosen as a chairman of the Association "Polish Community".

Maciej Płażyński was married to Elżbieta Płażyńska and together they had three children: Jakub, Katarzyna, and Kasper.

Plazynski devoted himself entirely to the struggle for the rights of Polonia where she was discriminated against.

Recently he spent a lot of time in the Belarusian courtrooms defending Poles living in Belarus who the Belerusian regime discriminated against just for being Poles. He wanted to bring the Poles from Kazakhstan. He was thinking about starting a national campaign, which was to end in civil repatriation. He wanted to force the Polish state to take financial responsibility also for the return of Polish compatriots from the Kazakh steppes. "It is a disgrace that we have abandoned these people. Shame for us politicians and disgrace to our nation," he explained. [410]

Since 2008 when he was president of the Polish Community Association to help Poles in the East he engulfed himself in it completely. Płażyński,

---

[408] https://en.wikipedia.org/wiki/Maciej_P%C5%82a%C5%BCy%C5%84ski
[409] Ibid.
[410] "Maciej Płażyński in love with the idea of showing off-u" by Zofia Wojtkowska, 12-04-2010 http://polska.newsweek.pl/maciej-plazynski--zakochany-w-idei-popis-u,56614,1,1.html

contrary to his calm public image, was a political fighter. He could seek a compromise when it was really worth it. He never accepted compromise at any price, even if it cost him the loss of the highest positions.[411]

He had already shown the nature of the warrior in 1981, when he led the occupation strike at the Gdansk University. "We were terribly irresponsible," he said. Probably as great irresponsibility was his involvement in the 1980's in the political Movement of Young Poland, and in 1989 Congress of Liberals. It was a dangerous game, but Płażyński liked the risk. And terribly he disliked the lack of freedom. [412]

---

[411] Ibid.
[412] Ibid.

Major General Taduesz Ploski
Military Ordinary of the Armed Forces

Tadeusz Płoski D.Sc., Ph.D. was born 9 March 1956 in Lidzbark Warmiński. He was ordained a priest for the Archdiocese of Warmia in 1982. He studied Canon Law at the Catholic University of Lublin and later obtained a Doctorate.

As a priest he served the Polish Bishops as a Canon lawyer. In 1992 he was assigned to minister to the faithful in the Polish military. Even in the military he served as a correspondent for Vatican Radio and Catholic News Sources. In 1995 he was appointed dean of the Vistula Military Units of the Ministry of Interior. Five years later, he was chaplain of the Government Protection Bureau.

Fr. Ploski published 150 articles about Canon Law and was a highly regarded expert on pastoral care and law in the military services. He was appointed the Military Ordinary of the Polish Armed Forces on 16 October 2004. In this role he oversaw the spiritual needs of the Polish Armed Forces and the priests attached to them. [413]

In the sermon he had prepared for the Saturday Mass in Katyn, Ploski wrote, "The truth can be a great burden, a source of peace, a fulcrum, the reason for indecision ... The truth is more important than happiness. Is it possible to be happy without truth?" [414]

In 2004, when John Paul II appointed him to the post of Military Ordinary, in an interview with Olsztyn "Gazeta" he told why he was attracted to the military: "I was fascinated, especially with the marches, songs, and military drill. My studies and seminars were very similar to military service. They both required discipline." [415]

When he completed Postgraduate Studies at the Operational and Strategic National Defense Academy in Warsaw, ("general's school")

---

[413] Two Bishops and Four Priests Also Killed in Tragic Polish Plane Crash by Deacon Keith Fournier 4/12/201 Catholic Online http://www.catholic.org/news/international/europe/story.php?id=36129

[414] "bp Tadeusz Płoski," by Katarzyna Wiśniewska 11.04.2010 Wyborcza.plGazeta Wyborcza Raporty http://wyborcza.pl/1,75402,7759250,bp_Tadeusz_Ploski.html

[415] Ibid.

he was the first military chaplain who finished the course. "Colleagues from that time, mostly colonels, looked at him stressed. They wondered among themselves about 'the man from the Vatican'. But once they met him, their attitude has changed," said the journalist of " Gazeta " Maciej Nowakowski. [416]

In the book "Who's Who in the Church," Polski gave his motto in life: "He does not need rules, who has character." [417]

In public statements he was principled, often using strong words to defend Christian values. During the dispute over crosses in schools after the judgment of the European Court of Human Rights in Strasbourg he said: "We cannot remain indifferent to the destruction of our heritage contained in the sign of the cross." [418]

But those who knew him stressed that he looked at people with understanding. "I have not heard from his mouth a bad word to people far from the Church or not living to the end according to the catechism. He tried to understand them. He knew how to work with people regardless of their beliefs," said a fellow priest. In November, he began a second term working in the Council for the Protection of Struggle and Martyrdom.

"He was very energetic, open and cheerful," said Father Antoni Skowronski, chancellor of the Diocese of Elku. "At the same time he was also very concerned about the affairs of the homeland and the army." [419]

---

[416] Ibid.
[417] Ibid.
[418] Ibid.
[419] "Wspomnienie: Biskup Tadeusz Ploski kochał wojsko i Ojczyznę," by Katarzyna Chojnowska, 10 Apr 2010, Gazeta Wspolczesna Wiadomosci http://www.wspolczesna.pl/wiadomosci/elk/art/5711648,wspomnienie-biskup-tadeusz-ploski-kochal-wojsko-i-ojczyzne,id,t.html

Junior Warrant Officer Agnieszka Pogrodka-Weclawek

Member, Government Protection Bureau (BOR)

Agnieszka Pogródka-Węcławek was born 15 December 1975 in Piaseczno. She grew up in Mount Calvary, then lived in Czersk, and then in Warsaw. In 1998, she joined the BOR as a civilian employee. In 2002 she became a BOR officer. In 2009 she graduated from the School of Social and Economics in Warsaw. [420]

Agnieszka Pogródka-Węcławek, was dubbed "Cleopatra" by Marek Krupa, a photographer for Prime Minister Leszek Miller. "She combed her hair a little up and then down. That gave her the appearance of the Egyptian queen," recalled Captain Jarosław Świderek, a retired BOR officer. "Agnieszka really wanted to have a child. I know that they were trying. A child probably would have been born in the next year," he said. [421]

Grażyna Kwiatkowska a friend of Pogródki-Węcławek, recalled that two days before her death Agnieszka told her she had been in a new jewelry store on ul. Mikitiwskiej and she found a four leaf clover charm for her bracelet. [422] On it, she had engraved the name of her husband, Albert. She wore the bracelet on the plane to Smolensk on April 10. [423]

"She was the favorite female officer and stewardess of First Lady Maria Kaczynski. Although Agnieszka never boasted," said her close friend Grażyna Kwiatkowska. "Agnieszka like no one had access to the First Lady. It was a close contact." Grażyna said she regretted that the image of her friend which appeared in the media in the official BOR uniform with

---

[420] https://pl.wikipedia.org/wiki/Agnieszka_Pogr%C3%B3dka-W%C4%99c%C5%82awek

[421] "Była ulubioną stewardessą Marii Kaczyńskiej, 19 Apr 2010, Fakt24 http://www.fakt.pl/Byla-ulubiona-stewardessa-Marii-Kaczyńskiej,artykuly,69644,1.html

[422] "Uśmiechem umiała zjednać sobie pierwszą damę," {She smiles she could win a first lady} by Anita Czupryn, Polska, 13 Apr 2010 http://www.polskatimes.pl/tag/agnieszka-pogrodka-weclawek-maz/

[423] "Była ulubioną stewardessą Marii Kaczyńskiej, 19 Apr 2010, Fakt24 http://www.fakt.pl/Byla-ulubiona-stewardessa-Marii-Kaczyńskiej,artykuly,69644,1.html

a serious face did not reflect what it was every day. She was always smiling, and perhaps that smile endeared her to the First Lady. [424]

Agnieszka Pogródka-Węcławek worked for BOR eight years, but worked in the same office much longer - since 1998. First, she worked as a civilian employee in the finance department. In 2002, she became a female officer and began to fly as a flight attendant. General Mirosław Gawor, former head of the BOR, remembered Agnieszka as a hardworking, friendly and ambitious girl. She finished college, taking a lot of courses, and recently had begun to talk of returning to school. She was a perfectionist in her work. She was great and succeeded in everything. And so happy; so in love with her husband. She met her husband, Albert Weclawek at work as he was also a BOR officer. They were married in 2005.

Grazyna Kwiatkowska revealed that since Saturday {April 10} her head still pounded with the same thoughts and questions. "I have flown on this plane 18 years, I knew it so well. Although I breathed a sigh of relief when the wheels of the plane touched the ground, and heard the distinctive rumble of engines. So I think: where was Agnes sitting? Maybe in the middle, between the kitchen and the third salon, because there usually would sit the stewardess. Or did she have time to catch a friend by the hand? I think: what were her last words? Was she aware that this is the end? I'm tired of these questions, to which after all there is no answer. I will never know...." [425]

---

[424] "Uśmiechem umiała zjednać sobie pierwszą damę," {She smiles she could win a first lady} by Anita Czupryn, Polska, 13 Apr 2010 http://www.polskatimes.pl/tag/agnieszka-pogrodka-weclawek-maz/

[425] "Uśmiechem umiała zjednać sobie pierwszą damę," {She smiles she could win a first lady} by Anita Czupryn, Polska, 13 Apr 2010 http://www.polskatimes.pl/tag/agnieszka-pogrodka-weclawek-maz/

Vladimir Potasinski
Commander in Chief, Special Forces

Vladimir Potasinski was born on July 31, 1956 in Czeladź. He graduated from the General Staff Academy of Mechanized Forces Officers. He was the commander of the Polish Special Forces. He had a rich experience implementing military tasks outside the country.

In the complex conditions of the Iraqi mission he established himself as an excellent leader and organizer of the work of the multinational headquarters and the activities of subordinate units and subunits. His high professionalism and devotion to duty earned him special respect and recognition among both Polish soldiers and allies.

Vladimir Potasinski began dating his future wife in January 2009. "We wasted so much time," he said later, recalling the failed attempts at matchmaking. They had only been dating for two months when Potasinski decided this was the woman he wanted to marry. All was meticulously planned for his proposal: a cozy restaurant, a huge bouquet of red roses, a diamond ring were waiting. But that day he had to be in Warsaw. He had several meetings, the last with the chief of staff, General Gagor. And here he ran into bad luck, because everything was delayed. Potasiński informed his supervisor that must be in Krakow, "It's a matter of life and death", asking to be released from the meeting. General Gągor said, "Wait a minute," and brought champagne and offered a toast for the success of the mission of his life. [426] Said Marta Potasińska, "I am a mature, sensible woman. And I agreed to get married after a few weeks of knowing him. I did not hesitate. I knew he was the man with whom I wanted to spend the rest of my life." In June (2009) they married. And from that moment on they were inseparable. As the general was leaving for a meeting, she rode with him. At the request of her husband she gave up working so they could spend more time together. He showered her with flowers at every opportunity, without any special occasion. On a lazy {April} Saturday he

---

[426] "Mijają dwa lata od tragedii pod Smoleńskiem. Jesteśmy u bliskich ofiar," by Katarzyna Janiszewska, 10 Apr 2012, Gazeta Krakowska, Fakty24
http://www.gazetakrakowska.pl/artykul/549965,mijaja-dwa-lata-od-tragedii-pod-smolenskiem-jestesmy-u-bliskich-ofiar,id,t.html

promised that he will not leave…that we will be together for the rest of the world. But he could not keep his word. Why? They wanted to build a house. Huge, made of logs, covered with shingles, with many guest rooms. They had already bought the land for the house. Now his wife is alone to build the house. They had planned to plant a tree on that Saturday but the general was invited to Katyn. He wanted to go there. But he was also a little angry that it happened this Saturday--that was to be the time shared with his wife. Late on the Friday before he flew to Smolensk they celebrated the purchase of their land with dinner, wine, and conversation about their plans. They were starting a new life. On Saturday, he woke up in blissful happiness saying, "It's going to be a beautiful day." [427]

If not for the catastrophe in Smolensk, Colonel Ryszard Jankowski believed that Poland would have been the sixth country in the world to have an allied Special Forces unit. General Potasiński dreamed of the creation of the Polish special forces. "He talked about it very often, almost without interruption. It motivated him to work even harder. He believed deeply that the Polish flag will be waved really high," said Jankowski. In his last farewell Jankowksi wrote: "General, sleep peacefully. We will continue your work." [428]

---

[427] Ibid.
[428] "Mieli tyle do zrobienia, ale nastąpił Smoleńsk" by Paulina Korbut, Maria Mazurek, Magdalena Stokłosa, 10 Apr 2013
http://www.gazetakrakowska.pl/artykul/802327,mieli-tyle-do-zrobienia-ale-nastapil-smolensk,id,t.html

Andrzej Przewoznik

Secretary General of Council for the Protection of
Monuments to Struggle and Martydom

Andrzej Przewoźnik was born 13 May 1963 in Jurkow. He was a Polish historian and served as Secretary General of the Council for the Protection of Struggle and Martyrdom Sites since 1992.

Przewoznik graduated with a history degree from the School of Philosophy and History at the Jagiellonian University in Krakow in 1988. In 2002 he graduated from postgraduate studies in the field of defense of the state from the Department of Strategic and Defense National Defense Academy in Warsaw.

In the years 1981-1989 he was involved in the "Solidarity" movement. In his role as General Secretary of the Council for the Protection of Struggle and Martyrdom he achieved numerous successes, including the cemetery and a monument to the victims of crime in Jedwabne and an effective long-term battle for the restoration and re-opening of the cemetery of Defenders of Lviv. [429]

Journalist Konrad Piasecki wrote of Przewoznik:

"He lived and worked with frantic activity. He got up early, so making an appointment with him for a morning interview never caused a great problem. From dawn he worked at home, then drove to the building of the Council. The work forced him to travel frequently in Poland, in Europe and in the world ... Mostly, however, he frequented the East, where he built the Polish monuments, restored cemeteries and, commemorated the tragic moments in Polish history--most of all this cursed Katyn to which he devoted so much heart and energy. It was he who forced the Russians to agree to create a Polish cemetery and monument to those murdered in the Katyn forest. [430]

"A few years ago I came to his office for a brief conversation. That's what struck me then, the movement, noise, commotion that prevailed in

---

[429] https://pl.wikipedia.org/wiki/Andrzej_Przewo%C5%BAnik
[430] "Andrzej Przewoźnik: Wojownik o katyńską prawdę," by Konrad Piasecki 08-04-2015 Newsweek (Polish) http://polska.newsweek.pl/kim-byl-andrzej-przewoznik-sylwetka-andrzeja-przewoznika-,artykuly,360682,1.html

his office. Ringing telephones, running between rooms, and the guests... The long name of his function could give the impression that he had the quietest job in the world. Secretary of the Council for the Protection of Struggle and Martyrdom ... It was a Polish paradox. The role in reality was like treading on hot coals. Andrew Przewoznik had an unusual tact, sensitivity and delicacy in maneuvering between the expectations of politicians, the requirements of diplomacy and historical emotions. He had to reconcile the conflicting interests, to be a link between the - often warring - veterans' organizations, soothe the wounds of Polish history and build another memorial site...He was a phenomenon in Polish public life. He embraced his role eighteen years ago and held it continuously until Saturday morning. And he could be dismissed at any time by one signature from the prime minister. Of Przewoźnik it certainly cannot be said that he had a flexible spine and adapted to the changing winds of policy. Oh no ... He had strong views, which he loudly expressed and earned a large group of enemies.[431]

"It was said of him that he was 'sick of Poland.' This had a double meaning because he was her patient, not only because he was a sincere patriot, but also because through his work he paid with serious heart problems. After several difficult anniversary celebrations he landed in the hospital in serious condition but again, answered phones and spoke in a whisper as you left that he would call you in a few days. He threatened that he would change jobs, but probably only once seriously tried to abandon the Council. It was in 2005, when he was one of the most serious candidates for the President of the Institute of National Remembrance. He hoped to win the competition for this position.... He made no secret of suspicion and resentment towards his rival, Janusz Kurtyka...They went together to meet their tragic fates when on April 10 at Okecie they boarded the plane. Though they probably sat far apart and exchanged only a handshake, they died at the same time ..." [432]

His death in Smolensk brought an end to many of his plans. He failed to finish a book about the Katyn massacre he was working on in the last years of his life. His colleague completed it. He dreamed also of

---

[431] Ibid.
[432] Ibid.

the creation of an institution whose purpose would be to study the history of the Borderlands and the fate of the Poles in the former territory of the Republic. He wanted to strengthen cooperation between museums in the country. Even in 2010, Andrzej Przewoźnik planned a trip to Kharkiv and Miednoje. "I could not slow down my husband. But soon we had finally found a haven for our family," explained Jolanta. "Andrzej loved the forest and we wanted to build a house in a forest somewhere. The heart of the house was to be the library where Andrzej, buried in a pile of books, would work." {3} Jolanta remarked on how many devoted friends they had. "Surely he looks down and is surprised how many people out of respect for him now help us." [433]

He is survived by his wife Jolanta and two daughters - Joanna and Julia.

---

[433] "Mieli tyle do zrobienia, ale nastąpił Smoleńsk,"Paulina Korbut,Maria Mazurek,Magdalena Stokłosa, 10 Apr 2013
http://www.gazetakrakowska.pl/artykul/802327,mieli-tyle-do-zrobienia-ale-nastapil-smolensk,id,t.html

Krzystof Putra
Vice Marshal of the Sejm

Krzysztof Jakub Putra was born July 4, 1957 in Józefowo, Suwałki County. He was a Polish politician, a member and one of the founders of the Law and Justice (PiS) party. He served as a Deputy Marshal of the Senate from October 27, 2005 until November 4, 2007. He later became a Sejm member (from November 5) and PiS candidate for Sejm Marshal.

A member of Solidarity during Communist rule, he was a worker in Białystok from 1975 to 1994. He was also a Sejm Member from Solidarity (1989–1991). As one of the Deputy Marshals of the Senate he was regarded as a *de facto* leader of the upper house.

He was married and had eight children.

A very experienced man with a hallmark mustache, he was formerly a member of the National Broadcasting Council, a great social worker, a man of great heart.

Putra described his family roots in this way: "I come from traditional family roots. My little Lithuanian grandfather, Zygmunt had a mustache and could sing beautifully; he was a remarkable man and that is why I remember him. He always would recite to me the fairy tale 'With Fire and Sword.' In it the mustachioed Longin Podbipięta had a great sword, and cut the three heads in one fell swoop. When I met my wife, I read her 'With Fire and Sword' aloud. My father has no mustache. But all the men were considered extremely strong people, physically strong and under such hard conditions." [434]

He was the son of a farmer. "Good, cheerful, very modest and nice man, just a nice neighbor behind the fence," said Krzysztof Putra's neighbors form Jozefowo. Residents add that Krzysztof Putra and his father did a lot for the local community. Among other things, they donated land for the construction of the local church and helped in the construction of the temple. Since 1980, Krzysztof Putra, regardless of the associated dangers, was active in the work of the "Solidarity" movement.

---

[434] "Osierocił ośmioro dzieci!" 14 Apr 2010, Fakt, http://www.fakt.pl/Osierocil-osmioro-dzieci-,artykuly,69178,1.html

His friends remember him as a man fundamentally true to his principles. But not always serious; he loved to remember the old days of service in the army, he had an excellent memory for jokes, but he'd repeat the same one several times ... He had a sharp tongue, which sometimes came out toward his political adversaries. Once when Roman Giertych (of Poland's League of Polish Families Party), was invited to a TV program together with Joachim Brudzińskim and Krzysztof Putra (both PiS), Giertych remarked: "I'm on this program in a difficult situation, because the gentlemen came as a pair." Putra, without thinking blurted out: "I have more sons and daughters than you have electorate." Very often he referred to his unusually large family: "I'm racing with Lech Walesa as to who will have the largest number of children," he said on another occasion. [435]

"He has come a long way from an ordinary worker to the Deputy Speaker of the Sejm and the Senate," said Robert Tyszkiewicz, head of Podlasie PO. Tyszkiewicz remembered Putra as an extremely consistent politician, fundamental and true, though often liked to joke. "As when he won the PiS party election in Podlasie 2007. He bet his famous mustache, that he would shave it if he won and conscientiously the day after the election he shaved it. Soon, however, the deputy speaker grew a mustache again, because, as he said, "In the house without it they would not accept me." [436]

He liked to talk about his family and was proud of them. Mariusz Kaminski remembers how Putra, after the birth of his youngest son Paul in 2000, for five years retired from active politics. In the house at the time there were four small children and he found that his place was with his family. But he often regretted that his work often took him away from his family. "Politics requires a huge sacrifice, and honestly wanting to do something - you have to choose: either family, or politics. Inevitably a man gives up his Saturdays and Sundays," said Leszek Dec, Director of the Suwalki Special Economic Zone. [437]

---

[435] "Putra, jakiego nie znamy," by Magdalena Kleban, Helena Wysocka mkleban@wspolczesna.pl, 16 Apr 2010, Wspolszesna.pl
http://www.wspolczesna.pl/magazyn/art/5712332,putra-jakiego-nie-znamy,id,t.html
[436] Ibid.
[437] Ibid.

Father Ryszrd Rumianek
Rector, Cardinal Stefan Wyszynski University

Ryszard Rumianek was born on November 7, 1947 in Warsaw. He studied at the Higher Metropolitan Seminary in Warsaw and at the Academy of Catholic Theology. He was ordained in 1972. After two years of work and catechetical ministry in the Assumption of the Blessed Virgin Mary parish in Konstancin he was sent for specialized Bible studies abroad. [438]

In 1977 he obtained a bachelor's degree at the Pontifical Biblical Institute in Rome. Then he studied in Jerusalem in the Studium Biblicum Franciscanum. He obtained a Doctor of Theology degree 1979 from the Gregorian University in Rome.

In the years 1979-1982 he was the prefect of seminarians at the seminary in Warsaw, and for the next 12 years he was deputy director of the same seminary.

Since 1990 he associated with the Theological School of the Academy of Catholic Theology in Warsaw and he was a lecturer at the university. In 1998-2001 he headed the Department of Biblical Studies and since 2001 the Department of History of the Bible. He received the title of professor in 2002.

In 2002 he was vice-rector of The Cardinal Wyszyński University (UKSW) for general affairs and research, and three years later the rector. At the same time he continued to conduct classes on the Pentateuch at the School of Theology. During his tenure he also launched brand new schools of international relations and archeology and he also established a Centre for Education and Interdisciplinary Research. [439]

Rumianek left many scientific papers, including a translation of the comments on the Book of Ezekiel, with which he was fascinated. For many years he was a licensed guide in the Holy Land.

His motto in life was: respice finem (look to the end). [440]

---

[438] "Ryszard Rumianek, Rector Cardinal Stefan Wyszynski University," http://smolensk.muzhp.pl/portret/ks-ryszard-rumianek/
[439] Ibid.
[440] Ibid.

Arkadiusz Rybicki
Member of Parliament

Arkadiusz Rybicki was born 12 January 1953 in Gdynia. He graduated from Nicolaus Copernicus University in Gdansk where he studied history. In 1977 he was among the founders of the Student Committee of Solidarity in Gdansk. In 1980 he was engaged in "Solidarity" activities and in 1981, led the news agency the Press Information Bureau of the National Coordination Committee "Solidarity." During the martial law he was interned in Strzebielinek. In the years 1983-1988 he worked closely with Lech Walesa. He came from a large family. After the death of his older brother Henry he became the oldest of the boys and he drew all of his seven siblings into opposition and clandestine activities. [441]

Arkadiusz Rybicki, to his friends "Aram", ran parallel political and social activities. Though he graduated with a degree in history at the University of Gdansk, he was always drawn to politics. The spirit of the oppositionist spoke to him from his early youth. As a 17-year-old he was called to the struggle for independence. He co-organized and participated in the Movement of Young Polish events in August 1980. He was one of the most important advisers to Lech Welesa. In the government of Jerzy Buzek, he served as undersecretary of state at the Ministry of Culture and National Heritage. In the mid-1990s he was involved in film and television production. Since 2005 he was a member of the Civic Platform Party. [442]

Rybicki was also known for his activities in support of people with autism (which his son suffered from). He fought on several fronts. Firstly, together with his wife Margaret Rybička he participated in the Centre for Therapeutic School for Children and Youth with Autism in Gdansk.

---

[441] "Aram Rybicki w 1970 r. namalował napis: NIE ZAPOMNIMY KATYNIA 15.04.2010 http://wyborcza.pl/1,76842,7775020,Aram_Rybicki_w_1970_r__namalowal_napis__NIE_ZAPOMNIMY.html#ixzz43TWHYbjw

[442] "Aram – dokument o Arkadiuszu Rybickim." 28 Aug 2014, Redakcja http://www.polityka.pl/tygodnikpolityka/kraj/1590637,1,aram--dokument-o-arkadiuszu-rybickim.read

Second, after taking a job in the Parliament he coordinated the work of the Parliamentary Group for Autism. [443]

"He was quiet, modest, always kind and willing to help; an intellectual and a great scholar. A man who always discussed the merits and tried to understand the other side," recalled Agnieska Mazurczyk. [444]

His wife was Margaret Rybička, whom he married in 1976. He had two children, Magdalena and Anthony.

---

[443] Ibid.
[444] Ibid.

Andrzej Sarjusz-Skapski
President of the Federation of Katyn Families

Andrzej Adam Sariusz-Skąpski was born November 20, 1937 in Krakow. He was the president of the Federation of Katyn Families from 2006 to 2010. His father, Boleslaw Skapski was prosecutor at the Ministry of Justice in Warsaw before WWII and was murdered in Katyn.

In 1962 Sairusz-Skapski graduated from the hydraulic engineering program at the Technical University of Krakow. He worked as a surveyor and designer. In 1989 he co-founded the Krakow Association of Families of Victims of Katyn of Southern Poland. In the years 1996-2003 he was Vice Chairman of the Federation of Katyn Families, and in 2006 he was president of the Federation of Katyn Families. [445]

For several years, Sariusz-Skąpski helped Andrzej Przewoznik, Secretary General of the Council for the Protection of Struggle and Martyrdom to organize commemorations in Katyn. He was a supporter of peaceful investigation for reconciliation with the Russian nation not wanting to use the term "genocide" in reference to the Katyn massacre so as not to alienate the Russians. Their cooperation was necessary if all the circumstances of the Katyn massacre were to be revealed. Because of this stance, he was often at odds with some of the other activists in the Federation of Katyn Families, however they appreciated, his involvement in organizing the anniversary celebrations and the search for the historical materials about Katyn. [446]

He barely remembered his father who was murdered at Katyn. "Before the war, my father was a prosecutor. When he got an offer to work in the Ministry of Justice, the family moved from Krakow to Warsaw. Holidays before the war were spent in my grandfather's house in Zakopane," he recalled. "Here in August 1939 my father got orders to be accommodated in Dubno, where they had moved the office of the Ministry of Justice. When war broke out, the Soviets surrounded the village and my father was transported to Starobelsk. As a two year old, I stayed with my mother for two months in Lviv. A month later we returned to Krakow to a building

---

[445] https://pl.wikipedia.org/wiki/Andrzej_Sariusz-Sk%C4%85pski
[446] "Andrzej Sariusz-Skąpski," by Bartłomiej Kuraś 11.04.2010, Wyborcza, http://wyborcza.pl/1,75402,7760084,Andrzej_Sariusz_Skapski.html

on the Groblach Square." [447] That is where Andrzej Sariusz-Skąpski lived until his death.

"Only after the birth of my first daughter, I realized how much I lost," he told the newspaper "Gazetta". "I did not think that parental love could be so strong, that I so much needed a child...I joined the Krakow Katyn Families. After half a century of silence I was glad that I could openly talk to someone about it." [448] In 1989, when it finally became possible, he went with his daughter to Katyn. Since then he drove to the cemetery each year. On Saturday, April 10th, he went there on his last journey.

"'Jeśli zapomnę o nich - ty, Boże na niebie, zapomnij o mnie,' ("If I forget about them - you, God in heaven, forget about me") are the words of a heartfelt prayers whispered by generations of Poles. It was repeated for decades by women whose husbands were taken into Soviet captivity in 1939, where they disappeared without a trace, and the names years later appeared on the lists of the Katyn massacre," said Sariusz-Skąpska during mourning ceremonies at Pilsudski Square.[449] These words were also in a speech that he was supposed to give 10 April, the 70th anniversary of the Katyn massacre.

The daughter of Sariusz-Skapski recalled the words her father was to deliver at the Katyn ceremony: "We came with our children, grandchildren and great-grandchildren of the victims, to the graves of our fathers to convey to them our message: Keep an eye on this place, keep an eye worthy of the memory of your ancestors. Do not let this memory be appropriated by foreign persons, as is unfortunately often the case. Convey someday this message to your children. Let this memory last. I repeat once again and commit you - keep an eye on the place and the memory of your ancestors." "This appeal by my father did not reach those gathered at the cemetery in Katyn, but his message has given us all strength of will. Katyn Families will not let the pain beat pain. They will continue," she said. [450]

He left a wife, Janina and two daughters--Isabella and Magdalena.

---

[447] Ibid.
[448] Ibid.
[449] "Jeśli zapomnę o nich - ty, Boże na niebie, zapomnij o mnie" 17.04.2010 http://wiadomosci.gazeta.pl/wiadomosci/1,114873,7781951,_Jesli_zapomne_o_nich___ty__Boze_na_niebie__zapomnij.html
[450] Ibid.

Wojiech Seweryn
Representative of Katyn Families Association

Wojciech Seweryn was born August 31, 1939 in Tarnów. He graduated from the School of Fine Arts in Tarnów, and studied at the Jan Matejko Academy of Fine Arts. He immigrated to Chicago in the mid-1970s. His father was a 16th Infantry Regiment officer killed in the Katyn massacre when Wojciech was only a year old.

Seweryn was a respected artist in the Chicago area's large Polish community. He was the driving force behind a memorial to the Katyn massacre at the largely Polish St. Adalbert Cemetery in suburban Niles, Illinois, about 14 miles northwest of Chicago. "He had that obsession about reminding people about Katyn," said Jan Lorys, director of the Polish Museum of America in Chicago. "Some people were turned off by that, some were encouraged. But that's why he was flying {there on April 10}"[451]

Seweryn, who once worked in a Chicago-area auto body shop to make ends meet, was remembered as a loving family man. He was also known for helping several churches design sculptures and displays. He came to the US as a tourist, without the right of residence and language skills to work to provide the family a better life. His two daughters—Anna and Boguslawa—he left behind in Poland. He continued working two jobs, trying to support a family and supporting relatives. He also helped many of his fellow countrymen. After his death, his daughters were surprised when many people they did not even know, told them how much they owe him, how he found them a job, how he cared for them during an illness.[452]

Although his daughter knew that their father would follow them into the fire, they sometimes had the impression that he was not always present. They said to him: live among us or among the living! But he still thought back to Katyn. His daughter remembered how he told her he was going to get to Katyn and bring from there the land sanctified by the blood of his father, and then put up a monument to him. After emigrating to the

---

[451] "Chicago artist killed in plane crash in Poland," 10 Apr 2010 http://www.pjstar.com/article/20100410/NEWS/304109933

[452] "O śp. Wojciechu Sewerynie," *Tadeusz Święchowicz, 23 Jun 2012,* http://hej-kto-polak.pl/wp/?p=42753

United States, Katyn took on a new dimension. With a monument, the Americans would have to learn about the crime. "When I can build this monument, I can die in peace" - he said. [453]

He completed the first drawings for the monument shortly after arrival in the United States. He started fundraising, obtaining permits and leading construction.

In 1995, Wojciech Seweryn went to Katyn. He brought back the urn with soil from the land. In Chicago, Seweryn managed to gather a group of like-minded people. With the favor of the archdiocese he found a location for his momument in the cemetery of St. Adalbert in Niles, Illinois, which since the nineteenth century has been the burial place of the Poles from the northern suburbs of Chicago. In 2000 the construction began in earnest and Sweryn's dream began to take shape. The Granit Gallery provided to him a hall to work in for free. Because of the dust and the smell, he worked with the door open. Curious people came to see what was happening there. They brought him food and drink. [454]

In May of 2009 the Polish Primate consecrated and unveiled the monument. It depicts the Blessed Virgin Mary holding in her arms a dead soldier. Behind her, an eagle with outstretched wings and a cross of black granite.

In the morning on April 10 Seweryn boarded the Tu-154M aircraft flying to the ceremony at Katyn. He was deeply moved by the possibility of meeting with the president. Previously he planned to go to Katyn by train. He was invited on the government plane as the representative of Katyn Families. On Friday evening, several hours before the flight, he was on the phone with his daughter. He told her: "You know who I am honored to meet? I'm going with the president. He is hosting me. I feel like a king."[455] Setting out to Katyn, he was carrying a briefcase full of invitations to the Chicago celebration of the 70th anniversary of the crimes, which were to be held on 25 April. He was also taking certificates of recognition for the Poles associated with the Polish House in Smolensk.

Anna Wojtowicz, Seweryn's daughter said, "Dad was a practicing Catholic. He often said that the faith could give life. That's why he was able to carry out his projects and make him dreams come true."

---

[453] Ibid.
[454] Ibid.
[455] Ibid.

Slawomir Skrzypek

President, National Bank of Poland

Sławomir Stanisław Skrzypek was born 10 May 1963 in Katowice. He graduated from the Silesian University of Technology before getting his MBA from the University of Wisconsin-La Crosse. He obtained additional post-graduate degrees at Krakow University of Economics, the University of Silesia, Georgetown University and at IESE Business School at the University of Navarra. It was on 10 January 2007 that Skrzypek was appointed to the role of President of the National Bank of Poland.

Slawomir Skrzypek's career has been always tied to the Kaczynski brothers, Lech and Jaroslaw. He was particularly friendly with President Lech Kaczynski and it was Kaczynski's nomination that resulted in his appointment as the President of the Polish National Bank. He was 43 years old and his nomination came as a surprise to many who felt he lacked experience. His nomination to the position caused a wave of unflattering comments, including the questioning of the legality of his diplomas. [456]

In the months before his death, the NBP, under his leadership, was heavily involved in promoting the Euro and education on the benefits of monetary union. In September of 2009, his international career was made by one sentence from him: "Inflation will fall without lifting a finger by the Central Bank." The forecast was so accurate that the magazine Global Finance has distinguished Slawomir Skrzypek among the 30 central bank governors. [457]

In Katowice and Gliwice, Slawomir Skrzypek spent his youth raised on patriotic ideals of the early work of the opposition to communist rule in Poland. He was extremely talented, particularly in the area of physics and mathematics. When he studied civil engineering at the School of Civil Engineering Silesian University of Technology in Gliwice, he was one of

---

[456] "Sławomir Skrzypek: od eurosceptyka do euroentuzjasty," by Agata Pustułka, Wydawca newsweek.pl 11-04-2010 http://biznes.newsweek.pl/slawomir-skrzypek--od-eurosceptyka-do-euroentuzjasty,56532,1,1.html

[457] Ibid.

the organizers and leaders of the Independent Students' Association. For his opposition activity he was temporarily arrested in 1982.

Although his nomination to head the NBP was considered political by many, because of his close ties with the Kaczynski brothers, he did well in the position. The prestigious international financial magazine "Global Finance" declared NBP as one of the best managed banks in the world and the attitude of Skrzypek was assessed as better than the President of the US bank. In times of crisis, there had been pressure, recognizing that the market can cope with the problems. [458]

"He was an exceptional boss. Demanding much from others, but most of all from himself; he was honest, very devoted to the company," said Mariusz Siembiga, deputy director of the branch of National Bank of Poland in Katowice. He was extremely patriotic and brave and even though he had a stellar career, perhaps the greatest of our generation, he never forgot about his old friends. He maintained contact with us, and would often call. Today, when he died so tragically, I listened to media coverage. Western and American stations mentioned him as one of the most prominent financiers. It is a pity that the country could not always count on these well-deserved opinions." [459]

He left a wife, Dorota Skrzypek and three children - two sons and a daughter.

---

[458] "Sławomir Skrzypek zrobił największą karierę w swym pokoleniu," Dziennik Zachodni 2010-04-12 http://slaskie.naszemiasto.pl/artykul/slawomir-skrzypek-zrobil-najwieksza-kariere-w-swym-pokoleniu,376324,art,t,id,tm.html
[459] Ibid.

Leszek Solski
Representative of Katyn Families Association

Kazimierz Leszek Solski was born November 23, 1935 in Baranovichi. His father Kazimierz, as an artillery officer, with the Nowogródzka Cavalry Brigade was arrested in 1939 by the NKVD, imprisoned in the camp in Kozelsk and on April 17, 1940 murdered in Katyn. Kazimierz's brother Major Adam Solski was also detained together with him in Kozelsk and on April 9, 1940 was also a victim of the Katyn massacre

Solski graduated from the Department of Hydraulic Engineering at the Gdansk University of Technology. He worked with the Katyn Families Association since the 1980s. In 1990, thanks to the support of the library staff of the Technical University in Gdansk, he organized the "Photographic archive of memorabilia of murdered Katyn Families from Gdansk," which among others was viewed by Ronald and Nancy Reagan.

The trip to Katyn was the dream of his life. Now his wife Eve asks: "How could I deny him that?" She could not.[460]

"He decided to go on this trip at the last moment," said Jan Sawicki, a neighbor of Solski's in Sopot. "Initially there was a delegation of the Katyn Families. My daughter for two days before flying to Warsaw got him all the necessary documents. I knew him from the time of his studies at the Polytechnic. He was always pleasant, helpful, people liked him. He was about 75 years old, but he was still very active," said Sawicki. [461]

Maciej Lisicki, Vice President of Gdansk also remembered Solski. "Leszek was a tenant in a housing cooperative of which I was president. We had common interests. He told me about his father and uncle, who died in Katyn. When he learned that I visited Katyn, he wanted me to tell him every detail of my trip. A few years ago, he said he's moving out, because living on the third floor was hard on his feet, and there is no elevator. Then, when I was Vice-President again our paths crossed. His wife Eva Solska is a doctor in a leading oncological clinic. Once he came to me and asked: 'Mr. President, you have 15 minutes for me please?' He

---
[460] "Leszek Solski," 11.04.2010 http://wyborcza.pl/1,75402,7760020,Leszek_Solski.html
[461] Ibid.

drove me to his wife's clinic and showed me the mass of patients crowding the hallways. Then he explained that the clinic must expand; the marshal of the province had promised to help, now he was turning to the city authorities. Of course, we helped the clinic." [462]

He left a wife Eva, with whom he had two daughters-- Joanna and Hannah.

---

[462] Ibid.

Wladyslaw Stasiak
Chief of the Chancellery

Władysław Stasiak was born March 15, 1966 in Wrocław. He studied history in Wrocław University, and attended the National School of Public Administration in Warsaw in 1993.

He served as deputy director of the Department of National Defense and Internal Security. From November 2002 he was deputy president of the Capital City of Warsaw, in charge of the protection, public order and security, the activities of the Municipal Police and records of population, health, sports and physical culture. Then Lech Kaczynski spoke of him as his "sheriff". [463]

From 2 November 2005 to 31 May 2006 he held the position of Undersecretary of State in the Ministry of Internal Affairs and Administration responsible for the supervision of the Police, Border Guard and Government Protection Bureau. He was secretary of state in the ministry from 24 August 2006, when he took office as the head of National Security Bureau and secretary of the National Security Council. From 8 August 2007 to 16 November 2007 he was the Minister of Internal Affairs and Administration in the cabinet of Jaroslaw Kaczynski. July 27, 2009 he was appointed head of the Presidential Chancellery.

"The last day we spent together it was my birthday," Stasiak's wife Barbara recalled to a reporter on the second anniversary of the crash. "I think it will always be associated with Władek, It was actually a celebration of our anniversary of meeting each other. Now April 10 I will always associate with my birthday, which was beautiful, because one of the gifts that I got from Wladek, was that he came home a little earlier. He was usually very busy. He worked from morning to night, and sometimes half the night. This time he came home early, which for him, in this case, meant around 8pm. He brought me a cake... My favorite cake - chocolate

---

[463] http://www.se.pl/w 1iadomosci/polska/wladysaw-stasiak-44-l-szef-kancelarii-prezydenta-lecha-kaczynskiego-zginal-pod-smolenskiem_136045.html

raspberry. He liked the cake also; it reminded him of childhood. His grandmother would bake it. [464]

"Ever since I first saw him, I knew that this man is unique. I know it may not sound objective coming from the mouth of his wife, but then I was not his wife. I saw the first time a man around which floated an aura of righteousness and strength. Later it turned out that he was even a man of great sensitivity and openness to people. They are all with each other harmoniously united: this strength and this sensitivity, it all together was very special and I always thought that he is an unusual man. I still think so. Many people also tell me this."

"{When I think of my husband} I imagine him in mountain boots, backpacking, walking in the mountains, and I think these are the Tatra Mountains...Wladek travelled a lot; he had a great knowledge about the history and geography of basically any place on earth. I sometimes joked that I was going to catch him on something he didn't know, but I never succeeded. Always he knew, or at least heard about various things I asked about. [465]

"We agreed that the one who went first, would give the other a sign... {after his deth I received such a sign}It was a dream.... A beautiful dream, in which my husband invited me to dance, and then smiled and said, 'We will finish this dance someday.' It was a beautiful dream; it was a dream, bright, full of hope, full of optimism." [466]

---

[464] "Barbara Stasiak: Obiecał, że jeśli odejdzie, da znak. Przyszedł do mnie we śnie," 9 Apr 2012, RMF24, http://www.rmf24.pl/tylko-w-rmf24/wywiady/news-barbara-stasiak-obiecal-ze-jesli-odejdzie-da-znak-przyszedl-,nId,596924
[465] Ibid.
[466] Ibid.

Ensign Jacek Surowka
Member, Government Protection Bureau (BOR)

Jacek Surowka was born in 1974 in Krakow. He served in the BOR for nine years. But beyond the protection of the president, in his free time he worked as a volunteer helping disabled children from the Warsaw Rehabilitation Centre "Helenów." Staff at the center remember him as a frequent visitor. "He was able to spend his holidays or adjust his schedule in the BOR, if you needed help," said Anna Pawlikowska, guardian of the resort Helenów. "Children eagerly came up to him. Though they were disabled these children wanted to hear about his passions: motorcycles and photography...they could listen for hours," said Pawlikowska.[467]

In the memory of the pupils of the special school he was always seen as "good father Jack." "His work with disabled children consumed him to the point that he changed his current field of study and decided to train in the care of intellectually disabled," said Beata Jarczewska, deputy director of the facility.[468]

"He was our friend who we could always count on. He was able to talk with each and every individual to establish a bond. He shared with us the energy he never lacked. He brought joy and humor, with jokes that everyone loved. Always cordial, he never showed fatigue...he always helped wherever there was a need.

"The kids loved him. He spent hours telling them about his passions, such as cars and photography—he taught them how to take pictures. In the beginning he was for them like a big brother. With time, however, when he learned how to better take care of them he was for them something more - a caring father. He always said the children made him look at life differently. They waited for Jack, for each visit," added Beata.[469]

---

[467] "Surowka, Jacek Pożegnanie oficerów BOR, którzy zginęli pod Smoleńskiem," by Wojciech Grejciun, Piotr Machajski, 23 Apr 2010, Wyborcza.plWarszawaWiadomości z Warszawy http://warszawa.wyborcza.pl/warszawa/1,34889,7809189,Pozegnanie_oficerow_BOR__ktorzy_zgineli_pod_Smolenskiem.html

[468] "Se.pl wiadomości polska Jacek Surówka: Był dla nas jak dobry tata," 15 Apr 2010 http://www.se.pl/wiadomosci/polska/jacek-surowka-byl-dla-nas-jak-dobry-tata_136522.html

[469] Ibid.

Aleksander Szczyglo
Head of the National Security Bureau

Aleksander Marek Szczygło was born 27 October 1963 in Jeziorany. From 1978-1983 he attended the Station Technical College in Olsztyn. In 1990 he graduated from the School of Law and Administration, University of Gdansk. In 1996, he completed a course for government employees from Central and Eastern Europe organized by Georgetown University (classes were held at the University of Wisconsin).

He was first elected to Polish parliament in 2001 and subsequently reelected on 25 September 2005. Both times he was a candidate of the Law and Justice party. From 7 February 2007 until 16 November 2007 he was Minister of National Defense in the cabinet of Jarosław Kaczyński. From 15 January 2009 until his death he was the chief of the National Security Bureau. [470]

"He was professional and disciplined all the while never lacking a sense of humor," so said his colleagues from the party. He was one of the closest associates of Lech Kaczynski. But a better word might be "ward" or "student".[471]

Alexander Szczygło first saw Kaczynski when he studied law at the University of Gdansk in the 1980s when Kaczynski taught there. His colleagues from those days remember him as a completely independent person. During the first presidential elections on the door of his room he hung a poster of Tadeusz Mazowiecki. In a place where everyone supported Lech Walesa, this was an act of courage. [472]

Then he fell under the charm of Lech Kaczynski. He joined with him in good times and bad - he owed to him his education, career, and perhaps loneliness. When Kaczynski was president of the Supreme Chamber of

---

[470] https://pl.wikipedia.org/wiki/Aleksander_Szczygło
[471] "Ty masz żonę i dziecko, a ja mam swojego prezydenta" by MarcinWojciechowski, Slawomir Sowula, 10 Apr 2010, Wyborcza.plGazeta WyborczaFakty Smolenskie http://wyborcza.pl/1,105742,7754410,_Ty_masz_zone_i_dziecko__a_ja_mam_swojego_prezydenta_.html
[472] Ibid.

Control, Szczygło became head of his office. When Kaczynski was leaving the Chamber, he sent him to study in the United States. [473]

Aviation was his passion. He laughed that he missed his opposition activities in the People's Republic because when in August 1980 as a 17-year-old he honed his skills as a glider pilot. He remained faithful to this passion. He earned a pilot's license in private aircraft. He proudly wore on his lapel a military eagle - a souvenir from the period when he was head of the Defense Ministry. So maybe the legal profession and politics was not his greatest dream. [474]

"He was my mentor, and I, like several other young people from his immediate surroundings, called ourselves 'Szczyglo's child'" said Paul Lulewicz, an employee from his parliamentary office. "On the outside the man seemed very aloof and stern. But we, his colleagues, knew his other face - an understanding boss with a sense of humor." [475]

Lulewicz once asked Szczyglo, why he did not have a wife and children. "He told me then that 'you have a wonderful wife and a child, and I'm your president. This was the path I chose and I will keep it to the end. I would not be able to reconcile a family life' he said. "He was a great patriot who has dedicated his life to working for the benefit of our country." [476]

Aleksander was the youngest of six siblings. "He was so much our darling: the most loved, the most spoiled," said Krystyna Bieńkowska, Szczyglos's older sister. As I recall his life, studying, learning, work, politics. He did not even have time to start a family," she sighed. "Although the family was proud of his career, at home he would not talk politics. Our father always said that work and politics should be left on the doorstep." [477]

---

[473] Ibid.
[474] Ibid.
[475] Ibid.
[476] Ibid.
[477] Ibid.

Jerzy Szmajdzinski
Vice Marshal of the Sejm

Jerzy Andrzej Szmajdziński was born April 9, 1952 in Wraclaw. He graduated from the Wrocław University of Economics in 1975. In the years 1973-1990 he was a member of the Communist Party.

In 1988-1990 he was vice-president of the Polish Olympic Committee

He became a member of the Sejm in 1990, and in his second term Szmajdziński was chairman of the National Defense Committee and in the third term a deputy chairman of that committee. He was Minister of National Defense from 2001 to 2005, elected to the Sejm on September 25, 2005 and was a candidate for President of Poland in the 2010 election.

In the headquarters of the Democratic Left Alliance, on Rozbrat Street in Warsaw a legend circulates of the last visit of Jerzy Szmajdzinski. Fellow Sejm member Ryszard Kalisz related the story. "The last time I was there I asked one of the porters. He told me that when Szmajdziński would leave the building, he was always at ease, talking with them. But on the Friday before the tragedy it was different. Jurek leaving this time turned to them and only repeated three times: 'Goodbye to you'. It looked as if he was saying goodbye forever to the place where he spent about 20 years of life." [478]

"I do not recall him ever raising his voice to anyone. Even in politics. How often I've seen him try to scowl, but I knew that he was acting, it so poorly came out," said Stanislaw Pelczar, Szmajdziński friend of 30 years. "The day before his death, it was his birthday and we could not even talk because he was busy. What was Jurek really? Just good. And with such determination. It was hard to catch him out of balance." [479]

Former Member of Parliament John Chaładaj was a witness at the wedding of Margaret and Jerzy Szmajdzińskich. "We knew each other 34 years; he called me his best friend. I called him on Friday to wish him a

---

[478] "Jerzy Szmajdziński czuł, że nie wróci z podróży do Katynia? Kalisz: Jakby żegnał się na zawsze,"19.04.2010 Se.pl, http://www.se.pl/wiadomosci/polska/jerzy-szmajdzinski-czol-ze-nie-wroci-z-podrozy-do-_136731.html

[479] "Jerzy Szmajdziński," by Jacek Harłukowicz, Wyborcza.plGazeta, 10 Apr 2010 http://wyborcza.pl/1,75402,7752875,Jerzy_Szmajdzinski.html

Happy Birthday, and he just apologized that would not be able to attend an event, because he was flying to Smolensk... He was a good man; if he had to say something bad about someone he just did not say anything at all." [480]

He was married to Margaret Sekula-Szmajdzinska and had two children: Agnes and Andrew.

---

[480] Ibid.

Jolanta Szymanek-Deresz
Member of Parliament

Jolanta Szymanek-Deresz was born 12 Jul 1954 in Przedborz. Initially she studied at the University of Lodz but after two years moved to Warsaw. In 1977 she graduated from the School of Law and Administration at Warsaw University. She worked in the District Court for the Capital City Warsaw. In 1987, after passing the bar exam she joined a law firm. In the years 1979-1990 she belonged to the Communist Party. From 3 January 2000 she held the position of Undersecretary of State in the President's Office, and since June 13, 2000 served as a chief of the Chancellery. On December 23, 2000 she was re-appointed to the post which she held until October 18, 2005. [481]

On September 25, 2005 she was first elected a member of parliament fifth term of office of the district of Plock from the Democratic Left Alliance (SLD) party. In parliamentary elections in 2007, for the second time she received a mandate in the parliament as a candidate from the SLD party. Since June 1, 2008 she was Vice-President of the SLD. In 2009, she unsuccessfully ran for the European Parliament. [482]

She came from a family of lawyers. Her father Tadeusz Szymanek was a judge of the Supreme Court and the president of the Chamber of Labor and Social Insurance.

The following is from a Polish Newsweek article on Jolanta Szymanek-Deresz in that magazine's Tribute issue to the victims of the Smolensk crash:[483]

> *"She was a wonderful, charming wife and a good mother. And what delicious fried pork chops! She was also a great tennis player. When she and her husband played doubles they were unbeatable.*

---

[481] https://pl.wikipedia.org/wiki/Jolanta_Szymanek-Deresz
[482] Ibid.
[483] "Jolanta Szymanek-Deresz: Perfekcjonistka," by Krystyna Szelestowska, 8 Apr 2015 http://polska.newsweek.pl/5-rocznica-katastrofy-smolenskiej-jolanta-szymanek-deresz,artykuly,360692,1.html

Those who had worked with her for a long time always said that she never raised her voice.

In 2005 she decided to fight for a parliamentary seat. She liked new and difficult challenges. She was a perfectionist. She was raised and educated in the big cities - Lodz and Warsaw – as an intellectual but she faced the people from small towns and their problems.

There was a time when the SLD seriously considered her participation in the upcoming presidential election as a candidate for the SLD. When the convention in December elected Jerzy Szmajdzinski, she agreed to manage his campaign.

She loved family life and active leisure time. Her free time, which was not much, she spent with her husband on trips in Poland, nurturing a garden and meeting with friends over a pint of good beer. She loved the Czech literature, and in rare moments of quiet listened to classical music. [484]

She was married to Paul Szymanek. She had a daughter, Catherine and a son, Dariusz Lewandowski, an actor.

---

[484] "Jolanta Szymanek-Deresz - professionalism and sensitivity," Style.pl http://www.styl.pl/magazyn/news-jolanta-szymanek-deresz-profesjonalizm-i-wrazliwosc,nId,272422&usg=ALkJrhgzVEmtgPM9A4iRXHRzreNRckJqug#.googleusercontent.comutm_source=paste&utm_medium=paste&utm_campaign=chrome

Isabela Tomaszewska
Director of Diplomatic Protocol in Chancellory of President

Jolanta Izabela Tomaszewska was born 13 September 1955 in Kwidzyn. In April 1979, she graduated from the Institute of Archaeology, University of Warsaw, receiving her professional degree in archeology. In the years 1979-1998 she worked as a research assistant at the Institute of Archaeology and Ethnology in Warsaw; in the 80s and 90s she served as assistant editor of the magazines " Archaeologia Polona "and "Polish Archaeology." [485]

From 1998-2006, she was an employee of the Press Office of the President of Warsaw. In 2006 she started working in the President's Office, where she served as director of the President's protocol team. In the President's Office she was the closest collaborator of Maria Kaczynski helping her to organize conferences, interviews, and social activity. [486]

Izabela Tomaszewska, head of the presidential protocol team, called her husband on a satellite phone from the Tupolev aircraft on the morning of April 10th. Jacek Tomaszewski said it was a constant habit of his wife. Whenever the plane took off, she called home to inform him and after landing sent a text message. But this time was a little different. "The phone call that I received about 8:19 on Saturday 10 April, was not from her phone. It was a probably a satellite phone of the President," said her husband, adding that the conversation did not last long. "She told me just: 'I'm on the plane.' I asked the question: 'Just now? After all, you were supposed to take off at seven.' She did not answer my question; in the background I could hear voices and all that. And of course I did not get a text with the message: 'the eagle has landed'" said Tomaszewski. [487]

She had a husband Andrzej Jacek Tomaszewski who was also an archaeologist, a son Philip, and a grandson, Emil.

---

[485] https://pl.wikipedia.org/wiki/Izabela_Tomaszewska
[486] Ibid.
[487] "Interrupted the conversation with the victim disaster," 13 May 2010, Fakt24.pl, http://www.fakt.pl/Przerwana-rozmowa-z-ofiara-katastrofy,artykuly,71850,1.html

Warrant Officer Marek Uleryk

Member, Government Protection Bureau (BOR)

Warrant Officer Marek Uleryk was born 6 Jan 1975 in Żninie and grew up in Dziewierzewie. He was in the service of the BOR 12 years, initially guarding the Presidential Palace, and later briefly serving in the protection of presidents Aleksander Kwasniewski and Lech Kaczynski; then he was entrusted with taking care of the safety of the wife of the President- Maria Kaczynski.

He was a parachuting instructor who made thousands of jumps. Once a member of the club Zawisza Bydgoszcz he won many medals in skydiving. In 2002 he was Polish champion in the parachute pentathlon (night and day jumping, shooting, swimming, and running). [488]

Jolanta Karmowska teaches math at the local school and remembered Marek Uleryk. "I remember him from the time of the Volunteer Fire Brigade. He already worked in the State Protection Office and I was in the youth team of the TSO. We organized firefighting competitions. Marek was the soul of the company. This cheerful, happy man...and now in a coffin. So hard to believe it." [489]

"To me it does not make sense," said Maria Kordys one of Uleryk's three sisters. "I live in a world where our brother is still alive. After all, he was with us at Easter for a long time. He arrived on Saturday... He was soon to come to Dziewierzewie on an extended vacation because he had not been there for a half a year. He wanted in October to prepare for the defense of his thesis as he was finishing law and administration at the University of Warsaw. He made a date with a friend to go fishing, because Marek was an avid angler." [490]

---

[488] "Paweł Janeczek, oficer BOR, był mężem znanej dziennikarki TVN Joanny Racewicz. Zginął z prezydentem pod Smoleńskiem,"(mag) Echo Dnia, 14 Apr 2010 http://www.gazetalubuska.pl/artykuly-archiwalne/art/7849199,pawel-janeczek-oficer-bor-byl-mezem-znanej-dziennikarki-tvn-joanny-racewicz-zginal-z-prezydentem-pod-smolenskiem,id,t.html

[489] "Piękny miał pogrzeb Marek Uleryk, ale strasznie tak zginąć jak on," by Adam Lewandowski, 24 Apr 2010

[490] Ibid.

In Dziewierzewie he visited his classmates and several others with whom in his youth he played football. He did not talk to them about business matters. Nobody knew he would be in Smolensk. One could only guess that if the First Lady was flying he would as he is one of two of her personal BOR officers. "He talked warmly about the First Lady," said Fr. Alfred Lugiert, parish priest in Dziewierzewie. "She took care of these BOR workers, sending two through college. It's beautiful, that in the presidential palace he found his second loving family. Ms. Kaczyńska was like his second mother, so he called her. She was very respected." said Zbigniew Sosnowski, Deputy Minister of Internal Affairs and Administration. {Marek} had the nature of a true athlete. He amazed others with his physical condition. While at work he was calm and balanced, but had a private passion for extreme sports. His element was air. He was a parachuting instructor and twice won the champion title in Polish military parachute pentathlon. He lived a very brave and interesting life." [491]

Colonel Slawomir Bogackim, deputy head of the department of protection of BOR, supervisor of Mark Uleryk remembered him as a quiet man, a great athlete, and a friend. "Part of our family is missing. Because among our officers we make friends and meet not only at work. In the presidential plane crash in Smolensk we lost nine such wonderful people. Almost every tenth victim of the accident was ours. [492]

---

[491] Ibid.
[492] Ibid.

Anna Walentynowicz
Legendary Co-founder of Solidarity Trade Union

Anna Walentynowicz was born on August 15, 1929 in Rivne in Volyn. Orphaned at the age of ten years, she went to work as a maid and spent years with strangers who took her in. After World War II she worked on a farm near Gdansk, then in a bakery and margarine factory. In 1950 she became employed in the Gdansk Shipyard as a welder and crane operator. She continued to work there, with a few interruptions, until 1991.

Anna began her quest for justice by speaking out publicly when one of her supervisors stole money from the workers' bonus fund to win a lottery. Instead of reprimanding the corrupt supervisor, the system turned on her and she was harassed by secret police.

In 1978, she joined the then just forming Free Trade Unions of the Coast. She was a member of the editorial staff of the organization's publication "Coastal Worker" and dealt with the distribution of leaflets and the organization of celebrations of the anniversary of the Polish 1970 protests. Her apartment became a focal point and meeting place for members of the FTU. She was systematically harassed by Polish government Security Services, once detained for 48 hours, searched, punished with admonitions and threatened with a gun.

For participation in the illegal trade union she was fired from work on 7 August 1980, five months prior to her planned retirement. This management decision enraged the workers, who staged a strike action on 14 August, defending Anna Walentynowicz, and demanding her return. On the third day of the strike, 16 August 1980, management granted Lenin Shipyard workers their working and pay demands. Lech Wałęsa and others announced the end of the strike.

In September 1980, she became a member of the presidium of the Intercommittee of the Independent Self-Governing Trade Union in Gdansk.

After martial law she was interned first in Fordon, then Gołdapia. Upon her release she co-organized hunger strikes, participated in numerous meetings in churches, and wrote personal protests and statements to the government. In December 1981, the court sentenced her to a year and three months in prison (which was suspended for three years) for, among other things, "Continuation of trade union activities and organizing protest action." In December 1983 she was again arrested, this time in Katowice for an attempt at laying the "Wujek" plaque commemorating dead miners.

While remaining active and outspoken, after 1989 Walentynowicz distanced herself from various political parties allied with the new Solidarity. She felt the new Solidarity elites abandoned the workers and ordinary people, not living up to the core Solidarity values of social justice. Walentynowicz avoided anniversary celebrations organized by the new Solidarity. In 1995 she wrote an open letter to Wałęsa. In 2000 she declined an honorary citizenship of the city of Gdansk.

In a 1985 interview, Walentynowicz said:

"We must not wait passively. A free Poland is our aim, but no one will give us that freedom. Our passivity will result in their murdering more and more of us, in more and more people suffering. We must educate, because even when a free Poland is achieved, the nation will be so exhausted that there will be no one to lead it.....Our aim should not be to secure a somewhat thicker slice of bread today, even if this would make us happy; we must not forget what our real aim is. Our main duty is to consider the needs of others. If we become alive to this duty, there will be no unjustly treated people in our midst, and we, in turn, shall not be treated unjustly. Our day-to-day motto should be: 'Your problems are also my problems.' We must extend our friendship and strengthen our solidarity." [493]

---

[493] "Don't Wait for Instructions: An Interview with Anna Walentynowicz [from: Biuletyn Dolnośląski, no. 1(59) (January 1985)]" (PDF). Polish Underground Extracts (11). 31 July 1985.

Teresa Walewska-Przyjalowska
Vice President "Golgota Wschodu" (Golgotha of the East) Foundation

Barbara Maria Teresa Walewska-Przyjałkowska was born September 10, 1937. She was a long-standing employee of the Department of Automotive and Construction Machinery, Warsaw University of Technology, had a doctoral degree and was an engineering specialist in automation and industrial robotics.

She was associated with the Warsaw parish of St. Bobola in Warsaw-Mokotów. In the early 1990s she founded, and since 1997 has been president of, the Association for the Propagation of Worship, St. Andrew Bobola. One her initiatives was the installation of the image of Our Lady of Kozielska--painted reliefs made depicting the NKVD camp at Kozelsk--in the sanctuary of St. Andrew Bobola in 2002. In 2003, this image was blessed by Pope John Paul II. [494]

Through the activities in the life of the church she met Father Zdzislaw Peszkowski, who was working in the Foundation "Golgota Wschodu" ("Golgotha of the East"). In 2006, she was head of the organizing committee of the international conference on "Truth, Memory, and Identity -Katyn Golgotha of the East", which took place on 28 September 2006 in the building of the Sejm. After the death of the President of the "Golgotha of the East" Foundation --Father Peszkowski-- in 2007 out of respect for the chaplain of Katyn families Teresa did not formally accepted the position of President but functioned instead as the vice president. In this capacity, she organized meetings and conferences devoted to the Katyn massacre. [495]

---

[494] https://pl.wikipedia.org/wiki/Teresa_Walewska-Przyjałkowska
[495] Ibid.

Zbigniew Wasserman
Member of Parliament

Zbigniew Wassermann was born 17 Sept 1949 in Krakow. In 1972, he graduated from the School of Law at the Jagiellonian University in Krakow. After graduation, he started working in the prosecutor's office and served as District Prosecutor in Chrzanow, Jaworzno, Brzesk, and Krakow.

After the resignation of Lech Kaczynski from the post of justice minister involved in the activities of the Law and Justice Party in September 2001 Wassermann was elected Member of Parliament of the fourth term from the PiS party in the Krakow district. In the IV Sejm he served as Deputy Chairman of the Committee on Justice and Human Rights and the Chairman of the Commission for Special Services. September 25, 2005 in the parliamentary elections Wassermann was re-elected member of parliament in the district of Krakow. In October of that year, he was appointed Minister-member of the Council of Ministers. In July 2006 he was re-appointed to the post in the government of Jaroslaw Kaczynski. He was reelected to parliament in 2007. [496]

"Obstinate, stubborn and suspicious of policies... He knew how to win, lose and forgive. He was just maybe too busy to take care of his image," said Zbigniew Wassermann's friend Joseph Pilch, president of the Krakow City Council. [497]

"He worked hard, was often gone, so I always waited and now I'm waiting too, and he's not coming back," said Wassermann's widow Halina. She remembered that there was a chance that she and her husband would be able to spend more time together. "My husband was considering withdrawing from politics," she said. "He wondered if he should take part in the next elections or to stay at home. Although perhaps he would regret it; perhaps at home he would have been bored, because a good rest comes only when we work," she added. "I did not want him to fly that day to Smolensk. He was weakened after an illness, he had no strength, but it was mandatory--to pay homage to the heroes, he had to go, even with his last

---

[496] https://pl.wikipedia.org/wiki/Zbigniew_Wassermann
[497] "Zbigniew Wassermann," by Wojciech Czuchnowski, Wojciech Pelowski 10.04.2010 Wyborcza.pl http://wyborcza.pl/1,75402,7754816,Zbigniew_Wassermann.html

ounce of strength. A few days before the flight he asked me to send him his passport. To this day I wonder that maybe if I said that I cannot find it, maybe if I had not sent it he would not have been able to fly," she said. [498]

Zbigniew Wassermann was married to Halina and had three children: daughters Agata and Margaret and his son Adalbert.

---

[498] Ibid.

Wieslaw Woda
Member of Parliament

Wieslaw Woda was born August 17, 1946 in Paleśnica. He graduated from the Agricultural University in Krakow. Since 1997 Woda continuously held a parliamentary seat, representing the Polish Peasant Party. [499]

"The most important things in his life were family, politics and bees. In that order," said Woda's younger brother Andrzej. On the family farm in Paleśnica were some orchards and a few bee hives. Their parents' ambition was to ensure the education of their children which was difficult because the farm was small, and there were eight children (seven boys and one girl.) Woda was the third born. "It was not an easy childhood," said his brother. "Every day, summer or winter, we had to ride our bikes to school in Brest because our parents simply could not afford bus tickets." Woda's father was an activist in the peasant movement. "He taught us the true history of Poland. We knew about Katyn from childhood," said Andrzej. "Wieslaw began to operate in the peasant movement in 1969. Politics was important to him. He liked power, a sense of being able to have an impact on different things, but ministerial positions he did not care for." Woda was offered the post as minister of agriculture, but did not accept it. [500]

"He was on the one hand extremely solid and well-prepared in his work but on the other hand, aggressive and desiring for power…But you could always rely on him…If he pledged to do something, he always kept his word. He always consistently demanded compliance with the statutes of our party," said Member of Parliament Janusz Piechocinski. [501]

"Wiesiek was very principled. If he saw that something was wrong, he tried to remedy it, even when it came to the little things," said one of his closest colleagues in the parliament, Eugeniusz Klopotek. [502] "Woda was irritated, for example, by the fact that the Express Train from Warsaw

---

[499] https://pl.wikipedia.org/wiki/Wies%C5%82aw_Woda

[500] "Wiesław Woda: lider małopolskich ludowców," by Marek Bartosik, 11 Apr 2010 http://www.gazetakrakowska.pl/artykul/243189,wieslaw-woda-lider-malopolskich-ludowcow,id,t.html

[501] Ibid.

[502] Ibid.

didn't stop at Płaszów railway station (where it should stop). He was driven up the wall by the escalator at the Central Railway Station in Warsaw which was in fact not moving. He struggled hard with Polish State Railways. And finally he succeeded. Ever since then, his Polish Peasant Party colleagues have been saying the following epigram about him: "Woda's railway achievements were: stopping the train and moving the stair". [503]

To take a relaxing break from politics, Woda went to the care of his bees. When he was tending them, he was at peace. Sometimes he would go to his apiary in Kasinka but he also had a couple of hives in the garden of his house in the city center. "Now I see those of hives of his. One is still very traditional, carved in a tree trunk. They are now there by themselves," said his brother Andrzej, the day after his brother's death. [504]

His family and doctors tried to dissuade him from traveling to Katyn. Recently, he was beaten in the street by a hooligan who broke his facial bones. He was awaiting an operation. But he told them "I must go. Maybe I will never have the chance again." On Saturday morning, he got into the TU 154 departing to Smolensk. [505]

Wieslaw Woda was first and foremost a family man, dedicated to his wife and children, always sacrificing for them. "His youngest granddaughter was born a little before his death. If he were alive, I'm sure he would be a great, loving grandfather," said Kazimierz Sady, Director of the Malopolska branch of the Volunteer Fire Brigades. Sady knew Woda when he served with him in the Fire Brigade in the 1970s when they quickly became friends. [506] "Though Wiesiek later held even the highest positions - deputy, governor, President of the Malopolska PSL- he was not ashamed to wear the uniform of a firefighter. He was there where people needed him," said Sady. And he added that Wieslaw Woda had no enemies.

---

[503] Ibid.
[504] Ibid.
[505] Ibid.
[506] "Mieli tyle do zrobienia, ale nastąpił Smoleńsk," by Paulina Korbut, Maria Mazurek, Magdalena Stoklosa, 10 April 2013
http://www.gazetakrakowska.pl/artykul/802327,mieli-tyle-do-zrobienia-ale-nastapil-smolensk,id,t.html

He liked everyone. "He often advised me, we talked a lot. After his death, I miss it. So when I have problems, or stand before a difficult decision, I go to Rakowice, to the Avenue of the Meritorious where Wieska's grave is. There I have with him an internal conversation." [507]

---

[507] Ibid.

Edward Wojtas
Member of Parliament

Edward Wojtas was born 1 Mar 1955 in Wolka Modrzejow. He graduated from the School of Economics, University in Lublin. From 2005-2006, he was Speaker of the Lublin province. In the 2007 parliamentary elections Wojtas won a seat from the PSL party for the Lublin district.

His friends say he was a soldier of the Peasant Battalions--his patriotism instilled by his father and the popular movement.

Jan Lopata, Lublin PSL deputy, was friends with Wojtas for 25 years. "Despite the fact that Edzio had many important functions he always had sensitivity to the suffering of others." [508]

Lucjan Orgasiński, a spokesman for the Lublin PSL remembered, "When petitioners came to him and he did not know how he could help, he just pulled out a wallet. I witnessed, as there appeared a 50-year-old man who had fallen; he had no help; he had family, dependents, terrible depression, tears in his eyes. Wojtas said: 'You wait a minute.' He reached into his pocket and gave him a few bills. He did it not ostentatiously, but in reflex to such helplessness and with compassion. Then he got him a job at the warehouse." [509]

"Wojtas was deputy director of the Department of Health in the 1990s, and an economist at such a position was not uncommon. He had already had intensive training in health economics, counting hospital costs, and preparation for deep reform of health care financing," wrote Marek Wojtowicz, President of STOMOZ. "Edward understood perfectly these problems. Friendly, always smiling, always with a new joke on his lips, he became at once the soul of each meeting of the Association of Healthcare Managers (STOMOZ). Even with successive promotions in his brilliant career as a public servant he did not change." Addressing Wojtas' widow Alina, Wojtowicz said, "remember always that your husband, like no other, proved every step of the way that a high government official can

---

[508] "Edward Wojtas (1.03.1955 - 10.04.2010)," by Paweł Reszka, itjg 09.04.2011 http://wiadomosci.gazeta.pl/wiadomosci/1,114892,9404965,Edward_Wojtas__1_03_1955___10_04_2010_.html
[509] Ibid.

be a normal, smiling, modest man, listening carefully and respectfully to suggestions and requests, and even criticism of subordinate managers from the front line. I remember him so." [510]

"The man had an extraordinary personality, he was an amazing polymath, expert on local government and the state economy," wrote Aleksander Dopliński, PSL deputy. In discussions, he was always kind and open. At the party meetings he was the initiator of many bills. He was amazingly calm, a man with whom no one has ever had any conflict - this is extremely rare, especially in politics. His death is a huge blow to the entire peasant movement. He always had a great desire to act - initiated many folk celebrations in the Lublin region, with which he was associated. He instilled in us the love of country and respect for another human being." [511]

He is survived by his wife Alina, and two daughters, Monica, an economist, and Margaret, a lawyer.

---

[510] "Zaszczepil w nas milosc ojczyzny"
http://www.sluzbazdrowia.com.pl/smolensk/sylwetka.php?o=92
[511] Ibid.

Pawel Wypych
State Secretary in the Office of the President

Paweł Wypych was born 20 Feb 1968 in Otwock. He had served as Deputy Minister of Labor and Social Insurance. From 2005 to 2006 he was Secretary of State in the Ministry of Labour and Social Policy and in 2007, Undersecretary of State in the Prime Minister's Office. From 2009 he served as the Secretary of State in the Chancellery of the President of Poland.

His passion was scouting. For 12 years he was an instructor in the Scouting Association of the Republic (ZHR). Another passion was his car—a 1987 Citroen. "Everyone wants in life for a bit of madness. One flies in space, the other collects money, and I have my Citroen," Wypych laughed in an interview with {Polish news agency} "SE". [512]

Paweł Wypych was married to Malgorzata Wypych and had two children.

His widow Malgorzata remembered her husband in an interview with Agnieszka Nowakowski, four years after his death. [513]

"Paul has always been an activist. As I left to marry him, my friends said, 'You know that this is an activist, and involvement in social issues will always be the most important to him.'

"He was an excellent organizer. On the occasion of the visit of the Holy Father John Paul II he organized the so-called White Service. It was a service of scouts in the place where the meeting was held with the pope... He liked a challenge. If there was something to do and everyone said that it absolutely can not be done, he always said, 'Well, okay, we try.'

"Always he told me that the family is most important to him, {but he worked so much} it seems to me that Paul fell into the trap of lack of time. Working for others and family is just very difficult to reconcile.

"Following his release from the post of chairman of the Labor and Social Insurance Ministry, Paul was out of work. He did not know what to

---

[512] http://www.se.pl/wiadomosci/polska/pawe-wypych-42-l-prezydencki-minister-zginal-z-para-prezydencka-w-smolensku_136052.html
[513] "ROZMOWA Z MAŁGORZATĄ WYPYCH" Interview by Agnieszka Nowakowska February 18, 2014 http://smolensk.muzhp.pl/malgorzata-wypych

do with himself...in the end, Prime Minister Jaroslaw Kaczynski mentioned it to his brother, who in turn knew {Paul} from working in the City, and in this way, Paul went to the Office of the President. In this way, he became a minister in the Chancellery of the Polish President Lech Kaczynski.

"As Minister in the Office he was able to make contact with the media. Certainly helpful here was his ability to talk with everyone...He had an uncanny ability to read between the lines...Paul was able to talk to any journalist, but repeatedly said: 'But Mr. Editor, I'm sorry--what are you talking about? You came with a specific question...and I do not think that's it.' He never gave up or got led astray by any of the media's attempt to disgress.

"Paul loved to sleep. He could fall asleep in every possible position and time... At the end of his life in connection with the various stresses it was different, but generally he laughed that any unused time for sleep is sometimes lost when it was most needed. If he was to be interviewed on the radio or on television, attend a meeting with the president or needed to prepare a speech, he could easily get up about five in the morning.

"When spending time with the kids very often he escorted Zuzia in the morning or later Chris to kindergarten. Although in their time together, when reading books to the children, rather than having them fall asleep, he entertained them for the next hour and a half and eventually they fell asleep. He would sit with Zuzka for her lessons, and play ball with Christopher Robin, who was still tiny. For as much as he could, he was a dad, but because of his different activities his time was limited." [514]

---

[514] Ibid.

Stanislaw Zajac
Senator

Stanislaw Zajac was born 1 May 1949 in Święcanach. He graduated from the School of Law and Administration at the Jagiellonian University. He held the position of judge, then practiced as a lawyer.

In 2005 he was elected deputy fifth term from the Law and Justice Party in the district of Krosno. In parliamentary elections in 2007, for the fourth time he received a mandate in the parliament. June 22, 2008 as PiS candidate he won the by-election to the Senate. He was deputy chairman of the PiS Parliamentary Club and president of the Senate Law and Justice Party, as well as chairman of the National Defense Commission.[515]

When he came to the small south eastern Polish town of Jaslo, his loyal and dedicated assistant, Wojciech Pielos was at his side. Outside of his family, Pielos was definitely one of the closest people to the senator. They had worked together for 12 years. "The mayor of Jaslo recommended me to work with the Senator," Pielos recalled. Zajac was in Warsaw everyday and so his contact with Pielos {who was in Jaslo} was limited mainly to phone and fax. A more detailed discussion of everything had to wait for the weekends. "And so I became a regular visitor at the Zajac home," said Piękoś. "The warmth of the house and the unique family atmosphere, which Alicja {the senator's wife} created, made me feel very welcome there. They always treated me like a son, sometimes referring to me as 'our son Wojtek.' And for me it was an amazing honor...Every day I learned something from him, I gained experience, I met the most important people in the country," said Piękoś. "Preparing his writings, speeches, congratulatory letters. The Senator was very meticulous, every document he carefully checked and corrected...I knew that everything has to be perfectly polished...In time, I learned to write using the language of a senator, and he adapted a little to my style and we understood each other

---

[515] https://pl.wikipedia.org/wiki/Stanis%C5%82aw_Zaj%C4%85c

almost without words. What I have achieved in my professional life I owe to him. [516]

But it was not only the knowledge and experience Piekos gained while working for Zajac. "Sometimes I catch myself on the fact that I took over from him his habits…His gestures, facial expressions, furrowed eyebrows, how to wear a jacket." [517]

"He was an amazing friend and benefactor of our school," - says Anna Grzesiak - Kaminska, Director of Primary School No. 4 in Jaslo. "When, in 2000 we had a school fire after the explosion of acetylene cylinders, thanks to his efforts we got 100 thousand złoty from a government grant to refurbish … And thanks to his intervention with the insurance company, we received full compensation, even though earlier we were refused." [518]

"Many times he helped us, always willing to sacrifice his time and energy on the education of young people in Krosno and Jaslo," said Francis Teleszkewicz, Chancellor of Higher Vocational School in Krosno. "He participated in the university ceremonies, but invaluable was his constant readiness to engage in new directions of education, teaching staff and student affairs. Although there were many intense social and political activities and serious problems the senator was always dealing with he always found time to talk or meet," emphasized Teleszkiewicz. [519]

Today, many people find it difficult to come to terms with the fact that it will never agian be possible to seek his advice. [520] Zajac was married to Alice and had two children.

---

[516] "Wspomnienie. Stanisław Zając angażował się we wszystko, co działo się w Jaśle i regionie," by Eewa Wawro, 12 Apr 2010, Nowiny24, http://www.nowiny24.pl/wiadomosci/jaslo/art/6079085,wspomnienie-stanislaw-zajac-angazowal-sie-we-wszystko-co-dzialo-sie-w-jasle-i-regionie,id,t.html

[517] Ibid.

[518] Ibid.

[519] Ibid.

[520] Ibid.

Janusz Zakrzenski

Actor

Janusz Zakrzenski was born 8 Mar 1937 in Przededworze to a religious landowning family with patriotic traditions. His father during World War I served in the 2nd Regiment of Cavalry Rokitniańskich. In 1945, his father was imprisoned and Zakrzenski stayed with his mother, an opera singer. In 1953 he started medical studies and took a job as a paramedic. After nine months in the ambulance service, he decided to change direction and began studying acting at the State Higher School of Theatre in Krakow, from which he graduated in 1960. He was an actor in the Slovak Theatre in Krakow (1960-1967) and Warsaw theaters: Polish (1967-1974), the New (1974-1984) and National (1984/1985). In 1985, he again became involved with the Polish Theatre in Warsaw. [521]

He played his last role on the eve of his death, April 9, 2010, in the Polish Theatre's production of the play "The Plague" based on the novel by Albert Camus.

He was married to Barbara, who died in 2014, with whom he had a son Martin.

His trademark was his mustache and impeccable manners. His audience will most remember him in his role as Marshal Pilsudski, which he portrayed on the screen, in the theater, and almost every year, during the celebration of Independence Day.

Zakrzenski was always drawn to art. "In our house there was artistic atmosphere," he said in interviews. "My grandfather painted, wrote poetry, recited; mother sang opera in Wroclaw. My childhood years were related to the Slovak Theatre, where she sang. Going to the theater was a duty." [522]

He believed in the social responsibility of public persons to treat their profession as a mission. "What is humanity?" he said "It is not isolation, not deafness, but friendliness and the opening of your eyes and ears to the other man." [523]

---

[521] https://pl.wikipedia.org/wiki/Janusz_Zakrze%C5%84ski

[522] "Janusz Zakrzeński, aktor prawdziwie polski," Krzysztof Kwiatkowski, Newsweek 13-04-2010 http://polska.newsweek.pl/janusz-zakrzenski--aktor-prawdziwie-polski,56624,1,1.html

[523] Ibid.

He happily engaged in educational campaigns and participated in a number of anniversary celebrations, during which he often returned in the role of Marshal Pilsudski. He promoted patriotic upbringing and the purity of the Polish language as a member of the program council of the Association of Pilsudski. [524]

In interviews, he warned against the modern pace of life and the collapse of values. About contemporary theater he said: "The rules are different than they used to. Actors compete, hurry. No one shows them the magic of theater traditions. Fewer and fewer people know how to express their thoughts."[525]

A few days before his death in the Smolensk crash, Zakrzenski lost his job at the Polish Theatre. The most painful thing for him was that no one thanked him for his years in the theater. The new president of the Federation of Polish actors Joanna Szczepkowska shared this information in "Gala"{magazine} "A few days before flying to Katyn he was released from the Polish Theatre in Warsaw. No one thanked him for his many years of work, no one shook his hand. He learned about it from the HR department. He got a card. He took it very hard," revealed Szczepkowska. [526]

Zakrzeński is not the only actor who lost his job at the Polish Theatre. The new director of the institution Andrzej Seweryn said there was real purge in this theater. But Mr. Janusz Zakrzeński of all was perhaps the longest and best-known and recognizable. On April 15 he was to celebrate 50 years on stage. But he flew to Katyn with a mission, with his trusted companion Wladyslaw Stasiak, the head of the Chancellery of President Lech Kaczynski. He was to read letters that some of the murdered Katyn officers had managed to send to loved ones at the graves of victims of Katyn. [527]

In the joint obituary with his deceased wife, Zakrzenski's son and sister Teresa shared his motto: Mors certa, hora incerta. (death is uncertain, its hour is uncertain) [528]

---

[524] Ibid.
[525] Ibid.
[526] Aktor "M jak miłość" przed śmiercią stracił pracę http://www.fakt.pl/Aktor-quot-M-jak-milosc-quot-przed-smiercia-stracil-prace,artykuly,69651,1.html
[527] Ibid.
[528] Ibid.

Gabriela Zych
Representative of the Katyn Families Association

Gabriela Lucyna Zych was born May 31, 1941 in Kalisz. She was a Polish social activist, founder (along with her husband, Leszek Zych), of the Association of Katyn Families in Kalisz and its President. Her husband Leszek (1928-2000), was president of Kalisz Katyn Families. He lost his father, Captain Stefan Zych, when he was 9 years old. Stefan Zych was a professional military officer in 1939. He went with a friend to muster with a unit in Przemysl. On the way, when refueling, someone stole their car. Then there was no information. It was only in 1943 that the family learned that he had been shot by the Russians.[529]

After her husband's death, Gabriela took over as president of the Association of Katyn Families in Kalisz.

Gabriela Zych was remembered as a person universally liked and respected, extremely active and optimistic that she has preserved memories for her grandchildren. In the memory of the people of Kalisz she remained a person of inexhaustible energy, very active and radiating optimism, though in compromised health and no longer young.

"She was a woman of great heart, and very busy," said Vincent E. Pawlaczyk, the President of Kalisz and Chairman of the Municipal Committee for the Protection of Remembrance, Combat and Martyrdom. "She always participated in the preparations for the local celebration of the anniversary of the Katyn massacre. People familiar with Mrs. Zych mention how she was proud and honored to be invited on board the presidential plane. She wanted to participate in the celebration of the 70th anniversary of the Katyn massacre. She considered it her life mission to save the memory of her father-in-law and the other victims of Katyn. Therefore, with great solicitude she gathered all the documents and historical materials about those tragic events. She initiated the construction of the Victims of the Katyn Massacre monument in Kalisz."[530]

---

[529] "Gabriela Zych," by Agnieszka Drzewiecka 11.04.2010 http://wyborcza.pl/1,75402,7759748,Gabriela_Zych.html

[530] "Kalisz: Gabriela Zych rok temu zginęła w katastrofie - jak ją zapamiętano?" by Daria Kubiak, 10 Apr 2011
http://www.gloswielkopolski.pl/artykul/390486,kalisz-gabriela-zych-rok-temu-zginela-w-katastrofie-jak-ja-zapamietano,id,t.html

"To tell the truth, after the death of Lech Zych our association existed only thanks to Gabriela," said Zofia Stefaniak treasurer of "Katyn Families" in Kalisz. "She was able to surmount any obstacle, reach out to each office, working for our common good. The most active members of the Katyn Families are elderly. The young, unfortunately, are not very drawn to this type of activity. Gabriela devoted a lot of energy to change it. The truth about the fate of Poles dying for this country she was trying to also pass on to others—to young people. She could tell about our history simply and beautifully. In this way, Gabriela Zych tried to rejuvenate the 'Katyn Family' and to forever preserve the memory of those tragically killed." [531]

They say about her that she could get along with everyone: both children and adults. Therefore, she managed to create a little Katyn family – for the great-grandchildren of the murdered officers she made membership cards, enlisted them to hold banners at the Katyn ceremonies, and she explained to them that you have to remember the people who lost their lives for the motherland. [532]

On the Thursday before the flight to the ceremony in Katyn, Gabriela was sitting at home with a stack of documents and photos from the war and post-war period, which her husband had accumulated with her throughout their life. Zofia Stefaniak visited her. "She said to me: 'Listen, I need all these papers in some order before I go. It's a pity that they do not fly with me. I do not have the energy, but I have to be at the cemetery.'" [533]

On April 10, 2010, she was flying to Katyn for the fifth time.

She had a son Przemyslaw, and daughter Isabella.

---

[531] Ibid.
[532] "Gabriela Zych," by Agnieszka Drzewiecka 11.04.2010 http://wyborcza.pl/1,75402,7759748,Gabriela_Zych.html
[533] Ibid.

Bibliography

"13th Airlift Squadron (Polish Air Force)," Wikipedia https://en.wikipedia.org/wiki/13th_Airlift_Squadron_(Polish_Air_Force)

"2010 Polish Air Force Tu-154 Crash," http://america.pink/2010-polish-air-force-154-crash_131047.html

"36th Special Aviation Regiment," https://en.wikipedia.org/wiki/36th_Special_Aviation_Regiment

Andrzekczak, Jerzy, "96 Koncow Swiata: Gdy runal ich swiat pod Smolenskiem" {96 ends of the world: when their world fell in Smolensk} Skrzat Publishing, 2011

Aviation Safety Network report, Flight Safety Foundation, https://aviation-safety.net/database/record.php?id=20100410-0

"Bielan: To nie prezydent wydał rozkaz. Klich: Bielan kłamie"{The President Did not Order; Minister Klich lying} Dżek 25.04.2010 Gazeta.PL Wiadomosci, http://wiadomosci.gazeta.pl/wiadomosci/1,114873,7810727,Bielan__To_nie_prezydent_wydal_rozkaz__Klich__Bielan.html

Cmentarz Katyński, 10 kwietnia 2010, filmyfrondowe, You Tube video, https://www.youtube.com/watch?v=jaQRxsTufHM

Champion, Mark, "Polish Flight Skirted Military Protocol," by Marc Champion, 15 Apr 2010, Wall Street Journal, http://www.wsj.com/articles/SB10001424052702303348504575184330003561878

CNN Crash Kills Polish President 10 Apr 2010 You Tube video https://www.youtube.com/watch?v=4yzRj9rmxO8

"Cockpit transcript confirms crashed Polish presidential plane's pilots pressured to land in fog,"Posted by blogfactory On April 07, 2015 http://blogfactory.co.uk/archives/4706

"CORRECTED-Polish radio says crew distracted before 2010 Smolensk plane crash"
7 Apr 2015, Reuters, http://www.reuters.com/article/poland-russia-smolensk-tape-idusl6n0x41g120150407

Czartoryski-Sziler, Peter, "The Picture of the Polish Flight Crew as Expert-Flyers Emerges: The Crew Cleared of Any Wrongdoing," for "Nasz Dziennik" ("*Bez zastrzeżeń do załogi*" *Czwartek, 19 lipca 2012, Nr 167 (4402))Translated by Jola D. with futher editing by Jan C.*
http://www.doomedsoldiers.com/Poland-pilots-and-crew-were-expert-flyers.html

Czuchnowski, Wojciech, "Incydent gruziński"{The Georgian Incident}, Renata Grochal 24.04.2010
http://wyborcza.pl/1,76842,7808706,Incydent_gruzinski.html

Day, Matthew, "Polish defence minister honours pilot who defied President Kaczynski" 18 Sep 2008, The Telegraph, http://www.telegraph.co.uk/news/worldnews/europe/poland/2983110/Polish-defence-minister-honours-pilot-who-defied-President-Kaczynski.html

Day, Matthew, "Polish family claims Russia 'mixed up' remains of Smolensk victims," 20 Sep 2012, The Telegraph, http://www.telegraph.co.uk/news/worldnews/europe/poland/9555681/Polish-family-claims-Russia-mixed-up-remains-of-Smolensk-victims.html

"Deaths record-Warsaw – Smolensk" November 6, 2012 http://okresprl.blog.onet.pl/2012/11/06/zapis-smierci-warszawa-smolensk/

"Dlaczego generałowie wsiedli do tupolewa," {Why were the generals on the Tupolev} 23 Feb 2013, Niezalezna, http://niezalezna.pl/38798-dlaczego-generalowie-wsiedli-do-tupolewa

Final Report from the examination of the aviation accident no. 192/2010/11 involving the Tu-154M airplane, tail number 101, which occurred on April 10, 2010 in the area of the Smolensk North airfield (the Polish report)

"Generał wrócił do Polski," {The General Returns to Poland} 16 Apr 2010, 22:32
http://www.tvn24.pl/wiadomosci-z-kraju,3/general-wrocil-do-polski,211731.html

Glen, Margaret, "Pilot Arkadiusz Protasiuk. Świetny pilot, który nie bał się tupolewów" {The pilot Arkadiusz Protasiuk. Great pilot, who was not afraid of the Tupolev}, Gazeta Krakowska, 14 Apr 2010, http://www.gazetakrakowska.pl/artykul/244235,pilot-arkadiusz-protasiuk-swietny-pilot-ktory-nie-bal-sie-tupolewow,id,t.html

Glinska, Pauline, "Samoloty nie miały przed nim tajemnic" {The aircraft had no screts from him} 10 Apr 2015 http://polska-zbrojna.pl/home/articleshow/15676?t=Samoloty-nie-mialy-przed-nim-tajemnic

Glowacki, Bartosz, "Polish air force dismisses five personnel following C-295 crash report," by, Flight Global, 14 Apr 2008, https://www.flightglobal.com/news/articles/polish-air-force-dismisses-five-personnel-following-c-295-crash-222917/

Gorska, Marcin, "Incydent gruziński oczami pierwszego pilota" {The Georgian incident through the eyes of the first pilot} 28 Apr 2010, Wyborcza.pl http://wyborcza.pl/1,76842,7821881,Incydent_gruzinski_oczami_pierwszego_pilota.html?as=2%20-%20ixzz41wrYQtnG

Herbert, Zbigniew, "Ocalales Nie Po To, Aby Zyc. Masz Malo Czasu, Trzeba Dac Swiadectwo,"{Were saved not in order to live. You have little time, you must give testimony}
Przesłanie Pana Cogito http://smolensk.muzhp.pl/portrety/

Hradecky, Simon, "Crash: Polish Air Force T154 at Smolensk on Apr 10th 2010, impacted trees on first approach" May 19th 2010, The Aviation Herald, http://avherald.com/h?article=429ec5fa/0008

"Identyfikacja ofiar katastrofy polskiego Tu-154 w Smolensku," {Identification of the passengers of the Polish catastrophe Tu-154 in Smolensk} Wikipedia, https://pl.wikipedia.org/wiki/Identyfikacja_ofiar_katastrofy_polskiego_Tu-154_w_Smole%C5%84sku

"Incydent gruzinski," {The Georgian Incident} https://pl.wikiquote.org/wiki/Incydent_gruzi%C5%84ski

Interstate Aviation Committee Air Accident Investigation Committee Final Report (Russian MAK report)

"Kaczynski plane crash explained: Full minute-by-minute reconstruction", YouTube video, https://www.youtube.com/watch?v=ucfMbPt8xRw&spfreload=10#t=676.562

"Kapitan pilot śp. Artur Ziętek" Opublikowano 12 października 2012, autor: emka
http://hej-kto-polak.pl/wp/?p=62929

"Kapitan prezydenckiego tupolewa nigdy nie ćwiczył na symulatorze jako dowódca"{Captain presidential Tupolev never practiced on the simulator as a commander}
13.10.2010, Wiadomocsi
http://www.se.pl/wydarzenia/kraj/kapitan-prezydenckiego-tupolewa-nigdy-nie-cwiczyl-_156566.html

"Kolejna zamiana ciał ofiar katastrofy smoleńskiej," {Another exchange of bodies of victims of the Smolensk disaster} 21 listopada 2012 http://www.rmf24.pl/raporty/raport-lech-kaczynski-nie-zyje-2/fakty/news-kolejna-zamiana-cial-ofiar-katastrofy-smolenskiej,nId,715696

Korbut, Paulina, et. al, "Mieli tyle do zrobienia, ale nastąpił Smoleńsk," {They had so much to do, but there was Smolensk} 10 Apr 2013, Gazeta Krakowska, http://www.gazetakrakowska.pl/artykul/802327,mieli-tyle-do-zrobienia-ale-nastapil-smolensk,id,t.html

Krzymowski, Michal, "Twarde lądwanie Specjalnego Pułku" {A hard landing for the Special Regiment} Dziennikarz działu Polska 09-11-2012 http://polska.newsweek.pl/twarde-ladowanie-specjalnego-pulku,97938,1,1.html

Kublick, Agnieska and Czuchnowski, Wojciech, ,'Tchórz" zabolał mnie najbardziej" {"Coward" hurt me the most} 29.03.2011, Wyborcza http://wyborcza.pl/1,76842,9337581,__Tchorz___zabolal_mnie_najbardziej.html

"Lech Kaczynski: Seventy years on, it is time the wounds of Katyn were healed", 12 Apr 2010, Independent, http://www.independent.co.uk/voices/commentators/lech-kaczynski-seventy-years-on-it-is-time-the-wounds-of-katyn-were-healed-1942938.html

Levy, Clifford, "Polish Crash Inquiry Looks at Decision to Land Jet" 11 Apr 2010, http://www.nytimes.com/2010/04/12/world/europe/12crash.html?_r=0

"Lista Pasażerów - obrażenia, rozpoznawanie," {List of passengers - damage recognition} zestawienia smolenskie," 12 Jul 2011, http://pomocnezestawienia.blogspot.com/2011/07/4-lista-pasazerow-obrazenia.html

Marianova, Alyona and Belovsky, Ignat, "Transcripts of last moments of Polish plane released" June 7, 2010, Gazeta.Ru, Russian Beyond the Headlines http://rbth.com/articles/2010/06/08/polish_plane_transcript_released.html

"Mirosławiec: Od katastrofy minęło sześć lat," {Mirosławiec: Since the disaster had passed six years} 22 Jan 2014, Lotnicza Polska, http://lotniczapolska.pl/Miroslawiec:-Od-katastrofy-minelo-szesc-lat,32471

"New Smoleńsk Air Crash Transcripts Released Ahead of Anniversary of Tragedy that Killed Poland's President" 9th April 2015 · Inside Poland. com, http://inside-poland.com/t/new-smolensk-air-crash-transcripts-released-ahead-of-anniversary-of-tragedy-that-killed-polands-president/

"Niezwyciezony w slalomie gigancie", {Invincible in the giant slalom} 30 Mar 2011 http://www.radiomaryja.pl/bez-kategorii/niezwyciezony-w-slalomie-gigancie/

Nolan, Liam, "The Continuing Nightmare of Poland's 2010 Smolensk Plane Crash," 1 Nov 2012, The Atlantic, http://www.theatlantic.com/international/archive/2012/11/the-continuing-nightmare-of-polands-2010-smolensk-plane-crash/264418/

"Pamięci Ofiar Katastrofy Smoleńskiej. Czwórkami do Nieba szli...– Agnieszka Podgródka-Węcławek, Włodzimierz Potasiński, Arkadiusz Protasiuk, Andrzej Przewoźnik" {Memory of the Victims of the Smolensk disaster. Fours go to Heaven ... Agnieszka Podgródka-Węcławek, Włodzimierz Potasiński, Arkadiusz Protasiuk, Andrzej Przewoźnik}01 Apr 2014 Redaktor: husarz, Solidarni 2010, http://solidarni2010.pl/27554-pamieci-ofiar-katastrofy-smolenskiej-czworkami-do-nieba-szli-8211-agnieszka-podgrodka-weclawek-wlodzimierz-potasinski-arkadiusz-protasiuk-andrzej-prze.html

"Pamietamy o Zalodze tupolewa—Andrzej Michalak"{Remembering the crew of the Tupolev-Andrzej Michalak} http://3obieg.pl/pamietamy-o-zalodze-tupolewa-andrzej-michalak

Pietraszewski, Marcin, "Kapitan pilot. Arkadiusz Protasiuk,", PAP, 11 Apr 2010, Wyborcza.pl,
http://wyborcza.pl/1,75402,7760220,Kapitan_pilot__Arkadiusz_Protasiuk.html#ixzz417HPjVe7

"Pilot-in-Command at the time of the 'Georgian Incident' Defends General Błasik and Captain Protasiuk", SCND: April 24, 2015, http://www.smolenskcrashnews.com/polish-pilot-defends-general-blasik-and-captain-protasiuk.html

"Pilot, który ODMÓWIŁ Lechowi Kaczyńskiemu lądowania w Gruzji: Było niebezpiecznie, ale prezydent ROZKAZAŁ lot do Tbilisi," {A pilot who REFUSED Lech Kaczynski landing in Georgia: It was dangerous, but the president ordered the flight to Tbilisi} 29 Mar 2011, Se.pl, http://www.se.pl/wiadomosci/polska/pilot-ktory-odmowil-lechowi-kaczynskiemu-ladowania-w-gruzji-bylo-niebezpiecznie-ale-prezydent-rozkaz_177965.html

"Pilot o locie z L. Kaczyńskim do Gruzji: Miałem wrażenie, że walę głową w mur"{Pilot flight from L. Kaczynski to Georgia: I had the impression that bang his head against the wall}
29.03.2011 From Gazeta.pl Wiadomosci http://wiadomosci.gazeta.pl/wiadomosci/1,114873,9337823,Pilot_o_locie_z_L__Kaczynskim_do_Gruzji__Mialem_wrazenie_.html

"Pilots in Smolensk crash that killed Polish president pressured to land in fog," 7 Apr 2015, The Guardian, https://www.theguardian.com/world/2015/apr/07/pilots-plane-crash-smolensk-polish-president-pressured-land-thick-fog

"Plane Crash Kills 20 Polish Officers," Associated Press January 24, 2008, Military.com http://www.military.com/NewsContent/0,13319,160664,00.html

Osiecki, Jan, et.al, "PLF:101, Ostatni Lot Raport o Przyczynach Katastrofy, {The Last Flight: root cases of the crash} http://www.plf101.pl/ksiazka_spis_tresci.asp

"Poland to charge two Russian officials over Kaczynski plane crash," World, 27 Mar 2015, Reuters, http://www.reuters.com/article/us-poland-russia-smolensk-idUSKBN0MN1BZ20150327

"Polish AF Tu-154 Crash in Smolensk (Part2) Airliners, http://www.airliners.net/forum/viewtopic.php?f=10&t=1023279

"Polish Air Disaster 2010—A Review," 25 May 2010, Above Top Secret, http://www.abovetopsecret.com/forum/thread575066/pg1

"Polish Radio Says Passengers Drinking Alcohol Before Smolensk Plane Crash," 7 Apr 2015, Reuters, The Moscow Times, http://www.themoscowtimes.com/article/518725.html?utm_source=feedburner&utm_medium=feed&utm_campaign=Feed%3A+themoscowtimes%2Fnews+%28The+Moscow+Times+News%29.

"Polish Tragedy in Smolensk: Final Moments on Cockpit tape." http://www.biega.com/polish_tragedy_2.html

"Polish Tu-154 crew ignored eight 'pull up' warnings" Flight Global https://www.flightglobal.com/news/articles/polish-tu-154-crew-ignored-eight-39pull-up39-warnings-342638/

Pronina, Lyubov and McQuaid, David, "Polish Pilot Pressured to Land Before Kaczynski Crash," 12 Jan 2011, Bloomberg, http://www.bloomberg.com/news/articles/2011-01-12/polish-pilots-under-pressure-to-land-before-kaczynski-crash-russia-says

"Przeczytaj stenogramy z rozmów kontrolerów" {Read transcripts of controllers conversations} 19 Jan 2011, TVN24, http://www.tvn24.pl/wiadomosci-z-kraju,3/przeczytaj-stenogramy-z-rozmow-kontrolerow,212876.html

"Przygotowania do 'katastrofy smoleńskiej' – dobór załogi", {Preparing for 'Smolensk catastrophe' - the selection of the crew} 12 Nov 2014, http://noweczasy.salon24.pl/615100,przygotowania-do-katastrofy-smolenskiej-dobor-zalogi

Puhl, Jan, "The Polish Gadfly: A Lawyer's Quest for Clarity on the Smolensk Plane Crash" 4 Jan 2014, Spiegel Online International, http://www.spiegel.de/international/europe/

berlin-lawyer-stefan-hambura-questions-smolensk-plane-crash-burials-a-875779.html

"Putin and Tusk remember Poland's Katyn massacre," AFP News Agency, YouTube video, https://www.youtube.com/watch?v=-g8JmVmEPjA&feature=player_embedded

Rao, Dinesh,MD, "Crash Victims exhumed Due to Flawed Autopsies", http://www.forensicpathologyonline.com/home/the-news/crash-victims-exumed-due-flawed-autopsies

Ruba, Magdalena, "Piloci krzyczeli: Jezu, Jezu!" {Pilots shouted: Jesus, Jesus!} 13 May 2010, Fakt24 http://www.fakt.pl/Piloci-krzyczeli-Jezu-Jezu-,artykuly,71784,1.html

"Russio-Georgian War", Wikipedia, https://en.wikipedia.org/wiki/Russo-Georgian_War

Shuster, Simon, "Russian and Polish Tensions Rise After Crash Report," 19 Jan 2011, Time, http://content.time.com/time/world/article/0,8599,2043130,00.html

Smith, Alex Duval, "Will Poland Ever Uncover the Truth About the Plane Crash that Killed the President?" 7 Feb 2016, The Guardian, https://www.theguardian.com/world/2016/feb/07/smolensk-plane-crash-lech-kaczynski-poland-russia

Smolensk Crash News http://www.smolenskcrashnews.com/about-smolensk-crash-news-digest.html

"The Smolensk Disaster: New Revelations and Old Accusations," April 10, 2015, Notes from Poland, https://notesfrompoland.com/2015/04/10/the-smolensk-disaster-new-revelations-and-old-accusations/

"Smolensk disaster victim identification," 29 Oct 2012, http://dvi-forensic.blogspot.com/2012/10/spotlight-smolensk-disaster-victim.html

"The Study Protocol Plane Crash near Miroslawiec, January 23, 2008," https://pl.wikisource.org/wiki/Protokół_badania_katastrofy_lotniczej_pod_Mirosławcem_-_23_stycznia_2008

Tu-154 Russian Investigation Timeline, http://www.mak.ru/russian/investigations/2010/tu-154m_101.html#metka1

Szary, Wiktor, "Poland relaunches inquiry into 2010 presidential jet crash in Russia" Feb 4, 2016, World Reuters, http://www.reuters.com/article/us-poland-smolensk-macierewicz-idUSKCN0VD1JM

Szymowski, Leszek, "Zamach w Smolensku",{The Coup in Smolensk} Bollinari Publishing House, Warsaw, 2011

Wegrzyn, Natalia and Gawlik, Pawel, "Lech Kaczyński: jesteśmy tu po to, by podjąć walkę" {Lech Kaczynski: we are here to take up the fight} 12.08.2008 http://www.rp.pl/artykul/175569-Lech-Kaczynski--jestesmy-tu-po-to--by-podjac-walke.html#ap-1

"Wieża nie informowała, że TU- 154 schodzi z kursu" {The tower was not aware that the TU 154 goes off course} 18 Jan 2011, TVN24, http://www.tvn24.pl/wiadomosci-z-kraju,3/wieza-nie-informowala-ze-tu-154-schodzi-z-kursu,159217.html

Wise, Jeff, "Pilot Error to Blame in Smolensk Crash," 12 Apr 2010, Popular Mechanics, http://www.popularmechanics.com/flight/a5579/smolensk-plane-crash-error/

"World leaders can't get to Poland for funeral due to ash," by the CNN Wire Staff

April 18, 2010 http://edition.cnn.com/2010/WORLD/europe/04/18/poland.funeral.laders/

"Żegnaj panie majorze..." {Goodbye, Sir...} Kurier Poludniowy, 30 Apr 2010, http://www.kurierpoludniowy.pl/wiadomosci.php?art=5451

"ZOBACZ STENOGRAMY, zapis ostatnich sekund tupolewa: Uderzenia, krzyki ".....rrrrwaaaa!" - koniec zapisu" {SEE Transcripts, record of the last seconds of the Tupolev: blows, screams, '....rrrrwaaaa!'— End of record} 2 Jun 2010 se.pl, http://www.se.pl/wiadomosci/polska/komorowski-w-stenogramach-nie-zadnych-sensacji_141369.html

About the Author

The author in Warsaw, Poland, 2011

Linda Boris is a retired Medical Service Corps Navy Commander, retiring from the Navy in 2000 after 25 years of service. Born and raised in Southern New Jersey of Polish-American ancestry, Linda has a special interest in genealogy and Polish history.

Printed in Great Britain
by Amazon